Dedication

This book is lovingly dedicated to
my dear friend, Linda Graf
and to my husband, Rod McKay

Now let us do something beautiful for God.
--St. Mother Teresa of Calcutta

Table of Contents

Preface

The stories that became this book began in emails to Linda Graf while she took care of her widowed mother during the last six years of her mother's life. Though Linda was an only child who never married, she and her mother were never close. Her mother was domineering, and Linda believed she was a disappointment to her. At 89, her mother fell often and feared she could no longer live alone, but was terrified of going into a nursing home. Linda quit her job, sold her own house, and moved in to care for her mother. I admired Linda for her loyalty and sacrifice; however, I knew she was embarking on a lonely, difficult, probably often thankless mission. To brighten her days, I sent daily emails about life with our horses on our little Kansas farm. Linda loved horses, and I hoped my stories would provide a pleasant diversion. As time went on, she encouraged me to put my stories about life with our horses into a book. When I asked her *what* I could write, I received a large yellow envelope full of strips of paper—paragraphs cut from my emails. She wrote: "This is the beginning of your book."

I knew Linda for over 30 years. We met when she was Children's Librarian at the Prescott Public Library in Prescott, Arizona in 1979. She had Master's Degrees in English and Library Science. She loved and knew books. Our children, ages 3, 5, and 7, attended her *Story Hour* every Saturday. She recommended books perfect for their ages and interests, and ignited a lasting love for reading in each of them. Every week we came home with a stack of books. Linda became a friend of our family, and we invited her to dinner at our home. She had a sweet, soft voice and was very humble. One might think she was afraid of her own shadow, but she had strong beliefs, intelligence and determination. She demanded much of herself and of others. If I became discouraged with writing, she reprimanded me firmly: "Maybe the only failure for any of us is not using the gifts God gives to each person, no matter how small they seem. Keep writing and you'll be just where God wants you, watching intently for Him in each moment, listening to Him, and sharing His beautiful world as you see it with other people. It is hard work and lonely too, but your stories could help people in ways you won't even begin to understand. So many people who cannot love or be loved by others, can feel and cherish the love of an animal, even in a book or magazine, and be strengthened and healed by it."

Right after her mother died, Linda suffered a mild stroke. She lived five more years. She read my entire manuscript, made suggestions, and wanted to read it a second time after I edited it. In April 2011, Linda was diagnosed with nearly Stage IV ovarian cancer; she underwent surgery, and lived less than a month. After Linda died, I put my book away for a long time. The book seemed to refuse to be written.

Years passed. I worked on my manuscript occasionally and gradually achieved a form acceptable to myself, and I think, to Linda. I dedicate this book to Linda in gratitude for her friendship, and for her unrelenting encouragement through the writing process. I secondly dedicate it to my husband of over 46 years, Rod, the forever horseman, who brought me to contemplative living by building me a country home, and giving me horses. Through our years together, Rod gave me a closer glimpse of God. Bearing and raising children gave us our first glimpse of God. In our later years, through living with His horses, God gave us a deepening realization of His love, and an understanding of His expectations through life with these magnificent animals: humble submission to His Will in *all* circumstances.

This book is the celebration of a simple life with horses as friends--without ribbons and trophies. The stories span 15 years, from the purchase of our first horse in January 1997, through December 2012. Though usually a "date person" I removed the dates to make the book timeless. This book is the story of the 9 horses who graced our property, my transition from city to country woman, the major role horses played in this transition and in revealing God's plan for me through my simple, hidden life in the country.

--Mary Barbara McKay

Chapter 1

A Horse before a House

The way we bought our first horse would probably make the expert horse buyers either laugh themselves silly, or shake their heads in disbelief. Our lack of preparedness to "house" the animal after purchase would undoubtedly baffle nearly every horse owner, though there may be a few who may have done what we did, with or without our success.

This is how my life with horses began. After we bought forty acres of Kansas farm land to build a country home upon, but before we even started building our house, my husband, Rod, found an ad for a horse in the newspaper, The Kansas City Star Want Ads. The overture to horse ownership went like this: "Oh, Mary Barb! *'Eight month old, thoroughbred filly for $300!'*"

I did not realize this ad and his entreating exclamation would be the beginning of my life with horses, and the purchase would radically change my life forever. Ironically, on New Year's Day, the first day of a new year, I was about to begin a new life *again*. Since marrying shortly before my twenty-third birthday, change had become nearly a constant in my life. Now, however, through our first horse and the eight others who would follow, God was going to use these magnificent creatures to teach me about Himself, about my strengths and weaknesses, about my husband, about friendship, about life and death, and about what He wanted me to learn to apply through our simple, quiet life in the country.

Rod liked to read the newspaper *Want Ads*, precursor to *Craig's List* or *e-Bay* on the Internet, for tractors, airplanes, horses, auctions—almost anything. I never thought of combing the Want Ads unless I was in need of something specific, never just for fun.

Living and working in cities nearly all twenty-six years of our married life, we never even *thought* of buying a horse before. We definitely did not *need* a horse now. However, we did now own forty acres of bare farm land where, eventually, we hoped to have a home, and, once we had some sort of enclosure, the horse could be kept on our property. Rod would be the primary homebuilder, while I worked as a nurse. For the years leading up to the purchase of this property, we deposited one salary in the bank each month. We paid cash for our property, and continued to pay for our house and everything we bought for our country home the same way. We used the money from my job to pay our living expenses while Rod built our house.

As a boy, Rod helped his parents add on to their home, and he converted a garage into a third bedroom and utility room for the house we owned in Texas. However, he had never built a home from foundation to finished, live-in product. I think some of my family, and maybe some of his thought it would be *the house that Rod built*: never completed, a dream we abandoned. The house in itself was a huge project, and now we were thinking of adding the care of a horse before we even started construction. The horse was definitely a diversion, a "recalculation," a "taking the scenic route" instead of going straight to our destination.

Buying farm land and building our own home was the start of "a new life." In our years together we made many new starts. We grew together through our changes, and, with God's help, raised our three children into accomplished, capable adults. Now that all had left home, we, the proverbial "rolling stone," finally stopped rolling. It was time to gather moss and let it grow. The first bit of moss, it turned out, would be a horse, and our decision to buy one set a precedent: horses would have a major role in our lives hereafter.

Practically speaking, we now had *space* for a horse, but no physical "place" to keep her from wandering away. Our forty acres was not fenced, except on the east and north boundaries where our neighbor's one hundred-twenty acres bordered ours with a barbed wire fence that was over 60 years old. There were no barns, no sheds, no shelter of any kind on our property, and it was winter. Winters in Kansas are a much more serious event than winters in California, our home for the previous 11 years.

Owning a horse now seemed sort of crazy, but not as crazy as it would have seemed any other time in our life. Fear of "biting off more than we could chew" should have been the main red flag of caution, but it didn't seem to occur to either of us. We owned the land; that seemed to be the biggest requirement for horse ownership. Rod grew up with horses on his parents' ranch in eastern Oregon; he practically rode a horse before he could walk. He and his siblings rode horses every night after school to gentle them into good riding horses for friends of his father. He knew how to train horses and knew how to provide for them. I always loved horses, and wanted one of my own, but my father said I could not have one because we lived in a city. It was time consuming and expensive to drive me to a stable to take lessons, to care for the horse, and to feed and board the horse year round. Maybe he was afraid I'd lose interest, as children often do.

I had no idea all this purchase would involve and demand. However, Rod frequently quoted his father's saying: "If you *wait until you can afford to have kids*, then you will never have them." Using the same *if-then* logic, I thought, *if* we waited until everything was "perfect" for buying a horse, *then* we might never buy one. Life is never perfect this side of heaven. We have to take chances: enjoy the good times, learn from the bad, and trust God to take care of us in every situation. To me, a horse seemed to be part of "the good," and God would take care of the rest.

Rod wanted to look at the horse before someone else bought her, but he also wanted to go to a building materials auction. I knew nothing about building materials or auctions, but I *could* at least *look at* a horse. Thus, the job of *inspector* fell to *me*. Truthfully, I felt poorly equipped to make this decision, though I loved horses. Rod was the one raised on a ranch; he grew up with horses, and his father, an expert horseman himself, said Rod had a "good sense" about horses.

We have a photo of Rod, less than six months old, sitting on a horse-- actually held there by his father who ducked behind the obliging animal. Several months later, the same "Baby Roddy" once crawled out to a horse his father was training and pulled himself by the horse's leg. It was the first time he ever hoisted himself up to a standing position. His mother and father both held their breath as they watched their upright firstborn successfully cling to such a dubious support. The untrained horse stood completely still; he seemed to understand there was a child at his feet. He patiently waited until little Roddy let himself down and crawled away. I always hoped Rod's parents rewarded that gentle equine with praise, pets and a bucket of grain. Yes, Rod definitely had almost inborn

3

horse sense coupled with much experience. He seemed to instinctively know how to understand and be one with the horse.

Sending me to look at the filly seemed to be an example of sending a city girl to do a country boy's job. It was something often, though unintentionally, repeated as I was initiated into country life. For sure, I thought, Rod could do this better than I!

Baby Roddy held on horse by his father

Readily I agreed to take our daughter, Veronica, a senior in college who was still home for Christmas vacation, with me to look at the filly. Veronica, nearly finished with her studies, double majoring in physics and English, was very logical and intelligent. She was the perfect person to accompany me. She would keep me from making

4

an impulsive, stupid decision. Rod gave us some pointers on horse conformation and health, and we left to answer the advertisement.

When we called on the ad, we learned a couple in Missouri had purchased the filly from a friend who bought her at an auction. The little horse had been separated from her mother to be saved from slaughter. The buyer called the filly "Star" because of the small, faint triangular white star on her forehead. She explained Star was a full thoroughbred; she had papers and could be registered with The Jockey Club. The owner said she had received several calls, but so far no one had come to look at the little horse.

Rod admired thoroughbreds for their intelligence and beauty; his father bought a former thoroughbred racehorse stallion, Foxy Beau, to improve his ranch horse stock. Rod loved riding Foxy. I remember seeing him ride and work him the summer we met. They actually seemed to talk to one another as I watched them from the other side of the arena fence. My husband's affinity for the breed, finally owning a piece of land, and the reasonable price were all factors that made us believe *we really could do this*. Three hundred dollars for the happiness of taking her home seemed like a good deal.

Veronica and I circled into the couple's home on their gravel driveway and immediately we could see the bedraggled bay filly in her furry winter coat standing alone in a corral; the couple's other horses were across the fence. Little Star looked lonely, but she walked right up to us as if greeting us. Her instant friendliness settled the question.

Not having the gift of dickering, I quickly wrote a check for the asking price, and said we'd be back with a trailer to pick her up as soon as possible. Veronica and I then drove into Kansas City and had a celebratory lunch together. I was so excited about our new horse I couldn't stop talking about her. I was like an exultant child. I remember telling her over and over that our new little horse was *beautiful*. Almost every little horse is beautiful to me; and *this* one was particularly so because now she was ours.

Veronica rationally said, "No, Mom. She is more like the little ugly duckling who will become a beautiful swan. She is not beautiful, but she will be." Veronica suggested a new name too: "You should call her 'Isolde' for the story of Tristan and Isolde;

5

because Isolde was dark, and beautiful." The lovely name seemed to suit our new addition. *Isolde* it was.

When I look back now at pictures of our first little filly standing alone in her furry winter coat, having survived separation from her mother at an auction yard, and having already gone through three owners, I know Veronica was right. Isolde was not pretty then, and she was probably not worth $300. She was probably not the best choice for us. For anyone with any sense of the practical and prudent, this was not the "right" time for us to buy a horse, especially such a young one. On the surface it made no sense. We should not be here: we had no trailer, no shelter, and no fence. We had nothing except the land on which to keep her, a man with exceptional horse-sense (Rod), and the desire to have her. We were daring to take a risk on a diversion in a new life that had really not even started; we were jumping far ahead of ourselves and off course. Perhaps it was another example of "going-off -half-cocked" on another "wild goose chase." Heaven knows we chased a lot of wild geese in our life together.

In our defense, I can only say that I had the intuition this little horse would somehow change our lives forever. Looking back on the purchase of our very first horse, I believe it was a blessing, not a mistake. We "made it" because of, or in spite of, this little mare. The world did not end, we did not *lose everything*, and this little horse made a profound difference for the good in both our lives. She became a beautiful, joyful departure from our work; she gave us profound insights into God's amazing creation, into ourselves, and into life itself. God gives us what is best for us, even if we do not recognize it at the time, or even ever in our lifetime. God's path is frequently a way that remolds and reshapes our lives and our reason for living to bring us closer to His design for us. "Yet, O Lord, you are our Father; we are the clay, and you are our potter; we are the work of your hand." (Isaiah 64:8) I think God put the ad for Isolde in the paper that New Year's Day and knew we needed *this* horse in our lives in Kansas right then, not at some later time. Hopefully she would say the same, if she could speak. Our daughter's prophecy eventually came true, too; our unattractive rescued filly really did become beautiful.

On the tenth of January Rod and Veronica set out to get our new filly. However, when they went to the rental agency to pick up the trailer, the man behind the desk told them it was frozen to the ground and could not be moved. *Frozen to the ground!* Winter in the Midwest is a stark, cold reality: ice storms, frozen ground and machinery, blowing snow, huge drifts and low temperatures are the norm. We definitely *were not* in California anymore!

Not to be deterred, Rod and Veronica decided to go to the farm without the trailer just to visit our new filly. As soon as Rod entered the pen, the little horse walked right up to him. That was the beginning of a lasting partnership: Rod and Isolde. Veronica again predicted truly: "She'll always be Dad's horse!"

In later years when Rod could walk up to Isolde anywhere and anytime and pick up her feet; or when he could always get her to trot beside him when he put her in a halter and lead rope and began to jog, he would smile and say: "We go a long way back."

Before he and Veronica left the farm without her that day, Rod helped put our little filly between some barns for wind protection; it was zero degrees with a hard north wind blowing.

Finally, on January 14th Rod and I rented a trailer and drove to pick up our Isolde. Rod constructed a sixty-foot round pen using metal cattle panels 48 inches high with welded four-inch squares, and set it up near the trees at the northwest corner of our property to give her a windbreak. He placed our auction-purchased farm machinery outside the pen on the north side to help protect her from the strong winter north winds. This was all the protection we could offer our new little horse. It was a far cry from the elaborate stables some thoroughbreds are privileged to call home. However, Rod's family never kept their horses in barns or stalls, and the eastern Oregon winters of his childhood were *not* mild.

Positioning the truck and trailer in the snow, and loading our new horse, proved nothing short of an ordeal. I knew nothing, then, of the natural claustrophobic nature of horses. I expected it might be difficult to coax a young horse into the trailer, but never did I dream it would take several hours of falls, cuts, food bribes, and many failed attempts. None of us knew how to quickly and kindly encourage this green little horse into the trailer. God finally answered our silent prayers and persuaded our new little filly to get into the frightening box. No one became angry or impatient; we were only sad that she felt such fear. At the end, we were all very tired, including little Isolde. We had her aboard at last.

We traveled the slippery sixty miles back to our property with our little cargo safe and snug. Isolde rode quietly. I felt sorry for her being alone, away from her mother, and in a small pen on our property. Our shaggy, fuzzy little horse looked so sad and forlorn there. Isolde was eight months old and we were her fourth set of owners.

Our elderly neighbor on the farm to the north offered his shed. I wanted to take him up on his offer, and thought Isolde would too. Rod, never wanting to trouble anyone, declined. Old Edmund, who sometimes told us stories of his eight work horses in terrible winters, added that he thought Isolde would be all right even not being in his shed. God knew what horses would have to endure in some winter climates, and designed their bodies to withstand very cold temperatures. The next morning it was a frigid, windy nine degrees; Isolde was covered with ice when Rod came to care for her. All that winter we made certain to keep plenty of hay in front of her at all times so she could eat and maintain a safe body temperature. Rod told me the process of digestion generated warmth in ruminant animals, and thus it was critically important to provide Isolde with lots of hay. He built a manger to hold her hay and keep her from walking on it, and fed her faithfully every morning and evening. The attention and the good food increased her trust and her growth. We became her friends, and she ours.

Our rescued first filly, Isolde, at 8 months

Chapter 2
A New Name and a New Home

Our first winter of horse ownership was frigid and wet. In early February we had over 3-1/2 inches of rain one day, and the night time temperature plummeted below freezing as the rain continued. Wetness adds insult to cold; snow is one hindrance, freezing rain seems to me, of all winter's scourges, "the most unkindest cut of all." Perhaps Shakespeare used bad grammar to make his listeners take note of exactly how traitorous Brutus' stab to Caesar was *Julius Caesar (III,ii)*. I borrow this description because freezing rain is to me the worst insult winter weather can give to man or beast. The nearly ever-present North wind seems to increase winter's abuse, and coupled with freezing rain it is intolerable to be outside. Poor little Isolde was soaked, shivering, and covered with ice. Rod brought out a blanket he had in his truck to cover her. Unacquainted with blankets, she spooked a little at it at first, but quickly accepted it. She sensed Rod's intentions were honorable; she knew he meant her no harm. She seemed thankful for the comfort that blanket provided.

From the very beginning Isolde seemed to know anything we did we did because we were trying to help her. She trusted us completely. Two different mornings Rod found Isolde lying on the ground in her pen with her front feet stuck through the squares of the cattle panels. She did not struggle; she just waited for Rod to come to help her. Trust and intelligence, two most obvious character traits in our little horse, were evident especially when she needed our aid. Throughout all of January, February and into March Rod carried water to her twice a day. He cleaned her feet and curried her, and taught her to accept hobbles made of burlap sacks so he could work on her feet without getting kicked.

On weekends we liked to walk Isolde with a halter and lead rope along the waterway at the north end of our property. She seemed to look forward to these little jaunts into the wide world outside her pen. I often thought that pen, though it did provide protection, must seem like a prison, but she never tried to escape it. She accepted her life with us and seemed to appreciate the care we provided, and, even at her young age, simply accepted the winter hardships we all encountered as a normal part of life.

Our new little horse taught us how we should be with the things God puts in our path in life—accepting, depending on Him to provide and take care of us. She amazed us both by being completely calm and unafraid when Rod drove the tractor into her pen to scrape out manure and old hay. The first time we prepared ourselves for snorting, bolting, rearing, or kicking, but it never happened. It was as if she knew the tractor was not brought in to harm her, but to help her. She trusted us fully.

In addition to caring for our new little horse, Rod was busy planning our house, preparing the foundation, and laying pipe for the sewage lagoon. The year before we bought Isolde, our first year in Kansas, Rod went to farm machinery auctions and purchased used equipment so he could plant and harvest soybeans. The first year he re-cooped the money spent on machinery in the sale of the beans. Some of the machinery, especially the tractor and front-end loader, he also used in building our house. After the second bean harvest we began growing our own hay to feed our horses instead of raising soybeans and buying hay.

I worked as a nurse for the home health care unit of a near-by hospital. My job was to help newly discharged patients adjust to life at home after surgery or a serious illness. Due to my work hours and to the house we rented being seven miles from our property, I did not get to see Isolde every day. Rod was the one who really knew her; he was around her daily and they naturally formed a special friendship which neither of them would ever fail to remember.

In mid-April, Rod finished fencing five acres on the southwest corner of our forty- acre plot. To me his accomplishment was a work of art: it was a giant, awesome sculpture. I *had* to take pictures of it. I paint and draw, but I could never create anything as magnificent as Rod's fence. He used posts, wire and the craftsmanship he learned from his father to make a splendid enclosure for our little horse. It was thing of beauty, precision, detail, practicality, and hard work. Rod did not yet have a post-hole digger for his tractor, so he dug each hole with a tool that looks like two shovels facing each other. It

11

was an arduous job alone. The fence's perfect straightness in spite of its immensity was amazing and impressive.

Later, when he was laying the individual pieces of ceramic tile for the floor of our home, he again showed his affinity for perfection and artistry. If all the pieces were not flawlessly laid, he was disappointed, and apologetically showed me the ones with defects. To me his mistakes were nearly imperceptible and very minor compared to the huge task he was so carefully pursuing. Not shown them, I would never even notice them. For Rod, I think the task was somewhat similar to landing an airplane: maybe the landing was not completely perfect, but he did everything possible to make it as perfect as he could. It is the same with everything he does, and so it was with the fence for Isolde, and tile for our floor. Rod made the best enclosure he possibly could for our first and our much loved little horse.

That April we also learned the Jockey Club rejected our first name choice of "Isolde" for our filly, as well as our second choice, "City Girl." Rod joked the second name fit me, as well as our little filly: neither of us liked muddy feet. The Club did give us our third choice: "Little Dorit." Rod liked the character from Charles Dickens' novel Little Dorrit, and that became our horse's new name, with one "r."

Isolde definitely noticed the new moniker. She cocked her head the first time I called her *Dorit,* as if to ask if I was *really* talking to *her.* I understood completely. It is exactly the way I feel when someone calls me *Mary* instead of *Mary Barbara* because the double name was what my family called me, and the only name I knew until I started school. Being called *Mary* has been my scourge and pet peeve ever since. However, our little filly was now on at least her third completely different name, and she was only one year old.

Finally the day arrived for us to transfer Dorit from her small pen at the northwest end of our property to her new five acre fenced pasture in the southwest corner of our forty-acre plot. We prepared ourselves for the chance she would bolt, rear, kick, try to run away, or refuse to come with us. Again she did none of these; she sensed our intentions were honorable and thus she relaxed completely. She did act somewhat unsure about her footing on the gravel road at first, but in no time she was walking as surely as she did on her daily walks with us, her best friends. She never once spooked, snorted, or tried to escape.

I walked along beside her, holding her lead rope, with a beaming smile on my face. What a simple thing to bring so much joy! Walking this little horse down the gravel road was not complicated. Little Dorit trusted us, so she was peaceful. We were bringing her to a new, larger, nicer home and it made me smile to think of the gift we were about to give her. It was like the excited anticipation I felt when we led our children to the Christmas tree when they were small. I felt grateful we could give them gifts we knew they wanted, and so anxious to see their bright, surprised eyes and hear their excited exclamations. Rod and I both knew Little Dorit would love her new home, and we also knew she had no inkling he had been preparing it for her. Smiles come easily for me around horses, and they did this day. I felt as excited as a child again-- full of expectation and sheer delight. Rod was there with me, but he let *me* lead her. Dorit walked calmly along with her trusted friends.

As soon as we closed the gate and released her into the pasture she began looking around, as if she could not believe what she was seeing, or believe she was really free to explore this great new world. She was *thrilled*! She ran up and down the fence kicking and bucking, then began galloping along it with her tail up, always returning to us as if to make sure we didn't need to reattach the lead rope and take her back to that sixty-foot round pen where she lived since January. Three entire months in such a small enclosure would make a person feel as if the closet door had opened to reveal a whole huge, unexplored house! Our jubilant horse was feeling much the same. She was so proud, so happy, and so free. She began pulling up mouthfuls of grass, eating tree leaves, eating *anything* green she could find. After every short venture away she always returned to us as if she was thanking us for this new spacious home and for the liberty to move about at last. I was amazed a horse would show such excitement and gratitude. Who ever heard of a horse saying "thank you?" Dorit clearly was.

Years later when I was reminiscing about how happy and excited she behaved when we first put her in that five acre pasture, Rod said: "The way Dorit acted was exactly how I felt when I first came here and began preparing to build our house." He said he felt as though

13

someone had set him free after being "locked up in a city" so long. He appreciated the fresh smell of the air, the blue sky, the many brilliantly colored birds, the shades of green of the trees, the earth beneath his feet, he said he even appreciated and marveled at the brilliant colors on the bugs he encountered. It was all part of God's wonderful creation that can be missed, hidden, removed, or ignored in a city. Until then, I never realized he felt "locked up." We'd lived in metropolitan areas nearly all of the first twenty-five years we were married except for the three years we spent in a house we bought on an acre of land three miles south of Belton, Texas. Even there we had Interstate Highway 35 nearly on our doorstep, and the town of Belton a very short distance away from us on a paved road. Until now, city life was my whole experience, the only way of life I knew, but this was not true for Rod. Yet he never complained. Cities then seemed to be part of *what we had to do* to make a living. Now we lived in the country it was time for me to learn to accept and to enjoy the quiet, hidden life of country living, to count it as a blessing, and listen to what God was trying to teach me.

Once when we were visiting Rod's family, his father turned to me with a smile and pointed out how happy, relaxed and confident Rod was doing things about the ranch. He said: "You can take the *boy out of the country*, but you can't take the *country* out of the boy!" I didn't know whether my father-in-law was criticizing me for being the one to take *his son* out of the country, or was complimenting his son who slipped back into country life as if he never left it. Rod returned to it as easily and naturally as he rode a horse, because he learned and loved it in childhood. He would never fail to recognize the aromas of his mother's freshly baked bread wafting from their country kitchen window, or forget the scent of lilacs in the spring, or the sound of Canada Geese flying overhead. He would never disremember how to milk a cow, how to ride a horse, or how to drive a team of workhorses pulling a wagon, rake or plow. These were skills and memories deeply rooted in his soul. Country was home, and home was country for Rod. It was evident in the whole way he acted and even carried himself.

In my case, the reverse was true. Being transplanted to our little farm in Kansas was as unpleasant and as uncomfortable to me as city life was for Rod. It was not easy for me to adjust. It took time, a long time. I felt as if I were breaking in tight new school shoes after going

14

barefoot all summer. I was suddenly a "new kid" in a strange school in a foreign land, in a class of students who grew up with one another. To me, this new remote country life seemed intimidating and lonely; it definitely was a *culture shock*. Adjusting to life in the country was one of the most difficult transitions I ever made. Even now I could easily slip back into city life, but I *would* miss the horses.

So many life experiences are like this. A new life, every time it begins— one's own birth, starting school, starting a new job, marriage, the birth of a child—all take time and effort, some adjusting, some putting away things that are no longer needed, acquiring new behaviors and habits required for the change as St. Paul writes in 1 Corinthians 13:11. : "When I was a child, I spoke like a child, I thought like a child, I reasoned like a child; when I became a man, I gave up childish ways." Giving up, putting away habits formed over nearly 50 years took me much time.

Some things cannot, do not, change any more than fingerprints change; some parts of me will always be *citified*. Horses have made my transition to country life more pleasant. Furthermore, these beautiful animals have supplied many missing links in my life; past and present—links I did not even realize were missing until I lived among these excellent creatures.

Alfred Lord Tennyson wrote the poem *Ulysses,* which I first read in high school, and loved so much that I memorized some lines and often applied them to my life at various times:

I am part of all I have met;
Yet all experience is an arch wherethrough
Gleams that untraveled world whose margin fades
Forever and forever when I move.

Old age hath yet his honour and his toil.
Death closes all; but something ere the end,
Some work of noble note may yet be done…

Come, my friends,
'Tis not too late to seek a newer world.

Though much is taken, much abides; and though

15

We are not now that strength which in old days
Moved earth and heaven, that which we are, we are—
One equal temper of heroic hearts,
Made weak by time and fate, but strong in will
To strive, to seek, to find, and not to yield.

Much was taken—my whole lifestyle--but much did abide. I had the same spouse, the same home country, the same faith. I was and am part of all I have met. It was not too late to seek a newer, untraveled world—that was what we were doing here. Probably over half our lives were lived, but we had more life to live. We had heroic hearts to strive, seek and find and not yield to abandoning noble works before we really tried to achieve them. Death would close our lives on this earth, but there was more before the end, as Tennyson wrote, "some work of noble note" through the purchase of these 40 acres of farm ground and our first horse. God was the Architect, the Designer. Rod said: "God built this house." He meant that because so many things seemed to fall into place as he made plans for building it that he believed God was definitely in charge of every step of construction. The first 6 months we lived in the apartments near the hospital where I worked; Rod went to daily Mass before coming to work on our house. He listened to EWTN Catholic Radio via short wave radio while he worked and often told me about Mother Angelica's solid, wise, godly, sometimes witty, but always compassionate truthfulness to her callers. God definitely was in charge, and He worked not only for Rod but also on and for me, and, I believe, continues to quietly work on everyone who comes to our home, humans and animals alike. Our little farm is a place of peace, quiet, love, faith and hope. Our sole purpose in this earthly life is to get ourselves and as many others as we can to heaven, thus, I believe, all Rod's labor was a "work of noble note" under God's careful direction.

Many parts, many life experiences, have made my whole life, but the whole was *not whole*, not complete, until horses became part of it. My life, and my understanding of the purpose of life, is fuller now. I believe I am a more complete person, better able to serve God and others because I live among our good horses.

Dorit's life, like mine, continued to change as she lived with us. Shortly after putting Dorit in her new residence, Rod and I moved the cattle panels that had served as her home those first three months to the new pasture. Now the cattle panels became our round pen, an enclosed area where Rod could work with Dorit to teach her. It was April and she had shed her furry, shaggy winter coat and was now a sleek bay yearling. The once ugly duckling had turned into the predicted *beautiful swan*, and her outward good looks reflected her friendly nature.

We were her only companions; she craved our attention. She was always very interested in what we were doing. She followed us as we carried each panel, and stood beside us as we fastened the panels to posts and secured the new corral inside her pasture. This friendly curiosity was Dorit's trademark, but sometimes it got her into trouble.

A few years later, when she should have been wiser, Rod added a single electric wire to the second strand of smooth wire fence in her pasture because, in reaching over the fence to get grass outside, she was ruining his lovingly and arduously constructed straight fence. Someone appropriately said: "The grass is always greener on the other side of the fence," and Dorit believed it absolutely. Dorit, inspecting new electrified wire with her velvet black nose, was quickly "zapped" by it. She snorted and jumped back. Then, as if she *did not believe* she had *really* been "bitten" by that thing, she crept slowly up to the wire a second time, and touched the hot wire with her muzzle and was jolted a *second* time! Rod and I could not believe it. We laughed and laughed that she would dare try to touch the fence again. Once was enough for both of us to be zapped by an electric fence, but Dorit was like an incredulous, inquisitive child reaching for a stove burner a second time to see if it was *really* hot! She did not try a third time.

Whatever we did in later days, no matter how many horses we had, Dorit always had to be right beside us, smack in the middle of things. Whether we were unloading hay, putting up fence posts, painting the fence, or cutting wood, she was forever at our elbows, wedging herself between us and whatever job we had, as if she were checking that we were doing it right, and offering to help. She took things from our pockets, picked up things from the ground and shook them, rummaged through empty cans and buckets, pulled things off the pickup truck bed and even managed to get paint in her hair if we were painting a fence.

Never having had a horse before, I was very surprised by Dorit's all too friendly attachment and curiosity. She always made me laugh. "I *never knew* horses did *that!*" I found myself thinking or saying frequently. I had never had such a relationship with any animal, nor had I realized horses were so intelligent. The laughter spontaneously rose up from within me and fluttered into the air like bubbles from a child's pipe or wand. She was the first, but would definitely not be the only horse to release such joy from my heart. I quickly realized that horses have a seemingly magical ability to heighten my sense of newness and beauty in the world around me. They make life a new adventure and allow me to view each day afresh. I found myself approaching middle age—if I live to be a hundred-- with confidence, gratitude and laughter--all generated by a cute little bay horse.

We never know what is ahead. Our attitude toward things that happen, how we react, and what choices we make determine whether we advance toward fulfillment and happiness, or desolation and despair. Horses led me toward the positive, toward a greater appreciation for the beautiful earth God made just for us: the amazingly gorgeous world with its plants, trees, and animals—all of creation for us to see, to love, to enjoy, and to share. All animals, but especially the horses, offer me a precious and profoundly real glimpse of God. I have come to see in all of nature an imperfect likeness of God Who created everything as a gift for us to enjoy and to give Him glory as we strive to climb life's ladder toward heaven. I am continually amazed and humbled before His exquisite, amazing creation. St. Paul writes in Romans 1:20: "Ever since the creation of the world his invisible nature, namely, his eternal power and deity, has been clearly perceived in the things that have been made."

Isolde in cattle panel "prison"

Little Dorit: A sleek Bay yearling

Rod building fence

Finished straightness of posts

Chapter 3
The Perfect Equine Gift

Our youngest daughter, Veronica, graduated from college that May with a double major in Physics and English, and was bound for graduate school. Her very ambitious goal was to obtain a Master's Degree and a PhD in both areas of concentration. We asked her if she wanted a new computer, which we knew she sorely needed; or a horse, which she did not need, for a graduation gift. She replied she knew she needed a computer, but she would really like a horse. Thus began our search for the perfect equine gift.

By Graduation Day we still had not found the best horse for her, though we had done some looking. When Rod gives a gift, he looks at all possibilities, and then makes his choice. He knows what he wants, and getting it is no simple task. As noted before, Rod is a perfectionist in everything, whether it is landing an airplane, laying a ceramic tile floor, or buying a horse. The perfect horse in this case would be the *best* horse we could afford for Veronica's gift.

Veronica spent the last week of July with us before starting graduate school. After we took her to the airport, we traveled to northern Missouri to look at a four-month-old thoroughbred colt we had just found advertised in the same newspaper that brought us Little Dorit. He was the great-great-great grandson of Seattle Slew, the 1977 Triple Crown winner. This tall, dark bay colt with a small round white star like a pinwheel on his forehead had large, round, gentle, alert eyes, and baby-soft hair. He was the most beautiful of all the horses we saw in months of searching. There was something regal about him, and his dam and sire. He was indeed the perfect gift for Veronica. He was called *Comet* because he was born March 22 that year, about the time Haley's Comet appeared.

Comet was owned by a genuine, friendly couple about Rod's and my age, we guessed, Linda and Jim, may both their beautiful souls rest in peace. We were amazed and impressed that their horses all "hung around" the barn as the four of us talked. They seemed like part of the family, at ease with their people and completely relaxed and unafraid of us as friends of their owners.

Rod liked Comet; he also liked his dam, sire, and older brother. Often finding it hard to choose between two, I wanted to buy both Comet and his yearling brother, but that did not happen. We wrote out a check for $800 for Comet alone, and made a date to return with another rented trailer to bring him to our home on August 4th.

Since it was August instead of January, no hazards of snow and ice faced us, but we still had the hazard of loading another green horse. Just like our little filly, Comet did not want to load into the trailer. Even when his dam was led into the trailer first, the little colt refused to load. Beside the fact he had never been in one, the partition in the center of the trailer made him balk. It was supposedly a "two horse" trailer, though I had my doubts whether even two foals, let alone two adult horses, could fit inside comfortably, or at all. Unfortunately, Rod and I had no opportunity to take a course in trailer loading since our experience with Dorit. Poor Comet was just afraid, and he did not want to leave his family and home. Once again it took several hours to load our new little colt. Finally, with Comet loaded safely and securely, we left Jim and Linda's driveway, and turned southwest. Comet nickered, and we heard his dam answer him. I thought his mother seemed to be calling: "Good-bye, baby son, good-bye. Good luck! I will miss you. Good-bye." Unless I was deaf, or had a heart of stone, I could not deny the truth of animal emotions at that moment. Even though I had never seen a colt parted from his mother, I knew he deeply felt the separation. He was only 4 months old. I thought: "Poor little guy! Poor mother! God protect our little horse! God get us all home safely."

Loading Comet had taken so long that it was nearing 9 o'clock and almost dark when we finally pulled the truck up to the gate of Dorit's pasture. No one had to tell *her* a thing. She could sense something exciting was about to happen! No doubt, she could smell another horse. Rod put a halter on her, and led her into the round pen inside her pasture; totally trusting, though still showing us that she was very interested in what was in the trailer, she went with him. Then he led Comet from the trailer into the same pen, and, as planned, I led Dorit out into her pasture again. We had decided it was best to leave the little newcomer there overnight rather than let him roam the unfamiliar, hilly pasture in the dark.

I knew little Comet would have a protector that night. As we left to return to our rented house in town, Dorit was standing alongside the pen right next to him. Nothing was going to pry her away from her new little friend. She was ecstatic to have another horse, and, I imagined that Comet, having just left his mother for the first time, found Dorit's presence and attention reassuring, even comforting in the darkness in that strange new place.

As the next morning dawned, Rod and I couldn't get to our property fast enough. It was barely light when our little car approached from the west. We could see the pen before we turned north on to our road: it was *empty*! No panels were knocked over. There was simply no horse in the pen. My heart sank. Our horse for Veronica was gone! As we drove the car on the grass to park it off the road we saw two horses standing side by side on the hill on the east side of the fenced pasture. What a perfect picture! Dorit and Comet were beautifully silhouetted against the rising sun. Comet, four months old, had jumped the 4- ½ foot high cattle panel fence to be with his new friend. Miraculously, he did not have a single scratch. We were astonished at our new little colt's ability, agility, and determination.

That afternoon Jim called to ask how Comet was getting along. His concern and kindness in telephoning impressed us both; he didn't just care about the money he made in selling his colt, he wanted his horse to be happy. We knew we bought a good horse from good people. When we told him about Comet's jump over the cattle panels, he told us that it must be in his genes: Comet's mother was a natural jumper.

We called Veronica to tell her about her horse that same morning. Of course, we had to brag to her about this four-month old wonder who jumped the cattle panels to be with Dorit, and did not get a scratch. Veronica hoped to learn to jump, and wondered if Comet's jumping ability might be an inherited gift. She wanted us to tell her all about "her baby," and wanted us to send pictures. This was before we had a digital camera, let alone a cell phone with a camera—before instant gratification---but we all survived. Comet's jumping ability survived too: four years later, renamed "Pascal," much larger and wearing a blanket, jumped a fence over five feet high from an uphill stance just to be with his friends at the barn near Veronica's school.

Dorit showered affection and attention on Comet, and he adopted her as a mother replacement; perhaps the new colt supplied the companionship she had lost when separated from her own mother too. She was definitely grateful to have another horse to share her pasture and her life. Never again did we see a solitary Dorit in the northeast corner of the pasture, head hanging in utter desolation. However, as much as Dorit loved Comet, she was not above stealing his food! He was smaller and ate more slowly. This was my introduction to the pecking order among horses; their hierarchy was no fable, but a clear reality. The bigger horse got the larger share unless someone intervened. We learned quickly that we had to feed one horse inside the pen, and one outside, to ensure Comet got *all* his grain. Later, when he was larger, the tables turned.

Pencil drawing of Dorit and Comet, first morning

Dorit with new friend, Comet

Now we were owners of two horses, and though I was no longer young, having horses made me, in some ways, *feel* young—maybe because I had wanted a horse as a child, maybe because they restored a sense of wonder and amazement I sort of "put away" as I became an adult. The horses inspired awe in me as I observed their intelligence, their trust, their loyalty, their humility, their desire to please. They were "just *such good animals*" Rod and I told each other often. Having a horse seemed to be the realization of a dream and a prayer, though it happened much later in life than I ever hoped or imagined. I had not outgrown my love for horses though by the time we could buy Isolde, I had nearly forgotten the dream of having my own horse. Like other dreams of my childhood, it faded, as it was gradually replaced by the realization it would probably never come true. As I grew older and faced very real obligations, my horse dream was folded up like the satin comforter I once *had to have* in order to sleep. I grew to live without it. Sometimes we come to accept there are just some things we want, but we cannot have.

Children always have hope; sometimes as adults we forget to have this precious virtue. Christ tells us to become like children, to have the simplicity and trust children have. Our horses' genuine simplicity and trust were obvious and beautiful.

As I began to know our horses, I found they gave me peace in troubled times, and joy in quiet times. They awakened in me a greater appreciation of the creative power of God, and His great gift in giving us not only the horse, but the entire grand world around us and every day in it. I thought back to the windy, sunny January day when we were brand new to Kansas, the year before we found Dorit. Rod and I stood together on our empty forty acres; we had not yet started building, but it was *our* land. He stood with his arm about my shoulder, and I with my arm around his waist. We heard the call of geese overhead, and looked up to see a "V" of Canada Geese majestically flying high above us to the southeast. They looked strong and free. We could hear the powerful, muscular whooshing sound of their wings as their call echoed in the distant cloudless blue sky. Apart from the sound of God's geese, it was utterly silent. Rod looked up, smiled, and exclaimed in awe: "Praise God!" It almost seemed as though God was calling us through His geese, and the geese were singing His praise. It was one of those moments when one feels very close to the Creator through the magnificence and wonder of His creation. Rod told me he remembered The Canada Geese flying over his home in Oregon. He remembered seeing them high in the sky, and hearing their far-off call. It seemed we were somehow united to that long ago, wonder-filled moment as we started a new life on our own piece of land in the country.

These days were a beginning of awakening into a new life: a life of appreciation for simple, holy beauties given us by God to love, to enjoy, and to use as a ladder to grow closer to Him. God made man master over all the rest of creation, not to reduce all the rest of creation to fearful submission, but for the animals and plants, the entire natural world to lift us up closer to Him. That first January when we saw the geese, we didn't yet have a horse, but God was preparing us. He was softly whispering to us, telling us to get ready. I did not know then God would soon begin to use our love for horses to begin to help us understand how to give Him greater glory and, little by little, to change our lives. The horses, and all the animals, I believe, are God's gifts to teach us how He wants us to be: accepting of and grateful for the life He gives us, using it the best we can. Horses teach me to strive for perfection; they teach me acceptance and humility, the acknowledgement of the truth. My spiritual journey with them began to unfold through these years, is still unfolding.

There was also something almost spiritual in the name selected for our newest horse. When we needed to send in the registration papers to the Jockey Club for Comet, Veronica chose the name *Pascal's Wager.* We thought it was a brilliant name especially for a thoroughbred horse. The explanation of the name is simple. The French mathematician and philosopher, Blaise Pascal, "gambled" that God exists because it is *the best bet.* He believed *if* we live our lives as if there *is* a God and a heaven, and we die and find the belief true, we have gained eternal life *in the good place.* Thus, we win. However, if we live a full, moral, upstanding life, and there is neither God nor heaven, we still have *really not* lost anything since we have the satisfaction of knowing we lived the best life we could. *Thus, we still win.* One should definitely hedge his bets when gambling with his eternal future; a hundred million years is less than the first second of eternity! It is indeed better to spend it in heaven!

The Jockey Club *hedged their bets* and accepted Veronica's first choice, *Pascal's Wager,* for the name of this great-great-great-grandson of Seattle Slew. Actually, there was no hedging at all; no other horse owner wanted that name. So, *Comet* became *Pascal,* but Rod and I continued to call him *Comet* for a time rather than make the abrupt name change we did with Dorit.

Pascal was playful in a gentle sort of way. He reminded me a lot of our son, Paul, when he was growing up, and of my husband, Rod—both of them big teases! I had to be prepared to laugh or I might either scream or cry. I realized now that I had to be prepared to laugh with a young horse, too. I've heard laughter is good for the soul, and Rod's father used to say, "Laughing is good for the belly." It disperses frustration, eases tension, and in general makes life easier. Looking back, I know I should have laughed more as a mother, as a wife, as a girl. Many people told me I took life *too seriously,* that I was *too intense,* and I know now that sometimes they were perhaps right. I believed I *should* take life seriously since it was the only one I had. I thought I better try to do my best. Now I know that doing my best is often enhanced and facilitated by laughter. With Pascal's antics I could just naturally burst out laughing and not worry about modeling "proper" behavior. He reminded me so much of Paul, yet he was a horse, not my son. I had also "mellowed out," as I aged.

Pascal was a real comedian. Once he took a big gulp of water, held it in his mouth until his head was over mine, and then let it run out on my head—something a grade schoolboy at a water fountain might do to another kid. Sometimes Pascal would open his mouth wide and hold his teeth and open mouth gently against my cap pretending he was going to bite me, but he never did. One day he found a Mountain Dew bottle in the pasture; in curiosity, he picked it up, and held it in his mouth in a way that looked as if he were drinking it.

Pascal was a kind horse too, if horses can be called kind. Our elderly neighbor had a black and white cat that liked to spend a lot of time at our place, and we liked her because she was friendly and kept the mice away from our house construction. She sometimes brought her freshly killed vermin right into the middle of our house project for our approval, or perhaps in an attempt to offer to share it with us. One morning, Rod found "Kitty" dead, lying in the dewy grass inside the pasture fence. While he was standing there looking at her, Pascal came up and sniffed her. Then he gently picked her up as if to try to make her stand up. Then he set her down again on the grass as if he hoped she would stand up alive again. He seemed sorrowful at her ended life, just as we were.

When we caught Pascal at feeding time, and led him, he liked to rest his nose against our backs, gently, just to let us know he was there, following closely behind. It was simply a friendly gesture; he never nipped or pushed at us. One cold morning I was breaking ice on the horse pond; I felt a gentle tug at my coat's shoulder. I turned to find Pascal there beside me. He just wanted to let me know he was with me. He patiently waited, and when I finished breaking the ice, he took a drink. He just gently wanted me to know he was there; he just wanted to greet me in his own special way. The first time Pascal saw Rod in his winter coat and matching fake fur trimmed hood, he had to gently grab the fake fur with his teeth—perhaps to tease, perhaps to test it and make sure it was not alive and able to harm him, perhaps to check and see if it was edible, or perhaps just to say:

"Good morning! I've never seen you wear *this* before!" Rod and I will always remember the gentle kindness of this very beautiful horse who later was fittingly nicknamed "*Buddy.*"

At times during his first winter with us, I thought Pascal was very lazy and maybe we should have named him "Ferdinand" after the bull in the children's story <u>Ferdinand the Bull</u> by Munro Leaf. Walt Disney made a wonderful cartoon of this story. This young bull loved to sit in the shade under the trees and smell the flowers until a bee stung him and made him run and bang furiously about the pasture. A passerby saw the fighting-mad bull crashing ferociously about, and thought he would be a fierce bull for the bullring. Once in the arena, gentle Ferdinand only wanted to smell the flowers. Pascal didn't smell flowers, but, I thought, he needed that bee to sting him to make him move! Some Sundays, just for fun, Rod and I took Dorit and Pascal for "walks" down the gravel road near our property. There was no traffic on Sunday afternoon, and it gave us a chance to get to know the horses, give them a change of scene and a bit of exercise. It seemed almost as if they were our huge pet dogs and we were taking them out for a jaunt. Rod took Dorit in her halter and lead rope, and I followed with Pascal. As I watched Rod and Dorit from behind, it appeared as if Rod looked at her and asked:

"Are you ready, Dorit?"

Doirt, immediately turned her head toward him. I could see their two profiles as they faced each other. She seemed to answer in her turn:

"Ready, Rod!"

"Okay, *let's GO!*" Rod seemed to tell her. Then off the two would dash down the road. They looked like two friends out for a sprint in gym class, or like teammates practicing their cross-country running. They both loved these friendly races together. If Rod begins jogging, Dorit picks up her trot beside him.

With Pascal at the end of my lead rope there was no such communication! He would not run a race, let alone start one. He seemed *very* far removed from his illustrious ancestor, Seattle Slew, as he planted his feet like huge roots and absolutely refused to budge. I needed a heavy-duty fishing pole with a huge bucket of grain or a bunch of carrots attached to the end of the line. I had no clue what to do to make him move forward or backward. Simple pulling, on the lead rope did *not* work. Usually Rod and Dorit ended up coming back to meet us, and once we turned around for home Pascal would slowly begin to move.

Veronica somewhat eased my frustration with my walking companion. She read the book we had given her about Seattle Slew and assured me that the 1977 Triple Crown champion had Pascal's traits—apparent laziness and a love for eating--maybe Pascal *was not so far removed* from his famous ancestor after all. Looking back, at those fun, simple times we experienced when we first began to live with horses, I felt peace and freshness, a zest and exuberance that I lost or "put away" after childhood. It was good to have a sort of second chance to live as effortlessly as a child and just enjoy the moment without concern about what someone might think, fear of running out of time, or of doing something wrong. Our horses would give these gifts of peace, freshness, friendship and trust to us in many ways as our lives with them continued, and we knew them more, and they knew us more.

Rod and Dorit out for a friendly jog

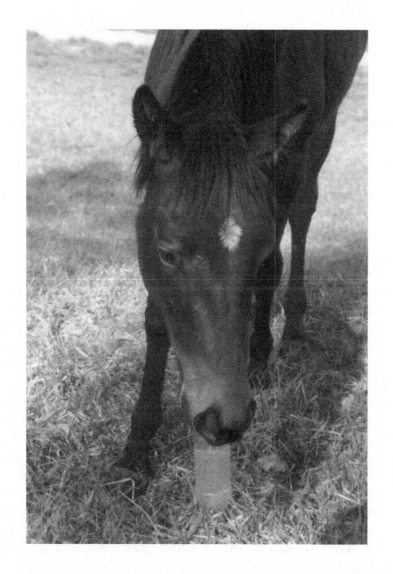

Pascal testing a Mountain Dew bottle

Chapter 4
Two Horses and a Shed

The first winter we had two horses, we worked constantly on our new little farm and country home. In between putting up the frame and roof on our house, and harvesting our soybean crop, making our dinner in the evenings after he returned to our rented house "in town," Rod also made time to build a run-in shed, a three-sided metal building, for the horses. Half of it was to serve for hay storage, and the other half as protection from snow, rain, and the hot sun for Dorit and Pascal. He even thoughtfully insulated their shed roof.

When Rod took a break from his shed building to eat his lunch, Pascal came to the window of the pick-up truck hoping for a handout: a piece of bread, or a carrot. Dorit was right beside him; she was especially fond of pieces of our homemade whole wheat rolls, but settled for carrots, or whatever she could get. During construction, our two horses followed Rod like building inspectors and generally got in his way: they pawed at the lumber, and chewed up whatever they could get their teeth on, managed to get their legs tangled in the measuring tape, then stepped on it and chewed it. They were very curious about the cement bags, and loved to shake them out when they were empty—sending dust everywhere. To make Rod's job even more difficult, they sometimes managed to tip over the buckets of water for mixing the cement for setting the shed posts. Dorit and Pascal usually left him alone for at least a little while, probably to wander off to nibble grass, but Rod said they returned every hour or so to check on his progress and to create more mischief. I have heard that curiosity is the opposite of fear in a horse. If that is true, our horses are definitely not afraid. They were terribly interested in everything we did, and in everything we had.

One day, shortly after the shed was completed, I was snapping pictures of the horses. I thought they were very photogenic, and I was always trying to get that once-in-a-lifetime photograph I could enlarge and frame, or use for a painting. When we finished playing with the horses and went home to our rented house "in town" for the night, I forgot my camera was hanging on a nail on the shed wall. Dorit and Pascal found it, and after examining it to be sure it would not harm them, they must have played with it—shaking and dragging it around. When Rod found it the next morning in the shed, it was covered with Kansas dust and dirt, and looked as if it had been the ball in a game. Rod later took it apart and tried to fix it for me, but it was never quite the same. Though it still took exceptionally sharp outdoor pictures, it never accepted a flash again, and the picture counter no longer functioned, though the film could be advanced.

That camera had been our first "big investment." We bought it when Paul was about a year old. After researching carefully which single lens reflex camera to buy, we saved for a long time and waited for a good sale to purchase it. We were *so proud* of our Minolta SRT 101. It was our prized possession. It had been our "friend" for over twenty-five years, and had given us hundreds of captured memories, and much, much pleasure. Even though I still used it afterwards for outdoor shots of the horses, and tried to keep mental note of how many pictures I had taken, I missed it terribly for other occasions. I took fewer pictures. At our daughter Catherine's wedding the following spring, everyone wondered why "Mom," the family photographer, didn't take as many snapshots? The reason was: *she* didn't have *her* camera.

I was becoming aware of some of the drawbacks of horse curiosity, and also of the need for me to try to always be one step ahead of them. Something I have yet to master. My forgetfulness opened the door to *too* great a temptation for Pascal and Dorit to resist. They had no idea they were doing anything they should not. In their minds they were just providing a secure environment for themselves—making sure the new object would not harm them. In spite of all their antics, Rod and I could always enjoy the horses' company—even if they nearly destroyed our treasures.

After spending his day working on our house, Rod rode each of the horses in the sixty-foot round corral that had been Dorit's first "home pen." He said each horse knew when it was his or her turn, and as soon as he finished with one, the other was at the gate waiting. We did not know whether they really liked and looked forward to being ridden, but they were used to the drill, and, no doubt, liked the attention. However, Rod said Dorit usually kept her ears back, a sign of anger or protest in a horse, the whole time he worked with her. Horses thrive on routine. It offers security. Over and over Rod and I commented to each other the horses seemed like images of the little children Christ told us to become in order to enter heaven: "Whoever humbles himself like this child, he is the greatest in the kingdom of heaven." (Matthew 18:4) Their humble, gentle acceptance of their lot in life, and their genuine simplicity was an example for us who at times can be impatient, angry, proud, or false. The horses are always themselves; they are always honest. Rod's father said: "You can't fool dogs and you can't fool little kids." I would add horses to the list of those who are not fooled. Our horses always seem to know exactly what we are about and what our mood is. As someone, whose name I never learned, observed: "God certainly outdid Himself when he created the horse."

Each night over dinner Rod would tell me not only what Mother Angelica said, but also about his adventures with the horses that day. I loved to listen. The horses removed our solitary existence; they gave us friendship and companionship, and brightened our lives. Since our children were grown and lived far away, the horses gave us a focus other than ourselves, and increased our appreciation for God's gift of His magnificent creation, particularly these beautiful animals.

One Saturday Rod asked me if I wanted to go alone to do our night care for the horses. It would be the first time he had not accompanied me. I felt I was entrusted with an *important job,* even though all I was doing was feeding our two friendly horses.

Dorit and Pascal met me at the gate when I drove up and parked the car. How flattering to have two such huge, exquisite animals so glad to see me! Just as I approached their gate Rod called me on the ham radio in the car. At the sound of his voice Dorit began peering inside to see if Rod was going to come out of the open car door. In my inexperience with horses, I thought she was terribly smart to recognize his voice, and felt a bit sad for her disappointment in not finding her buddy there.

Feeding the two horses alone was easy; I just did what Rod and I always did together. They knew the routine as well as I did. There was nothing complicated to complete, but doing it *all by myself* was thrilling to me, just as walking Dorit down the road to her new pasture was. The key was the horses knew and trusted me.

I tied each one in place; fed each one grain, and, while they munched, I curried and removed burs. I pet them and talked to them, before finally turning them loose in the pasture. Time spent was always peaceful and comfortable with the horses—like being with my family in a warm house on a snowy night with a cozy crackling fire in the fireplace, or like hearing the rain on the roof from safe inside a dry barn, or being with a friend I know so well we don't need to speak because we are at ease with silence. That sense of quiet understanding seemed ever present with the horses.

I think a horse contentedly munching hay makes one of the most relaxing, comforting sounds I have ever experienced. It continues to be one of the most soothing sounds and sights for me, and I know others have thought the same. I am mesmerized by it—just as I am when I stare at a campfire, or watch the tide advance and retreat on the shore. I love to watch them eat their hay. I lose all sense of time with the horses, which is good for them because they do not keep time, and enjoy all I give them. It is good for me because it lets me slow down, breathe, and think. They do not mind what I look like, they are not concerned with how much money I make, what kind of house I live in, where I went to school, or anything else extra about me. Horses know I am there with them and, know, because I am there, I care about them. They know I give them my best; in return they give me their best.

Mary Barbara with Pascal (L) and Dorit (R)

Beginning horse shed construction

Finished horse shed

Chapter 5
Completely Smitten

Pascal and Dorit were inseparable. As Dorit passed her second birthday, March 13th, and Pascal passed his first, March 22nd, the hormones began to awaken in both of them. Dorit and Pascal actually looked at each other with "moon-eyes," which was my mother's description of the coy way junior high school girls and guys looked at each other when they thought they were really "smitten" with one another. It was an apt description to apply to Dorit and Pascal. They playfully chewed one another's manes, rubbed one another with muzzle and nose, made contented sounds, and danced around together in preparation for breeding. Dorit almost batted her eyelashes at Pascal, and Pascal gazed back completely infatuated. Barely one year old, Pascal already had his illustrious ancestor's innate sense about when a mare is in season. Though Dorit certainly was crystal clear in her intentions, Pascal, for sure, could pick her out a mile away. It was spring, and this was how the horses instinctively continued their bloodlines.

Rod and I hoped to get a foal before we gelded Pascal, but our vet dashed those hopes. He told us we *definitely did not want to breed a two-year old mare.* He said breeding a horse so young would be akin to a pre-teen girl having a baby. We guessed he meant she would not know what to do, and would not care for the foal. He encouraged us to let him give Dorit a shot of prostaglandin to abort the baby if she had conceived. We did not like the idea. We did not want to do it. We did it because he told us to; but we felt badly about it. There would be no baby from Pascal and Dorit. It was time. Pascal needed to be gelded; he was becoming more and more a proud, rambunctious stallion and getting harder to handle as weeks passed.

Pascal's gelding operation was humane, much more humane than the gelding procedure I watched at Rod's father's ranch the summer Rod and I met. Pascal was given an anesthesia for the surgery, and woke up after everything was "over." However, afterwards, especially for the first few days, it seemed there was emptiness in his character, in his whole being, as well as the physical change. Something *was* missing, not only physically. He was different. It wasn't natural. Pascal had been becoming a "handful" as a budding stallion, and we knew gelding him would make him a more functional horse for Veronica, but it was sad nevertheless. It didn't seem right or fair. The vet irked us by commenting it was good we were gelding Pascal because he "wasn't much of a horse anyway, and only the *best horses* should be kept as stallions." I was horrified! I held my tongue, but I thought it was a perfectly atrocious, unkind, and unprofessional thing to say to the owners of *any* horse, let alone the descendant of Seattle Slew. Even if he thought it, he should keep his opinions to himself. I am sensitive about our horses—every one of them is exquisite. Anyone who does not think so, has no taste, period, and should keep his mouth shut. I sort of wished I had blurted out: "Pascal just happens to be the great-great-great grandson of Seattle Slew, 1977 winner of the Triple Crown! Don't you know a good horse when you see him?" Most people who see our horses do indeed say they *are* beautiful, including our niece who worked for two years at Calumet Farms in Kentucky—*the* Calumet Farms: home of nine Kentucky Derby winners, and two Triple Crown winners. I was convinced that our vet truly didn't know a good horse when he saw one. Interestingly, and much to my satisfaction, he retracted his appraisal when he came to issue travel papers the summer Pascal was three years old and leaving to accompany Veronica to graduate school.

When he saw the sixteen-hand glisteningly beautiful three year old Pascal who looked every inch of his Seattle Slew heritage and had the Triple Crown winner's laid-back, gentle temperament too, his exact words were: *"He grew up!"* There was no doubt in my mind he would have made a very wonderful stallion and would have sired the very best off-spring. Perhaps this vet would have admitted the same thing then.

Dorit and Pascal completely smitten

Several days after the gelding procedure, Rod decided to take Pascal to the north end of our property, near our home site, to use the hose to wash Pascal's sheath. Since his arrival over a year before, Pascal and Dorit had *never* been separated. Rod led Pascal out the gate, and up the gravel road. Dorit pranced along the fence parallel to Pascal and Rod, within the pasture, until the fence ended. When she understood Pascal would continue and she could go no further, she furiously charged back in my direction and began kicking and bucking, twisting herself into contortions that would make an Olympic gymnast jealous, and nickering loudly for her beloved buddy. She was throwing a temper tantrum! She continued to call to him, dash along the fence, and angrily paw the ground, buck, and jump until Rod and Pascal finally returned. During her angry exhibition she never came even remotely close enough to me to cause me any concern for my own safety; however, she definitely went to great lengths to demonstrate her displeasure. As soon as Pascal entered the pasture again, Dorit hurriedly sniffed him to make sure he was unscathed, touched her nose to his, and then the two of

Dorit throwing her temper tantrum

them galloped off up the hill away from the *mean* people who had separated them.

If I were to do the same thing now, I would put a lead rope on Dorit and let her walk with Pascal while Rod washed him off underneath, and then walked them both back to their pasture together. That was then and I did not have the understanding of equine minds I now have. That night I learned that "sweet" Dorit could hold a grudge and take revenge for an insult. When I went to bring her to the shed for her grain, she carefully backed up beside me, turned her head slightly to the side to make sure she had correctly judged my position, and quickly kicked me! She was so close to me that the full impact was blunted, but she decidedly did kick me nevertheless. It reminded me of tales of an old-time teacher administering a swat with a switch to an errant pupil. *Ready, aim, fire!* It was done, and that was the end of it. It was the first time she had ever shown aggression toward us, and seemed deliberate, malicious and premeditated. I was stunned! Until now, if Dorit backed up to us it meant she wanted her rump scratched—her tail-end was always her favorite place to be scratched. Tonight, however, she seemed just plain irritated with me for letting Pascal be taken away, and kicking was her way to express her resentment even hours after the fact. This happened again years later when she thought Rod was paying too much attention to another horse. Dorit was jealous: she walked out the gate, stood beside Rod, and kicked him. Both instances were "one-timers." Little Dorit, we now knew, had enough "brain" to remember an injury, brood over an insult, and take revenge, as well as recognize Rod's voice over the car ham radio. She definitely was not dull or dim-witted, nor was she very forgiving.

Dorit also seemed able to recognize a mistaken perception, and make deductions. Rod was rebuilding a gray Volkswagen pick-up for Veronica, and he had it parked at our house building site; from a distance it looked much like the white Volkswagen Rabbit car she saw him drive every day when he worked on the house and took care of her. Apparently Dorit had noticed the pick-up parked at the home site throughout Rod's work day, and "assumed" Rod was at the house. When he drove up to the pasture gate in the white Rabbit, she looked at it steadily momentarily, and then she turned and looked at the vehicle parked at the house nearly a quarter mile away. It was as if she was asking: "How can you be *here?* I thought you were up there?"

Late the same spring Pascal was gelded, one of the cats belonging to our elderly neighbor on the farm to the north had kittens. He said we could take any we wanted. We selected two sisters to be "mousers" for our horse shed: a calico, and "tortoise shell." We were only taking them a quarter mile from their birth place, so to attempt to trick them into not knowing they were close enough to walk home, we drove a half mile north, a mile east, another mile south, and another mile west, and then turned into our fenced pasture on the southwest corner where the horse shed was. We moved the kittens into the "hay side" of the shed where the horses could not enter, and fixed a large wooden box as private place they could hide, but could also leave at will. As we were settling them into their new little home, I looked up to see Dorit and Pascal's heads hanging over the partition, their eyes glued to the babies. No cat could have been more curious than our horses! They were quietly and intently watching the whole "settling in" of the kittens. What a perfect picture: the two horses' heads looking over the outside wall to observe the newest additions moving in. We named our kittens *Tiger* and *Paws*.

"Barn cats," those not allowed into homes, usually survived less than a year or two, we were told. They become the dinners of coyotes, raccoons, bobcats, and other varmints. We never noticed that our horses took up a real friendship with the cats, but we did notice the cats were always with them in the early mornings when we jogged by on our morning runs. We assumed they stayed with the horses for protection at night.

During the day, too, especially in the summer, Tiger and Paws were often nearby, lying in the horses' shadows to shade themselves from the hot sun. They always knew when we fed the horses, and they came with us like faithful little dogs. They ran up the posts and batted at the ropes with their paws as we tied the horses before feeding them. Then they perched on the fence and watched them eat as we curried them, removed cockle-burs and cleaned their feet. If we dangled a rope in front of the cats at other times they refused to grab at it; it was only fun to attempt to claw the rope if we were tying the horses up.

When Rod rode or worked with Dorit or Pascal in the round pen, Tiger and Paws always came to watch. They seated themselves safely outside the cattle panels; their heads neatly fit into an interlocking panel squares. They draped their paws over the panel wires so they looked like they were peeking out a doll house window, or sitting in box seats watching a rodeo. They were there to cheer Rod and the horses on. These cats were always there to see what was happening, to be part of the action, to be friendly, to be part of the family. Until now I always thought of only dogs providing this sort of companionship.

Even when we had additional horses, a new barn location, and a different feeding place the cats still ran alongside the hay cart happily, with their tails straight up. They still played "attack the rope" from atop the fence posts where we tied the horses before we fed the grain in their buckets. We didn't feed Tiger and Paws their food at the same time or place, but they knew we were outside *to do something*, and definitely wanted to be included. It amazed me that cats would be such loyal, faithful companions.

Chapter 6
Country Home and a Third Horse

We moved into our unfinished home in September, about two and a half years after Rod began building it. My mother died that August at the age of eighty-five. Mom was diagnosed with lung cancer in mid-July after a fall to her back brought her to the hospital. My father passed away of a massive heart attack 16 years before. Until her fall, mom drove her own car, did her own cooking, cleaning, and gardening, volunteered for the USO and a Catholic Charities Thrift Store. She was a docent at the museum for her city's Historical Society, attended monthly meetings of the Daughters of the American Revolution; she drove herself and two friends to Mass regularly, and played bridge three times a month. We knew she was getting old, but, until this incident, we did not know she was dying. Mom started smoking in her early twenties, enjoyed it, and refused to give it up.

After x-rays were taken of her back, cancer was discovered, not a broken back as she feared. The doctors said she had less than six months to live. Mom told us many times if she was diagnosed with cancer, she wanted "no chemotherapy and no radiation." Her instructions were simple: "Just keep me comfortable." Hospice Care was ordered, and a nurse checked on our mom in her home several days a week. My sister left immediately from Colorado to be with her; our brother lived only a couple miles away from mom. Near the end of July, I took Family Medical Leave, and went to stay with my sister and brother in our mother's home near San Francisco to help care for mom until the end. I expected to be away six months. Rod gave the required one month notice to vacate the house we were renting; he planned to "camp in" our unfinished house and continue working on it until I returned. Unexpectedly, Mom lived only three weeks; I was home by the middle of August.

During the last days of August Rod and I moved our necessities into our unfinished home, and all our "non-essentials" into a storage locker. Pascal and Dorit did not appear interested in our activity at

43

the house, but they knew we were there. I think they appreciated us being less than a quarter of a mile away, instead of seven miles, especially when they were hungry or wanted company. If we were late in getting down to feed them, Pascal watched for us, and as soon as he saw us walk out the back door, nickered to remind us it was time for his dinner. Rod said: "He's saying: 'Rod! Come feed me!'"

There was little the horses missed; they seemed to keep track of which cars came and went, and basically knew where we were at all times. It was a new experience to live at the same place where we kept our horses: it was so different to walk out in the mornings and see farmland and trees instead of the house next door, to hear the trains' lonely whistles in the evenings and early mornings instead of hearing cars driving past the house, or police sirens in the distance. It was peaceful to see the horses eating grass in their pasture from the windows of our *own* home. From that September through the end of March the next year I grabbed a quick glance at the landscape and our two horses as I hurried to my car and began the drive down the gravel roads to work. Some mornings I had to stop my car while I watched four or five deer, or sometimes ten or more turkeys, cross the gravel road in front of me. To a former city dweller, this was rather amazing and sort of funny. I often shook my head and laughed. It was certainly *different from anything I ever experienced!* I was beginning to gradually become acclimated and even take *some* pleasure in living in "the middle of nowhere," especially in the peace of those beautiful early mornings. I was beginning to appreciate country living as somewhat less an adversity and more of a privilege, at least in *some* respects. Perhaps I was a little bit like Duke Senior in Shakespeare's *As You Like It.* The Duke is describing the world he's been forced to adopt since being deposed and exiled by his villainous brother:

Sweet are the uses of adversity,
Which like the toad, ugly and venomous,
Wears yet a precious jewel in his head.
And this our life exempt from public haunt
Finds tongues in trees, books in the running brooks,
Sermons in stones, and good in everything.
I would not change it. (II,i,12-12-16)

My country life definitely was free from *public haunt,* and there was beauty that spoke to me of God and His love for me in all nature, especially the animals and their surroundings. There definitely was *good in everything.* The next April I resigned from my nursing job. Rod said he had our house finished enough to take a job, and work on the house in his after-work hours. He told me now *I could stay home.* Rod never thought I had to earn a salary to carry my "share of the load." While he did not try to prevent me from taking a job if I really wanted to work, he was happiest when I stayed home. Even with just two of us now, there was plenty to do especially in a country home. When we raised our children I usually stayed home. I held two teaching jobs each for 2 years, separated by seven stay-home-years, and twice worked as a substitute teacher during times Rod worked afternoon or evening shifts so we could trade times staying with our three children. We did some home schooling through the eighth grade year, and when Veronica started high school, I went back to college to get a second Bachelor's Degree in nursing. Becoming a nurse was a dream I nurtured for a long time, and finally had the confidence and stomach to tackle after we raised three children. After our son was working, and our daughters were in college, Rod and I both worked. We typically had different shifts and different days off. Rod was an airline pilot; I was a nurse. Often we were like ships passing in the night. To make as much money as possible was not a vow we made when we married, though the extra money always was attractive and useful. However, ever since we married we worked hard not to be covetous, and believed in our souls as St. Luke wrote: "Beware of all covetousness; for a man's life does not consist in the abundance of his possessions." (Luke 12:15) I really appreciated the dinners Rod had ready every evening when I came in from work; now I would be home for him. Rod liked to provide for his family; he considered it his responsibility. He also took very seriously Christ's admonition to live simply, to lay up "treasures in heaven, where neither moth nor rust consumes and where thieves do not break in and steal," rather than build-up treasures on earth. St. Matthew adds: "For where your treasure is, there will be your heart also."(*Matthew 6: 21)* Rod's treasure, God and his family, was always where his heart was. This was the basis for our lives when we married, and deepened during our time here.

45

One of our earthly "treasures," Pascal, was about to leave us. Pascal was Veronica's horse; we kept him for her three years; Rod rode and gentled him enough for her to begin riding him. Veronica began taking riding lessons shortly after we bought Pascal. Now she wanted to begin riding her *own* horse instead of schooling horses and board him at a stable near her school.

Besides riding Pascal, Rod taught him to load into our trailer. Even though Pascal was still a young, inexperienced horse, and a tall sixteen hands high, he was gentle for Veronica. She was not afraid to climb on his back while he was eating his grain at the entrance of the shed, and let him meander over to the hay feeder some twenty feet away without bridle, saddle, helmet or even halter and lead rope. Pascal was a green horse, but he and Veronica were friends, they understood one another—that made all the difference.

Anticipating Pascal's departure and remembering how lonely Dorit was before Pascal came, Rod and I began looking for a horse to replace Pascal as a companion for Dorit. The plan was to get an experienced horse I could ride since Dorit was *green*, and so was I. Over the years, I had occasionally ridden "bullet proof" stable horses and those on Rod's father's ranch, but never regularly. I lacked *hours in the saddle*. Rod's admiration for thoroughbreds convinced me they were the best. I would not consent to getting anything else, especially what Rod called "an old plug." I didn't know horses well enough then to understand that I would have loved even "an old plug," and the old plug would have loved me. I wanted a thoroughbred, a Lear Jet, not a Cessna 150—not for the speed, just for the form, beauty and intelligence. It was a demand that would bring me both regret and satisfaction. We think we live and learn; we think we make the transfer from one situation to another. For our sixth wedding anniversary, Rod gave me the money for flight ground school and flying lessons for my private pilot license. He wanted me to share his love of flying. I achieved the private pilot license, but I did not fly a Lear Jet. I should have made the connection; I did not. Thoroughbreds are Lear Jets; I needed a Cessna 150.

We departed one Sunday in April to look for another horse. We had been combing the Classified Ads that brought Dorit and Pascal for another thoroughbred, an experienced one. The ads brought us to a farm that had more horses than I have ever seen in one place. We ultimately settled on an 8-year-old thoroughbred grey mare, *Teeter on a Star,* or simply *Star.*

Even though in my heart of hearts I believed she was *too much of a horse* for me, I didn't dare go with my gut. How could I say I didn't want her, when I had wanted a horse for so long? How could I refuse a gift picked out for me? In addition to seeming offish and too high-spirited, I ashamedly I admitted, only to myself, I didn't *like* her *color.* I was prejudiced against my horse before I even knew her because of her coat and her unfriendly behavior. I wanted a friendly, darker colored horse with a white diamond on her forehead.

Though to me Star seemed far too advanced for an inexperienced person, I rationalized that Rod could gentle her for me, and then I would have a nice, well-mannered horse I could ride. She had been a racehorse, so she certainly had been ridden. However, I was not a jockey—another connection I failed to make. She did not need to be "broke to ride," but her riding experience was very different from mine. I naively told myself she was nervous because we were new people to her, and she *would* settle down.

There was another horse there much more to my liking, shorter, probably about fifteen hands high, a dark bay like Pascal. However, she was out of my league in a different way. This smaller, quieter mare was nearly twice Star's price, and we reasoned with Star we were getting two for the price of one: Star was pregnant.

A baby! I was very interested! Before working as a nurse in Home Health, I worked for almost five years in maternal-infant nursing: labor and delivery, nursery and post-partum care. It was my favorite area of nursing. I thought it would be exciting to have a mare give birth and to experience the birth and new life of a foal.

The month before we came to purchase her, Star had jumped the fence to be with a stallion. Nothing shy about her! She knew what she wanted. Star had powerful hind legs, and was just over sixteen hands tall. She seemed to not like, need, or want to be around people. The day we bought her, she ran away, head up and tail flowing out behind her, when anyone tried to catch her. It was a game for her; she seemed to be laughingly chiding: "*Catch me if you can!*" It did not seem like a game to me. I did not like it.

I thought: "If a horse does not want to be around me, why should I bother trying to *make* her be around me?" These were not good beginning thoughts for forming a friendship with my very first horse!

I told myself I did not *know* horses. Rod was the horseman; if *he* thought Star was a good horse, she probably was. I let myself be talked into something I did not want for fear of losing my chance to have a horse: fear of seeming unreasonable, ungrateful, too picky, or "a chicken." Trusting my own judgment would surely have made my introduction to horsemanship easier. Looking back, however, it seems to me that Star and I were meant for each other. I have often been one to learn things the *hard way.* Like Saint Paul, who was knocked to the ground and heard a voice, which turned out to be the Lord, saying: "Saul, Saul, Why do you persecute me?" (Acts 9:4) I too had to be knocked down to begin to listen to what the Lord wanted me to hear. Star would be His perfect instrument.

Rod awed the seller by climbing on Star's back without a saddle, without a helmet, and with only a bridle. He briefly rode her around the corral, and proclaimed: "She's a good horse. We'll take her." Hindsight is always 20/20. Had we known then what we know now our decision would have been different and we would have missed out on a lot of pain, sorrow and frustration as well as a lot of joy, love and fulfillment.

We never know what might have been had we taken a different road somewhere in our lives. We cannot see into the future, nor can we predict how we will handle the situations even if we *could* see them. Only God knows; that is best. I do not know what kind of person I would be had we not bought Star. I believe I am a better human being for my experiences with her. Star put me on a journey back to the true meaning of life. She changed my life forever, and continues to change it for the better, though it has been a twisted road with many obstacles and sharp turns. Hopefully I will be closer to God at the end. Star helped me realize I was not preparing adequately for the next life, and the next life is the one that matters.

A few days after we purchased Star, a young woman, Hannah, who worked for the horse farm, and who introduced us to the horses, delivered Star in a trailer. Dorit and Pascal together galloped toward the pasture gate, excited to meet the newest equine resident of the farm. Star, however, once released inside the gate, eluded them. It seemed as if she felt she was too good for them, as if she perceived them too childish and irresponsible, and not as if she were afraid or apprehensive about the unfamiliar place. Cantering around the five-acre pasture with her head high and her tail flowing out behind her, looking about her strange new surroundings, she seemed proud and beautiful, and though she perhaps seemed a tad bit nervous, she seemed completely and confidently in control of herself. She appeared to glide over ground effortlessly, and seemed more to float just above the earth than to run upon it. Nothing impeded her forward motion; she was absolutely sure-footed even her first time over a strange pasture. Hannah said: "She is doing the 'new kid on the block' thing. She'll be this way for several days; maybe a week or two before she settles down." As she left, she thanked us "for giving Star a good home." The weeks passed. Star did not settle down soon. The chase remained a game she loved and I hated.

Teeter on a Star

Chapter 7
Of Lear Jets and Cessna 150's

Star and Pascal vied for dominance: they were nearly the same height, and though Star was older, Pascal had been here longer. The question of which horse was "at the top of the heap" was open for grabs. Neither horse asserted him or herself savagely; it was rather an on-going tussle, a kind of "cold war." Pascal usually won, but always kindly; he gently called the shots, the others followed. The three horses liked to stand in the shade of a large tree at the north end of their pasture most summer mornings. Every afternoon about one o'clock, Pascal would give a loud nicker, and canter toward the shed to get out of the heat of the day and away from the flies. He was a dark bay, dark brown body, nearly black, with a black mane, tail and black socks. Like a black car in the sun, his coat absorbed the heat and he tolerated heat poorly. He was often the only horse covered with sweat at the end of a hot summer day. Star, a grey, did not mind the sun. Her coat reflected the heat just as a white car is cooler in the beating sun. Nevertheless, Star followed Pascal to the shade of the shed displaying her beautiful floating canter, and Dorit tagged along with them. There was room inside the east side of the shed for three horses had Star *let* Dorit enter, or had Dorit not been afraid of Star. We kept hay bales stacked on the west side, and there was a mid-line partition and walls north and south to enclose the hay. Dorit stood outside the shed in the sun while the other two stood in the shed. It was better, in her mind, to be hot in the summer afternoon sun near her friends, than up on the hill under a tree in the shade alone. I was beginning to learn horses' security is in the herd.

While Pascal and Star vied for dominance, he and Dorit were still best friends. He seemed to always want to be with her. Star stayed with them, but usually stayed a bit aloof though close enough to remain comfortable. She did take an instant dislike to Dorit, or more exactly, to Dorit's too forward attempts at friendliness, or maybe attempts at dominance. When Star arrived, Dorit nearly threw herself at her trying to be noticed, trying to be her friend, or perhaps trying to establish her place in the hierarchical ladder before Star took a place. Dorit, after all, was here first. Star did not know that, nor did she need or want to know it. Star was offish from the start. She was not mean, just disdainful, proud, perhaps a bit afraid and uncertain. She acted withdrawn, shy, reserved.

Hannah, the young woman who first introduced us to Star and later delivered her to us, called her "meek." I never thought of the word *meek* as descriptive of Star. Star was courteous, refined, and not prone to start fights. She did not flatten her ears back and point her nose in a disgusted manner to show her disagreement; in fact she actually seemed to try to avoid a conflict when she could—maybe that is what Hannah meant by "meek." However, Star was neither overly submissive nor spiritless; she was patient to a degree, but she expected things to be done right. As I began to know Star, I became convinced she had been either trained severely or abused. She seemed unaccustomed to kindness, patience, or love. Horses, any animal, humans too, do not easily forget harsh treatment. Years later a large loud truck thundered roughly by on the gravel road and made a noisy crashing sound which startled her; it was the only time I ever remember Star pulling back when tied. I gently reached my hand to her neck to pet her and reassure her everything was all right. In response to my raised hand, Star threw her head high and showed fearful eyes; she steeled her body as if I were going to beat her! She seemed still somewhat distrustful even as I managed to quiet her and pet her. Rod and I looked at each other and said "someone must have beaten the heck out of her" sometime in her life. She stood still for saddling, she put her head into a bridle or halter, and she did not bite or kick. However, she seemed to tolerate people because she had learned she *had to,* not because she liked being handled or ridden. When we approached her she ran away, obviously not anxious for our contact. Rod continued to say it was a game; but for me it never was a game.

I remember Rod handing me Star's lead rope the first day she arrived, and telling me: "You finally have the horse you have always wanted! Spend time with her!"

Sadly, though this would not be true now, then I was completely at a loss for *what to do* or say. I was a little afraid too because she was big, fast and offish. I remember Rod said his father always told him to *talk to* horses. I didn't know how. I thought horses were to just get on and ride: squeeze to go, pull to stop. It never occurred to me to curry Star, to comb her mane and tail, clean her feet, walk her around the pasture with just a halter and loose lead rope, and to just softly talk to her about anything that came into my head for weeks, maybe even months, before I ever attempted to ride her. I wish I had the attitude that it was *all right* if I never rode her but we were just friends—but I did not know that then. I did not know how to "get to know" her and become her trusted companion. I felt a bit inhibited at first about talking to our first child too. Babies, I learned as I grew into motherhood, *need* to be talked to, they thrive on it, and it quickly became natural for me. I did not know I also needed to grow into horse ownership—there was more than just riding. Horses need to be talked to, petted, groomed, to become trusted and trustful friends, I know now: friendship first, then ride.

Looking back later, Star did seem ill at ease—stiff, uncertain, shy, untrusting—just as I was. I didn't know then, and no one told me, that just to breathe deeply, groom her, and talk to her would have quieted both of us and begun the bonding process. We live and learn; hopefully we change and grow better with God's help. However, sometimes I make the same mistakes even when I thought I learned my lesson, and not only with horses.

Star remained aloof. She did not *want* to be caught. However, we did manage to catch her, always after a not-so-merry chase, and, once caught, she complied. Rod began riding her on the gravel roads in a saddle, and sometimes I rode her bareback in the pasture. She seemed to think the minute I was on her back she was supposed to *take off!* She had been a racehorse; she seemed to think she was still leaving the starting gate as soon as I mounted.

I *should* have listened to my gut, but I refused. My gut told me: "She is *too much horse* for you." I didn't want to seem ungrateful, but I wished we could take her back, exchange her for a less powerful, more amicable horse. Not having the courage to voice this desire, I hoped I could, with practice and perseverance, be transformed into Star's good rider, and truly thought I was giving that desire my best shot.

When Rod came home from work in the afternoon, he tried to teach me to ride the way he learned as a child. The "riding session" would begin with Rod boosting me up on Star bareback, with just a snaffle bit bridle. Immediately Star would *take off!* One particular afternoon I remember Star *took off* with me aboard. We raced twice around the five-acre pasture with me tightly hanging on to her mane, my legs clamped tightly around her. Twice we passed the galvanized tub full of water, each time I thought I was going to end up head first in the water tank. Miraculously, I avoided the headlong crash into the tub. Finally, after being a fearful idiot passenger for too long, I remembered *to pull one rein*. Pulling one rein gradually slowed Star, and she finally stopped. After that whirlwind race, what followed seemed like a slow motion sequence: as Star finally halted, I gently folded to the ground, unhurt. Rod ran up to me as I rose to my feet and said: "You did *so good*!" I did not think so.

Rod's father believed: "Anyone who has not fallen off a horse hasn't ridden much." I had never fallen off a horse until now. I accepted falling off a horse as part of the necessary learning process, part of obtaining the hours in a saddle. Rod's father also believed riding bareback was the safest way to learn to ride. There were no stirrups to catch the feet, no saddle to add extra weight and height to a fall, no saddle horn to puncture the stomach, or break the pelvis. He allowed none of his children to ride with a saddle until he or she could canter a horse bareback. That was the "learning plan" for me because it was the safest, and because at that time we did not yet own a saddle. I hoped I would eventually learn even to canter bareback.

We bought Star in April; in May I started taking riding lessons from a woman who taught dressage. I barely knew what dressage was, and had never ridden an English saddle. I wanted to learn to ride English because I thought it was more beautiful, and because I was certain I could lift an English saddle up on the horse's back, which was something I sincerely doubted I could do with a Western saddle. In preparation I began reading Sally Swift's book Centered Riding. I felt it gave me a great advantage as a beginner. I was so grateful for her straightforward insights and instructions that made riding make so much more sense.

I had seen my instructor ride; she was completely synchronized, smooth, coordinated, entirely one with the horse. I liked her and respected her, and she seemed to like me personally. Though I now realize she, just like Star, was too advanced for me, she agreed to

53

take me as a beginning student, and arranged for me to use her twenty-seven year old mare until I had a trailer to bring my own horse for lessons. At the time, as far as I knew, she was the only English instructor near us, and even she was over twenty miles away.

During the very first lesson she had me canter as she held the horse on a longe line. (Initially I thought the term was *lunge line*. According to Eleanor Blazer in her article "To Longe, Lunge or Lounge" on her website The Way of Horses, *longe* is the correct American spelling.) Later I wondered if she was trying to discourage me from learning to ride. Veronica called to see how my first lesson went. She was surprised when I told her I had cantered in my first lesson. She said she did not canter for the whole first semester when she began her riding instruction.

After two lessons my instructor told me: "You are gutsy! Most students will scream and yell and say: 'I can't do it!' But *you!* You just do what I tell you to do!"

I thought to myself: "Yeah! That is why I am here taking lessons and paying *you* money. I am supposed to do what *you* tell me. *You* are the teacher!" I suppose she thought anyone fifty-one years old learning to ride had to be either brave or crazy, or maybe a little of each. I just wanted to learn to ride.

Veronica said some riding instructors don't like beginning students. They prefer the accomplished ones who only need a few finishing touches to easily excel to perfection. In one of my "earlier lives" I was a secondary school English and art teacher; I knew it was rewarding, even fun, to have the honors students who were interested in the material, were quick to learn, and who wanted to do well. However, I quickly learned the average students were rewarding, even inspiring too. Sometimes the average students' insights into the material was even more profound than the "whiz-kids'" insights. The normal students discovered a joy in learning they never found before and brought a worked-for perspective to their understandings. I was never a whiz kid. Right now I just wanted a chance to learn to ride. That didn't seem like too much to ask of myself or of the instructor, but looking back, I wish I had started by first getting to know my new horse, and letting her get to know me.

Some teachers act as if they have never been beginners themselves, as if they were born knowing everything they know now. Perhaps it was so long ago that they have forgotten ever being a beginner. They do not know how to introduce their knowledge simply. "Simple words for big ideas" was advice our high school speech teacher gave us. Attempting to learn English riding from this very accomplished instructor was a giant step when I needed to begin with smaller steps—another Lear Jet when I needed a Cessna 150.

At the start of the cantering session, my instructor told me to hold the pommel, the upward-projecting front part of the English saddle, and to grab a piece of the horse's mane to help me keep my seat in the saddle; she told me to "scoop" with my hips and bottom. She did not expect me to be thrown from the horse, but I wondered whether she was trying to hurry me along because I was older, or perhaps attempting to discourage me completely. I was never instructed how to soften the impact of my back and bottom hitting the saddle, nor to relax and move with the horse rather than grip the horse and saddle with my legs and thighs while attempting to keep my back straight. I think younger students probably achieve the correct posture naturally. Catalogs sold padded riding underwear, so I assumed all beginning riders had bruised crotches, aching legs and backs, and took Ibuprofen at night for back pain.

In spite of all the things I did not know, somehow I was doing well at lessons on the old schooling mare and loving it. However, on Star I felt like I was about to fly out of the new saddle I had just received as an anniversary gift from Rod. Star was younger, taller, faster, and stronger than her schooling counterpart. She almost seemed to belong to a different species. It was as if I came home to ride a camel, or a giraffe, or a tornado on four legs. My instructor told me I had "natural ability," she was impressed with my posting trot and even with my canter at this early stage on the schooling horse, but in my new saddle on Star, nothing was the same.

Finally our trailer was complete; with it I could bring Star with me to the lessons. My challenges now seemed bigger than ever. I had never driven a truck with a trailer, let alone a trailer with a horse in it. The instructor's driveway was not *trailer friendly* for an experienced driver, not to mention a green one, nor was the busy twenty-mile stretch of two-lane state highway from our home to her turn-off made for an amateur to guide this kind of vehicle easily and safely. I knew I would need a lot of patient instruction in trailer handling before I tackled this job alone. As it turned out, I was stopped in the starting gate. Perhaps I was stopped from a worse collision than the one I met.

Chapter 8
Horse Riding On Hold; Pascal Departs

I kept riding Star, and I was becoming comfortable on her with a saddle, but I was a long way from the hours in the saddle that would give me the ability to react automatically to emergent situations. One day toward the end of July, Rod was teaching Pascal to load in the trailer for his move in August, and I wanted to practice riding Star. I saddled her, and was ready to mount. Star let out a huge sigh and sort of fluttered her lips. I lifted myself into the saddle. All seemed as if it would go well. We walked around the area, near Rod, the trailer, and the other two horses. I told Rod, "Just once more, then we'll quit for lunch." I would regret that ill-fated *just once more.*

While Star and I were riding on toward the house, Rod decided Dorit and Pascal were, as he said later, "in a bad place," so he moved them to the other side of the trailer. When Star turned around she immediately saw her two friends were gone, and bolted. My mind and body froze. I did not have the experience-honed ability to think and act quickly. I had fallen off Star, and considered it part of the hard knocks of learning to ride. As I had been instructed at my lessons, I grabbed the saddle pommel and her mane to prepare for the canter instead of trying to stop her racing forward momentum.

I saw terrible fear in her eyes as she catapulted herself into her highest "racehorse fear gear." I forgot anything about pulling one rein. I never considered "baling off"—it would have been like jumping off a speed boat at full throttle. Such "thrills" never interested me. I just hung on.

When Star swerved rapidly to miss some trees, I was thrown to the left and out of the saddle. My head in my new helmet hit the ground and its Styrofoam liner split, but it protected my head from the impact against the dry clay ground. In hindsight, had I indeed been bareback when Star shifted into high gear, I most likely would come off sooner and would fall from several inches closer to the ground which almost certainly would have lessened my injuries. After my "crash" I presumed I was unhurt. Just another fall that would bring me closer to being a rider, I thought, until I attempted to stand. Immediately I realized my right arm was not connected to my shoulder. Reflexively, I placed the palm of my left hand under my elbow to support my right arm. I knew I had broken my humerus, the long bone of the upper arm, as did a dear ninety-year old man I cared for as a Home Health Nurse just the year before. He slipped on the ice going out his front door to get his newspaper one January morning. He had to have physical therapy, but he recovered completely.

I called to Rod: "Rod, come here, I've broken my arm!"

Rod came. He looked at my arm, and felt it, and said: "I don't think you broke it."

There were no bones sticking out, no obvious abnormal bend in the arm as there had been when I broke my left forearm in a bicycle accident when I was nine years old. I, however, knew for certain it was broken. We returned to the house and began the process of calling the insurance company, calling the hospital, driving to the hospital, waiting for the doctor, having x-rays taken, waiting again for the doctor, and then waiting for the surgery—all the drudgery I had gratefully been able to avoid most of my life by being very healthy. Though my accident happened about 11 AM, I was ultimately not taken to surgery until over twelve hours later.

Sitting quietly in the car while Rod drove me to the hospital, I remembered asking patients to rate their pain: "On a scale of one to ten, with ten being the worst pain you can imagine, how would you rate your pain?"

"*This,* I now thought to myself, *has got to be a ten!"*

I had indeed broken my humerus, the upper part of my right arm, just below the ball and socket joint, and had also split the entire bone nearly to the elbow. Upon hearing the diagnosis, Rod, who seems always ready with humor to lighten up a tragic or tense situation said: "Is this supposed to be *humorous?*" Even I had to give a quick laugh. He was quick on horseback, and just as quick with the words. It is truly a gift to be able to inject a bit of comic relief and thus ally fear and discouragement when the going gets too rough.

To set the fracture, the orthopedic surgeon put two screws in the shoulder, a titanium rod down the length of the humerus inside the bone, which is hollow, and a third screw approximately a hand's width above my elbow, where the radial nerve crosses and continues down the inner arm to the hand. All precautions were taken. A blunt instrument was used to push the radial nerve out of the way while the final screw was placed, but the surgery left me with a damaged nerve and wrist drop. I could not raise my right hand; it limply flopped like a rag doll when lifted and released. At first the doctor thought the lack of wrist function was due to post-operative swelling, but function did not return when the swelling subsided.

New to horses, I had no experience with them being "herd bound." Until this time, I had no idea Star was extremely herd bound, and would prove that over and over again in years to come. I never blamed her for my ignorance or my injury. I was mad at myself for my inexperience and for not taking charge of the situation.

My children told me never to ride Star again. I believed *real* horse people *get back on* after they are thrown off, but, in my case, getting back on was impossible for quite a while. It seemed my horse riding days were over before they started.

I wore a brace to make my arm somewhat functional, though it was weak. I helped Rod daily with feeding and currying the horses, but being partially incapacitated was hard to accept. I was familiar with the Old Testament story of Job, but I never actually had to internalize it. I would have been angry had anyone reminded me Job's response that we must be ready to accept the evil as well as the good things the Lord sends our way: "Shall we receive good at the hand of God, and shall we not receive evil?" (Job 2:10) Intellectually I knew God allows suffering to bring about a greater good. It was only with God's grace that I gradually began to understand the purpose of life's trials, and this one in particular. I do not think I will ever truly "rejoice in my suffering," as St. Paul writes in Colossians 1:24, I am doing well if I remember to offer it up, to join it to Christ's suffering on the cross, when it comes my way. I learned many years before to endure disappointment, to not expect to get everything I wanted, but this was the first serious physical trial I ever knew. I did not regain full use of my arm for over a year. Rod broke his jaw in a freak accident at work in May, and my accident happened in July. We spent the rest of that summer and fall keeping doctors' appointments which made us both grateful for the good health we normally enjoyed, and grateful too for the little time we normally spent waiting in doctor's offices. My horse riding was put on hold with an unknown date to resume. It was discouraging; but I continued to admire the horses from the ground, help with their care and feeding, and look forward to Star giving birth to her foal March 1st. Rod said we should name the foal *Consolation.* It seemed an appropriate name. The birth of the foal would be a comfort and light in the long tunnel of a slow recovery.

Another bright spot in this disappointing arm ordeal was being able to travel with Veronica when she transported Pascal to his new home. The original plan had been for us to share the driving; but now I was a passenger--there only for companionship and help getting food and necessities during the long hours of driving. We left in the pre-dawn darkness after Veronica and Rod stealthily snuck Pascal up from the pasture and loaded him into the trailer without arousing the suspicion of his two pasture mates. He led willingly, and entered the trailer flawlessly. The hours of patient, repetitive training paid off. We immediately rewarded him with several carrots, bid good-bye to Rod, and each slid into our seats in the truck. Veronica started the engine, and the truck and trailer rumbled down the driveway on to the gravel road. Pascal settled in for his first extended trailer ride. Dorit suddenly discovered her buddy was gone and nickered a forlorn "Good-bye" or a "Where are you? Don't leave me!" to him in the darkness as we slowed to turn the corner and begin our journey to his new home. Veronica made the twelve hour trip carefully, expertly—just as she seems to do everything she does. We stopped frequently to check on our precious cargo and to offer him water. Now that Pascal was gone; Dorit and Star became pasture mates in a state of peaceful co-existence, not friendship.

Through the fall months I had various tests to decide if my nerve was severed. It was determined that there was no communication below the point where the final screw entered my arm, and I would need a second surgery to remove the screw near my elbow which either compressed, or had cut my radial nerve in two. My surgery was December 5th. Four days later, December 9th, Star lost her foal.

It was a Saturday morning, and Rod left for work at 5:15 AM after coming in to say good-bye to me. This day would be one of those times when I needed the man who was raised on a ranch, the man who best knows horses, and how to handle problems that arise, but he was not home. The "city girl," the fragile country transplant, who has no prior experience, has to take care of the situation as best she can.

This whole episode of the foal loss affected me so profoundly over the months following. It seemed to follow me like a ghost everywhere, to almost haunt me every day. I could not escape it. Finally, I realized I *needed* to write about it. When things affect me deeply I ultimately find I must write, paint, or draw to extinguish the shadows that seem to pursue me. Ultimately, I find I have to create to fill the void the tragedy has left within me, to bind up my soul, to release and quiet the emotions locked inside my being which seem to follow me everywhere. I was so moved by the grief I saw our horses demonstrate, especially Star, but Dorit too, in this sad circumstance, showed an immovable, determined, honorable support for her equine sister. I never knew animals grieved, but they truly do, and it is heart-breaking to witness. I felt utterly helpless as both horses continued to look to me to make things right—to breathe life into a dead foal. I really wished at that moment that I could bring her dead baby back to life for her.

The death of Star's foal was more horrible to me because it happened in winter when the whole earth is dead and cold. Poor Star! She suffered her loss alone, in the dark of night while we were safe in a warm house, sound asleep. I believe this turmoil, this tragedy, and all it entailed was the birth of my belief that it is <u>never</u> *just a horse!* I detest that expression! Horses do have emotions and are capable of love, fear, grief, jealousy and many emotions in a way akin to what people experience in comparable situations. Star's loss brought to mind the loss of my father, my mother, and the loss of our own child. All my losses led me to connect more closely with Star and grieve with her and for her. Her foal loss was one of those things that forever changed my life.

Finally writing about Star's loss was cathartic, healing. Awhile after I completed my writing, I sent the finished work to <u>Equus Magazine</u>; they printed my story in the February 2004 issue, #316, page 74. It is reprinted here with permission.

A Sorrow Shared

A previously standoffish mare and her owner forge a special bond
After a sudden loss

By 6:15 AM on that Saturday, I was in the garage on my treadmill—my way to avoid the chilly December winds and the eerie predawn darkness of solitary gravel roads. As I run, I find it peaceful to look out the window at our two horses, toy size in the distance, hazily silhouetted against the naked winter trees as the sky begins to turn light. This morning was no different. I watched as the horses wandered back and forth in their rolling pasture, just as they normally do. It looked bleak; snow was forecast for early next week. After my exercise, I ate my breakfast and dressed for the long walk out to feed the two mares, Star and Dorit.

Dorit, our little bay, had been the first resident of our country home. As a forlorn, fuzzy, stunted 10-month old she'd moved in before we'd even dug the foundation for our house. To keep Dorit company, we bought Star, an 8-year old grey Thoroughbred. The day we first saw her, my husband, Rod, had jumped on her bareback, ridden her around the pen and declared that she was a good horse. She had good confirmation, and she appeared strong and sound. Best of all, we were getting two for the price of one: Star was in foal.

Star was to be mine—the fulfillment of a lifelong dream. I had wanted a horse since I was 12, but my ambition had been derailed by growing up, marrying, raising children and living in cities. Now I was impatient to learn all of the things that had been out of reach for so long. In some ways, Star was the ideal first horse: It was obvious that someone had spent a lot of time training her. She did not bite or kick, and once caught, she stood still for grooming and saddling. She led well, and she was not afraid of enclosed spaces.

Star was a polite, no-nonsense horse—but she was not a pet. She seemed unaccustomed to kindness or affection and turned away if I got too close or gave her more than a few perfunctory pats. She tolerated people and she did what was asked of her, but she did not seek human interaction. She was also aloof with other horses. She was a loner who liked to keep her distance, and she had always been difficult to catch.

This morning proved to be as icy cold and windy as it had looked. I shivered as I walked down our long gravel driveway. When I reached the mailbox, Star saw me coming and nickered. That was unusual. Star rarely showed any anticipation of my arrival. She turned around and began walking toward the shed where I normally feed her. Immediately I saw that her hindquarters were covered in blood, and she was dragging a sheet of tissue behind her.

A sudden terrible chill filled my heart. "Oh, Star! You've lost your baby!" I said achingly out loud, though there was no one to hear me. What had gone wrong? The due date was three months away—it was too early for the foal to have survived. My mind raced. I wondered how I would ever find the foal in this five-acre pasture full of trees and hills. At the same time, I knew that the retained placenta was a serious problem that required immediate attention. She could hemorrhage or develop a serious infection if the tissue was not removed, and that could be very difficult.

When I got closer, I saw that Star didn't appear to be actively bleeding, so I decided to feed the mares first, then look for the fetus on the way back to the house to call the veterinarian. As I climbed through the fence, Star and Dorit met me, and we walked to the shed together. With tears in my eyes, I stroked and hugged Star's neck. This time, she didn't shy away; she just plodded along by my side and allowed my hand to rest on her neck.

I told star I was very sorry, and that I had lost a baby once and I knew how awful it was. I knew she didn't understand my words, but I hoped my tone and my petting would somehow convey my sorrow. She was only an animal, but I empathized with her loss. As a labor and delivery nurse, I had been at the side of women who had delivered stillborn babies and had offered what comfort and care that I could, but how does one console a horse?

I gave each of the mares their normal ration of hay and oats, then circled through the pasture on my way back to the house. In a small vale, much closer to the shed than I'd expected, I found a perfectly formed miniature horse, lying still and lifeless on the frozen ground. Beside it was a large, full bag that I assumed was the amniotic sac.

Suddenly I realized I wasn't alone. I turned, and there stood Star and Dorit. They had left their food to follow me! They both looked at the foal, and one at a time, each came up to sniff it. They stood still, looking down at the small body, then they both looked directly at me, seeming to ask if I could do something. I hugged Star again and petted her neck, then I stroked Dorit as well. I told them I was sorry I couldn't do anything to help the baby, but I wished I could. Reluctantly, I left them to call our veterinarian.

When he arrived, I opened the gate and told him where the foal was. He suggest that we first go and look at the foal, and as we walked, I said that I was afraid that maybe our being late with the rhinopneumonitis vaccine at seven months had caused the loss. At the site he went to the sac and opened it slightly. "There's your problem," he said. "You did nothing wrong. She was carrying twins."

Twins! That hadn't occurred to me! I'd been too saddened to examine the sac earlier and had focused only on the exposed foal. I knew horses only rarely carry viable twins to term.

Next we went to the shed, where we found Dorit standing near Star, as if protecting her. As the veterinarian drew equipment from his truck, he told me he would give Star a sedative, followed by oxytocin to help her uterus contract so that, he hoped, he'd be able to remove the retained placenta manually. Fortunately, the medication worked rapidly, and the tissue came out with little difficulty. He then rinsed out her uterus with 1,000 milliliters of saline mixed with the antibiotic gentamicin and gave her an injection of Banamine to treat the swelling and discomfort.

Throughout the procedure Star stood with her head hanging. She looked sad and alone. I continued to stroke her neck and tell her it'd be all right.

As the veterinarian prepared to leave, he told me Star would arouse in about 30 minutes and that I could feed her. I thanked him and saw him to the gate. After he was gone, I returned to the shed and stayed beside Star, petting her and talking to her as I curried away the dried blood. Dorit, who'd stayed nearby, now moved closer to the other mare and sniffed her. Dorit and Star had never been friends—they just sort of peacefully coexisted and met each other's herd instincts. Today, though, Dorit had never left Star's side.

As Star began to wake, I fed her some hay and stood with the two mares for a while, soothed by the contented munching. Earlier, I had seen vultures settling near the vale, and I went back out to take care of the fetuses before the birds could destroy them. On my last trip up from the house, I had brought a roll of heavy black trash bags, which

I took out to the site where the foals lay. The birds were still either in the trees or circling overhead. I doubled the bags and pushed each heavy, lifeless body into the plastic, hoping they'd be safe until Rod came home to help me bury them.

As I finished securing the last bag I felt breathing on the back of my neck and turned to see Star behind me, Dorit just behind her, at her side. Once again they'd left their food to follow me here. For what seemed like the hundredth time today I wanted to cry. Was she still hoping I could do something? Her sorrow seemed so real. I have witnessed people grieving many times, but this was my first experience like this with animals.

Again I hugged Star, stroked her neck and told her I was sorry. Then she turned and walked away. She looked so desolate. I wanted to run after her and hug her some more, but I knew I'd done enough of that. I let her go.

When Rod came home we buried the foals east of our house, well away from the horse pasture. That evening, when we went to feed the horses, Star led us once again to the vale where the foals had lain. For nearly a week afterward, I'd often see Star standing alone in that spot. I grieved for her, and I made certain that I gave her extra time each day, thankful that we had not lost her as well!

Perhaps it is my imagination, but I feel that Star and I have come to an understanding. She often walks up to me now and stands beside me, seeming to ask for pats and scratches. Sometimes she butts me with her head to tell me she's there, and she no longer pulls away when I put my face against her head and stroke her neck. Lately, when I jog by in the early mornings, she's even begun coming to the fence—something she had never done before. I fancy I may be the first human she's ever liked. Our friendship may have had a delayed start, but I'm certain it will continue to grow.

Star and Mary Barbara

Chapter 9
A Stallion Named John

With the loss of Star's foals, we began to think about taking Star to a stallion. We thought maybe we could sell future foals to generate a little money from our country home. We did not know the horse market was flooded. The only foals selling were those whose owners were in the right, very elite, circuit. We were not connected to this circuit, and selling our foals would generate contacts, but no serious buyers. We did not know that. We also did not know how very attached to our babies, and how fiercely protective of them we would become. We would become very careful, very particular of the kind of buyer we would allow to purchase them.

The fee for a thoroughbred stallion to breed one of our mares started then at about $1,000 or $1,500. Sometimes there was a live foal guarantee, sometimes not.

To my untrained, non-horse-business mind, it seemed it would be better to buy a stallion for $1,500 and have him breed both Star and Dorit, rather than pay $1,500 twice to have each mare bred. This reasoning inspired our search for *the* thoroughbred stallion we needed.

In early February that next year we found an ad for a two-year old thoroughbred stallion in the lineage of *Bold Ruler,* father of 1973 Triple Crown winner, *Secretariat,* and winner of the first two legs of the Triple Crown himself in 1957. The owner told us he wanted "seven-fifty" for him—we thought he meant $7,500, but he did not—he meant $750. We decided we *had* to see him.

As Rod preferred, we did not take the horse trailer to go for the initial inspection of the horse. That would be my way, but it is not his style. The owner lived approximately 150 miles northwest of us. When he took us out to look at his horse, he had probably eighteen horses scattering nervously around his many corrals and pens. He was very much into all the racing terminology, like *dosages,* and words that meant nothing to me, but not much into the care of the horses on his property.

The stallion he had for sale was a twenty-two month old chestnut thoroughbred with a white crescent shape on his forehead, and a slight Roman nose that I thought made him look masculine. He was small, for his age; he actually looked like a yearling except for his long tail. His coat was not pretty, even for a winter coat. From my study of human nutrition, I would have said he needed the B vitamins to help make his hair healthy.

He appeared to lack both good food and worming. In fact, none of the horses seemed to have been getting enough to eat. The owner seemed to think one flake of hay from a small square bale was quite enough for a horse for the day. The stallion's sister, also a chestnut with white marking on her forehead, I thought, gave me a woeful glance from across the fence. I wanted to take her too. This man with so many horses, a farm, lots of equipment, and an intense interest in horse racing had no clue how to look after and provide for them. He was certainly amiable enough, but he seemed addicted to gambling, to betting on and winning in horse races. Horses were something for him to use; they were not his friends.

I told Rod we should buy the stallion. We had two mares to breed, and his was a good price in light of the stallion fees we had encountered, and he was of good lineage. When we went inside to write the check to buy the stallion, I asked the seller what the horse's name was. He told us the day he was submitting the name to the Jockey Club, he was listening to the radio, and Johnny Cash was singing "A Boy Named Sue." The horse's name was *John's Sue*.

"So, what do you call him?" I asked. I feared this was a horse named "Sue." I could not believe anyone would give a horse such a name!

"John," he replied.

"At least you got *that* right!" I thought to myself. "What a stupid name for a horse!" Official name changes through the Jockey Club cost plenty. I knew we were stuck with the name, and we would certainly call him *John*.

We returned with our truck and trailer February 21 to load John and bring him back to our farm and our two mares, Star and Dorit. The seller had a loading chute for cattle that made loading much easier. John practically walked right into the trailer, and it was only *after* he was inside the trailer that he realized perhaps he did not want to be in there. He looked afraid, but he did not kick or bolt, and

68

actually seemed very peaceful once we began to drive. I imagined that the conditions John was leaving were not ones he would fight to maintain, in fact, he may have been relieved, even glad, to be taken from *this* place.

The day we first came to see and ultimately buy John had been dry, and rather warm, February day. Not so this day. Leaving the seller's farm, it began to snow thick white flakes so hard and fast that soon we were driving in a blizzard. Rod had placed boards in the stock trailer so our new stallion would not be too blasted by the cold wind on the trip home, but the wind was not the only hazard. There were times we wondered if the trailer and truck were going to slide off the road, and maybe none of us would make it home. Visibility was poor, the way was slick. We each prayed as we inched our way along the narrow roads. Then, about twenty miles from home the storm suddenly stopped. It was completely dry the rest of the way! Our part of the state did not receive any part of the storm we had battled. Snow and ice one minute, dry brown winter ground the next. We drove right out of the storm; we did not complain. It was like exiting a nightmare, or a tunnel without lights. "Praise God for the barren winter scenery with the sun shining!" I said to Rod.

When we finally parked our truck and trailer alongside the gate to the pasture where we kept Star and Dorit, the two thoroughbred "ladies" were very interested in the new horse who was about to join them. John exited the trailer quickly, and looked around at his new home. He did not appear fearful, he just wanted to EAT! We offered him the feed we gave Star and Dorit, but he was not interested; he just wanted to *eat hay!* It seemed like John had never been allowed to eat hay. He seemed to say: "Hay! Give me hay! I want *hay!* No treats, no grain, just *hay*, please and thank you!"   Never in his short life had John been allowed to eat all the hay he wanted, any time he wanted. Now he could. He must have thought he was in paradise.

Dorit was very aware John was *male* and she was *female*, and began pestering him at once. She jumped at him and squealed, lifted her tail and urinated. She was very obvious about what she wanted, but John seemed oblivious to Dorit's advances. All he cared about was food. Star, always the reserved lady, utterly disdained Dorit's brazen forwardness. Such boldness was not in Star's nature. She calmly raised her head, partially closed her eyes, revealing her white eyelashes, turned her head, and looked the other way as Dorit threw herself at John. Star seemed to be thinking either a reproachful: *"Whatever!"* Or perhaps she thought: "If you *must be so forward, so grossly obvious,* I choose not to look!" Star's estrus cycle had been shut down by her miscarriage of the twin foals in December and she had no interest in John.

The first two months we had John, from the last week of February through the end of March, *food,* not mares, in or out of estrus, was primary in his mind. The poor little horse had been starved!

In mid-March, we had the vet examine our new stallion. "He is definitely in need of some groceries!" the doctor said. His manner of expressing John's near state of starvation without actually saying so, struck me funny. *"In need of some groceries"*—for sure!

He gave us the name of a distributor for rice bran, and suggested we begin giving John rice bran daily to help him gain weight. He examined John's teeth, and set up a worming regimen in thirds rather than complete doses all at once. Apparently getting rid of all the worms at once can shock the horse's system, and can kill him. The last thing the vet did was to look underneath John. In a very matter of fact manner he told us John "would not pass a stallion inspection now." We wondered if we had thrown away $750 on an infertile stallion. We thought he was underdeveloped due to such inadequate nutrition all his life, but hoped if he was properly fed and gained weight, he would catch up in *all* areas.

In spite of this potential problem, we had much to appreciate. John had a gentle disposition, and conformation we liked: a short back, long legs, broad chest, and large bones. If we could resolve his stunted growth through care and feeding, he might have a chance to be the stallion for our mares, if not we would geld him and keep him. "He was a nice guy," we would so often say to each other in later years, and he was a nice guy from the very start. We were not the only ones who thought so.

John was even tempered from the beginning; though he was hungry, shy and somewhat fearful, he never took it out on us. He seemed humble, perhaps because he had been the "low horse on totem pole" at his previous home. Here he was the youngest, and the only male.

John was usually very humble, grateful, easy-going and content. One morning, however, he acted very unlike himself. When we walked down to feed the three horses, he acted very agitated: we could see the whites of his eyes, and both eyes were large and starry. He was tense, jumpy and "snorty"—blowing through his nose, making a sort of snorting, almost snoring noise, as horses do when something is unusual or frightening. Somehow John had gotten his too-long tail tangled in a large mass of brush—it seemed to be a small tree branch. He was dragging this large, branch-like weed in his tail, and the sound of it scraping behind him and pulling his tail was unnerving him. He acted like the devil himself was after him, and he was going to run first and ask questions later. Poor guy! The faster he ran, the more it pursued him. He shot by us at a fast trot headed for the north end of the horse pasture. Rod and I split up to catch him.

We didn't know how long he had been dragging this scary cargo in his tail, maybe most of the night, maybe just a few minutes. No matter, he was scared to death! John did not go very far at this time; he stopped on a small hill toward the north fence of the pasture, coincidentally, the direction I was walking. He stopped and looked right at me. I half expected at any minute he would take off again, but he just stood there watching me, and let me walk up to him. It seemed as if he wanted me to tell him everything would be all right. He was afraid, not threatening, just afraid. I thought he would take off again, but he did not. He just stood there.

My right arm was still in a brace due to the fracture and resulting nerve damage eight months before; I was "all thumbs" with the halter. The man who sold us John said John was "not halter-broke." We had not haltered him these first few days we'd had him; we'd just fed him and pet him, and tried to acclimate him to his new surroundings. I was afraid now the halter would scare him, but I had to take the chance he might accept it if I moved slowly enough. I walked up to John and slowly rubbed the strange thing on both sides of his neck, and on his head, and his face. I talked to him calmly, unhurriedly, softly as if he were a friend who was standing on a ledge of a high building about to jump-- someone who was afraid and needed help.

"John, I'm kind of new at this, and I'm kind of handicapped, but we need to put this on you so Rod can get the branches out of your tail," I said. To my surprise, John did not "cut and run," though he definitely had every opportunity to do just that. Instead, he just stood there listening to me talk, and letting me rub the halter on his neck and face. He might have been intently watching me as I slowly fiddled with that contraption; I don't know because I was looking more at the halter and trying to figure it out, than at him. No doubt he was listening to me, and perhaps the calm tone of my voice told him he had nothing to fear. Perhaps the kind way he had been treated here told him everything was all right and he could trust us. Maybe St. Michael the Archangel, Patron of horses and horsemen, was holding him for me. I wondered if John was thinking: "What the heck are you trying to do with that thing? Why is it taking you so long?" It would have been a perfect time for him to leave, but he did not. He seemed interested in the time I was giving him, and in what I was doing, more curious than afraid. He seemed to know I wanted to help him.

Slowly I was able to slide the halter over his head, fasten it, and pet him. Rod met me, and as I held John's lead rope and pet and talked to him, Rod tried to pull the sticks and weeds from his tail. John was afraid of the hurtful pulling, and would have none of it. He frantically side-stepped his hind end around and we could not keep him still long enough to remove the goblin from his tail. Finally we brought him down to the post where we tied him to feed him. Even with the full feed bucket in front of him he still circled round and round the post winding the rope many times around it. Rod finally managed to remove the debris; however, it was a maneuver we hoped to never have to repeat.

I always remember John as humble, willing and friendly. He was a bit awkward at first, especially in his mobility, but also in his emotions. He seemed amazed that anyone would like him, be kind to, and take time with him. He was fearful of not getting enough food, and fearful of not pleasing us. He always tried to cooperate; he wanted to be good. We certainly did not have an aggressive or impulsive horse on our hands; John just wanted to be safe, to please, and to eat.

Feeding three horses was more complicated than feeding two, especially since John needed so much more food than either Star or Dorit. I remember one feeding time Dorit, always hungry and curious, stuck her head into John's feed bucket as we were taking it to him. She popped her head out in amazement, and the whites of her eyes showed in surprise. She seemed to mentally ask: "You mean *he really gets that much food?*"

Rod read her expression, and said: "I *know,* Dorit, it *isn't fair,* is it? He gets so much food and you do not!"

Good-natured Dorit did not fight to keep John's food bucket; the food went to John, and he ate "the *whole* thing" humbly, gratefully. Dorit, always "an easy keeper," kept her weight effortlessly and needed little food to maintain it. She got fat too easily, dangerously fat on the food that the other horses ate without getting fat at all, and she was *always* hungry. I often thought she might lick the rubber right off the feed bucket. In later years we bought a grazing muzzle to control how much she could eat, but now she just got smaller portions of food than the others.

Since John needed to gain weight, and since he got a lot of food, we tied him alone at a post about fifty feet away from the mares who were tethered to posts on the front of the shed. He was utterly serious about his eating. During his meals, John frequently bent and raised his front right leg and pawed the air, sort of swinging it hurriedly back and forth, up and down, like a dog paddling in water. It seemed as if he imagined shaking his leg would hurry his food into his mouth, or as if standing on three legs somehow made it easier to get his food into his mouth. He reminded me of a child standing on his toes, lifting one leg and anxiously reaching for the cookie jar, or of someone at a boarding house extending his leg out behind him as he reached with a long arm for dessert toward the other end of a long table, or of excited children who jump up and down and clap their hands when they learn there is ice cream for dessert. He was just excited and impatient for the food to get into him. "I can't wait! Hurry-up! Hurry-up!" he seemed to be thinking. He ate with relish and intensity, and always, it seemed to me, with such a grateful heart. He still loved his hay best of all, but he seemed to know he had to eat the rice bran mixture in order to grow and live the life he was meant to live. I wondered if it appeared as ugly and unappetizing to him as it did to us. If it did, he never let on. We never knew what he thought of it, only that he ate it.

At first we called John "Little John" because he was so skinny and small, and the youngest of our horses, but he had big bones. His knees looked big, perhaps because the rest of him was so wasted. When I took a tape measure and measured around his knee and around Star's knee at the same place, however, the measurements were exactly the same. I hoped with good feed and care John could perhaps overcome his stunted size, and grow into the beautiful stallion I imagined. After all, Bold Ruler, father of Secretariat, was his great-great grandfather. That had to count for something.

John's coat was what is called sorrel or chestnut. He had a thick, bushy mane that I loved to comb while he was eating. I liked to watch the wind blow through it. To me our John grew more handsome by the day. He seemed to have such a mellow disposition. He was like a little boy who's been sick all his early life, but was now well, or like a child who is disfigured by disease suddenly being cured. His first two years had been so hard that now nothing could frustrate him. He could take everything in stride as part of life rather than an interruption. Being "at the bottom of the heap" may explain a great deal too. Two different people who have known horses well told me sometimes the bottom horse turns out to be the best horse of all, the calmest, and the most dependable. So far, John had done nothing to dispute this theory.

At times John looked awkward. He watched Dorit and Star, and followed them from a distance as if he were not really sure what he was supposed to do. He seemed sort of overwhelmed by the heavenly wide-open spaces he now inhabited with these two new friends instead of the muddy paddocks and wooden fences that had enclosed him and seventeen other unfortunate companions probably since his birth. I don't know anything for sure about his past, but only know how the situation appeared the first two times we saw him.

Sometimes he dared to wander off by himself. When Dorit nickered to him, he answered with a big nicker, and "galumphed" a funny, stiff half canter-half trot to join her. Those two soon became a "pair;" they "hung out," as kids say, and they seemed like kids, like two friends walking around the school yard together, sometimes talking, sometimes playing, always eating lunch together—almost "joined at the hip." I always thought that Dorit had ulterior motives for making John her friend. It seemed as if she knew that one day John would wake up and realize he was a stallion, and *she* was an available mare.

Dorit was five years old, John was nearly two, and Star was a more mature lady of nine. While the two younger horses enjoyed their games Star remained the reserved, stately, dignified lady, ever disdainful of Dorit's all-too-obvious advances toward John. Such antics were beneath her. When Dorit tried to encourage John to breed her, Star always turned her head, raised her long, delicate nose, partly closed her pretty, long white eyelashes in seeming shunning exasperation, and looked the other way as if Dorit's intentions were indecent to her, and as if she were above all that nonsense. Obviously she had forgotten she herself had jumped the fence to be with the stallion just before we bought her.

Easter that year we had some of the family join us for the weekend. Naturally, everyone wanted to see the horses. Rod brought Star into the north pasture separated only by a fence from the horse pasture, and some were taking turns getting on Star. After a while we took the saddle off, and Rod cantered Star around the pasture bareback, and stopped near the fence to talk to Dorit who was on the opposite side. John looked up from the grass he was eating and seemed startled and amazed to see a man astride a horse! We both saw John's surprise, and commented that it seemed John had never seen anyone ride a horse before. We began familiarizing John to people being on his back. The times our son, Paul, visited us with his family he held his little son, Matthew, on John's back while John ate. When John finished eating, Rod led him around the feeding pen at a slow walk, while Paul held Matthew on John's back. Matthew loved the ride, and it did not bother John at all. Matthew began his acquaintance with horses as a baby with Dorit before he was a year old; he was a "seasoned horseman" by the time he met John. When Matthew was two years old, his little sister, Maria was born, and as soon as she could sit up, Paul began holding her on the horses' backs for brief rides. Maria eventually loved all the horses, especially Star.

John continued to eat and to grow through April and May. Sometime the end of May and into June we began to occasionally see John attempt to breed Dorit, sometimes several days in a row. Her estrus cycle always returned about two weeks later, so we knew she was not in foal. If she conceived she would no longer ask John to breed her. In June we added a fourth horse.

John with Rod, Paul and little Matthew

John

Dorit with Veronica and Matthew abroad

Matthew petting Dorit

Rod bareback on Star with Dorit on left

Dorit and John "mane chewing" (grooming)

Chapter 10
A Fourth Horse: Winspiration

In my search for a horse I could ride instead of Star, I found a newspaper ad for a 15-year old thoroughbred mare. The owner was not yet home from work when I called, so I talked with her husband. Since the horse lived nearly one hundred miles away I wanted to be at least somewhat convinced she was a viable horse for me. I also wanted to make it clear I needed a gentle horse. I apologetically explained my situation: my fall, the surgically damaged nerve, the brace I still wore, the limited use of my right arm. The man listened kindly, and then said he thought his wife's horse might be just what I needed. He confided his wife was sorry to sell this horse, but had to because of recurrent health problems; she wanted a buyer who would love her and take good care of her. He added that this horse had had a foal, but it had died. His wife, he said, never got over the loss of the foal.

These people seemed to have the same attitude toward horses as I did. I made an appointment for the next afternoon to meet with his wife and see the horse. Veronica was home on a brief break from her work and schooling; she was glad to accompany me on another horse mission. She had been taking riding lessons for over two years and learning and experiencing a great deal. Actually, we both knew more than we had when we set off that winter day four years earlier to see the horse who became our Little Dorit.

From the moment we stepped out of the car at our destination, we were encircled with a cordial atmosphere that made us feel instantly welcome and accepted. Though they lived in a neighborhood of larger county plots with very nice homes, they were still country people—kind, sincere, honest, friendly. Their kitchen was adorned with actual photographs of horses as well as paintings and posters of horses, horse placemats decorated the kitchen table, and even the kitchen towels had horses on them. Without delay Ann took us to the barn to let us meet the beloved mare she had been bathing, clipping and combing to meet us. Her name was *Winspiration;* her loving owner affectionately called her *Winnie.*

The beautifully groomed chestnut horse with a white diamond glittering on her forehead turned to look at me as we entered, and I knew she had the exact look writer Gene Smith described as the look of her great-great grandfather, War Admiral in the Public Broadcasting System's special: *Seabiscuit: An American Experience.* Winspiration, without a doubt, had "that long, elegant, aristocratic, wide-eyed look of eagles." She was absolutely exquisite. No one could ever tell me *Winnie* was anything but beautiful. She had an impeccably chiseled, graceful, regal head that bespoke her aristocratic ancestry and made her appear younger than her years. She reminded me of pictures of Man O' War, her great-great-great grandfather on her mother's side, and it was evident she was doted upon and very affectionate. I knew instantly this was my long-sought-after equine.

In the course of our conversations I mentioned that we had a stallion that ran with the mares, and there was a chance of Winnie's being bred. My remark brought forth the incident her husband mentioned the day before.

Winnie had been in foal when she purchased her three years before. Ann had looked forward to the foaling anxiously; she and friends had camped out at the stall in shifts. The foal was nearly two weeks late. She said she determined to name the baby *Finally.* The morning the foal at last did arrive, she was already at work. A friend had arranged to stop by and check, and called to tell her that the foal had arrived.

Ann's face turned sad; she looked away and momentarily closed her eyes and held back tears. She told me she didn't know exactly what happened, but somehow Winnie stepped on the foal and it was dead by the time she arrived home in the evening. The stall was a large double one, so crowding was not the reason for the tragedy. There had been a lot of storms at the time, and some neighborhood kids had been setting off fireworks during those days. Ann thought perhaps the sudden sharp cracking of thunder, or perhaps firecrackers unexpectedly exploding near her stall spooked Winnie and she jumped on top of her baby. Since that heartbreak Ann, understandably, never wanted to breed Winnie again.

"I don't think I will ever get over it," she said.

My mind instantly flashed back to Star's loss of her twin foals: the pain of loss I endured with Star, and the grief I had observed in Star afterwards. Horses don't forget, just like women do not ever forget the loss of a child.

"I am so sorry! How awful! How horrible that was for you and for Winnie! I know I wouldn't ever get over it either," I offered in sympathy.

In a desire to make it very clear to Ann I totally understood her foal loss and the grief she vividly remembered, I recounted both the grief I had seen Star exhibit with the loss of her twin foals six months earlier, and my own devastation in her loss. Our joint foal fatalities created a bond of understanding and empathy between us: in our exchange, we understood much more than horses about each other because our *sorrow shared* spoke volumes about our attitudes toward life and towards our animals. Ann and Winnie's loss was horrible because the baby made it safely out of the womb completely well and alive; then a freak accident had taken the foal's life. Star's foals never had the chance to be born and live even for a short time. I don't know which was worse, but I know both were dreadful for horses and owners. Innocent life ended abruptly, unfairly, unnecessarily in both instances. It was crushing to consider. The shared tragedies cemented our friendship. Ann and I still email each other occasionally, and when I did write my story of the loss of Star's twin foals, Ann was one of the first to read it.

I was certain I wanted *this* horse; nothing could have changed my mind. I wrote out a check; and Ann gave me Winnie's registration papers, vet reports, and all other papers she had collected over the three years she had owned her. We traded home and email addresses, and she asked me to *at least* send a Christmas card and let her know how Winnie was doing. I assured her she would not be *just* a Christmas card recipient! I left feeling satisfied; I had finally bought *my very beautiful dream* horse at last.

As a young girl I wanted to own a chestnut horse with a white diamond on the forehead. I know I would gladly have kept and loved any horse I was given, but the red-brown horse with the white diamond was the one I rode in my day dreams, the one whose picture I doodled on my notebooks, the horse I hoped would somehow just show up at my house one day and I would be able to keep her.

I cannot pinpoint exactly why I wanted to own a chestnut horse with a white diamond on the forehead, but in reflecting on my past I have determined some clues for my specific longing. The first horse I ever remember was *Lady,* my cousin Candy's horse. Lady was a chestnut with a beautiful white blaze, and had been a show horse before my uncle bought her. All four of his children, beginning with Candy at age four, learned to ride upon the generous back of that gentle animal. By the time I was eleven, Candy had another *Lady,* a chestnut with a white diamond.

On one visit to their home in Tennessee, Candy and I slept in the hay loft because we both loved horses and more practically because our sleeping there made bed space in the house that usually slept six, and suddenly needed to sleep ten. Our parents knew the two horse-lovers would not mind sleeping in the barn. I loved the smell of the hay as we smoothed our sleeping bags over loose hay next to the square bales in the hay loft. I thought we were indeed lucky to sleep in the hayloft.

These images maybe lingered in my subconscious. They perhaps were the seed for a vision that I unintentionally, almost unknowingly nurtured for so long: my dream horse that was a chestnut with a white diamond. My perfect equine was tucked away in my memory, unrecalled, and nearly forgotten, for almost forty years. That cherished vision was lurking in the cobwebs of my mind, waiting to reemerge the day I met Winspiration: she opened the door of the dream I shut so long ago. It was like walking in and finding an old "best friend" smiling at me, waiting to take up our friendship where we left off. I felt like somehow I had known her and missed her all my life, and finally found her —this time for real.

In desiring a horse I followed a pattern in my family: my mother wanted a pony as a little girl. My mother's father, in what I always thought was a very cruel joke, put horse manure in her stocking and a note which read: "You *had* a pony, but he got away." Every time I heard that story as a child it made me sad and mad—sad for my poor mother, and angry with my grandfather for his mean attempt at an adult-sized joke on his little daughter. He passed away suddenly of a heart attack the year before my parents married, so I never met him and had the opportunity to ask him *why* he had done such a thing. Children do ask such questions. My brother learned that the scar above my father's left eyebrow was made by a rock his older sister threw at him. The next time we visited our aunt, the first thing my brother asked her was *why* she had thrown the rock at *his* father? Of course, she did not remember. Horse manure in a Christmas stocking hung up for an early January birthday was no joke for a little girl. I decided I would have been afraid of anyone who played such nasty tricks.

My mother told me her brother bought her "a riding habit" when she was in college at La Salle Junior College near Boston, Massachusetts but she never wore it. By then she was afraid of horses, and remained so all her life, though she always said she thought they were "beautiful to look at." However, a year after my mother's death, my brother sent me my mother's college scrapbooks. She had a newspaper clipping of students who were in the *LaSalle Seminary Riding Club*. My mother was raised in a horse racing town—Saratoga Springs, New York. My thought is that my mother never lost her interest in, maybe even love and desire for, horses. Her father's joke might have been the beginning of her conviction that she was afraid of horses—her own horse had run away.

My mother's younger sister, Mary Louise, whom everyone called "Cookie" beginning with an incident in her early childhood, the name stayed with her all her life--she even had "Cookie" printed on her checks. Cookie also wanted a horse as a child. Like my mother, Cookie never had a horse of her own either. However, when her first daughter loved horses, she made certain Candy had a horse. Aunt Cookie was always a friend to me.

Lady was Candy's special charge and pet. After Lady passed on, by the time we visited Candy's family when I was 11, she had "Lady II"—a chestnut horse with a white diamond on her forehead that seemed my prophetic image of Winspiration. Ever since those early days horses have been a part of my cousin's life, and they are still. They have helped her become the caring, hard-working, determined, happy woman she is. Candy and a friend give buggy rides for weddings and special occasions, she runs a bed-and-breakfast and has a knack for making every single person feel welcome and respected. It was Candy who cared for her mother in the last days of her life when she was diagnosed with Alzheimer's disease. I was not at all involved in my aunt's last days, but I think maybe Candy was somehow unconsciously returning the favor of the precious gift her mother gave her by introducing horses into her life.

Perhaps my mother and my aunt missed something vitally important in their early lives because they were denied horses; maybe horses would have made them different in some way big or small. No one will ever know. I believe horses can make us better people if we take time to listen to, and learn from them—if we let them teach us. I hope that I am a better person since horses came into my daily life; I know I would have missed a great deal had I been denied their company.

The day following my purchase of *Winnie,* Rod and Veronica and I returned with the trailer to bring her home. I could tell releasing Winnie was pulling on Ann's heart strings; she was about to cry as I put on a maroon colored halter to lead my new horse into the trailer. I empathized; I would feel the same way. Even if I completely trusted the individual who was buying my horse to give her an excellent home and the best care, it would not be easy to let her go.

"That halter looks so pretty on her," Ann whispered, choking back tears as she pet Winnie's nose for the last time. I invited her to visit us and see Winnie in her new home. She said maybe someday she would.

She emailed me a few days later: "Selling Winnie was one of the hardest things I have ever done, but knowing she has gone to a good home helps a lot." She commented that her Quarter Horse gelding had been depressed and missed Winnie. However, he was not completely alone—her stepdaughter had a pony to keep him company in Winnie's absence.

It was late evening when we reached home with our truck and trailer and our new horse. Star, John and Dorit stationed themselves at the north fence of their pasture like sentinels, carefully monitoring the entire process of the entry of the new horse into the pasture connecting to theirs, marking her every step, rustling through the grass and occasionally nickering to her.

We left Winspiration by herself that first night after giving her feed and water. She appeared content to be alone in her new pasture, and seemed quite satisfied with our grass. The three horses in the lower pasture trotted back and forth, east and west, straining their eyes, ears, necks and noses to gain knowledge of the new horse. It was as if an invisible barrier kept them from returning to the south end of their pasture, though I noticed Star gave herself breaks to eat grass—her curiosity was more subdued than John's and Dorit's.

Winnie ignored all three, pretending to not see them. She knew they were there, but she did not need them. She ate, walked leisurely around her new surroundings, and showed no sign of fear or of desire to be with the horses on the other side of the fence. There was none of the "new kid on the block" high-headed trotting around the edges of the pasture Star had exhibited. Each horse is unique, I was learning, just like each person is unique. Winspiration was amazingly calm, independent, and undisturbed by her transplantation. This trait of autonomy is one she always kept. She was almost always the first out in the mornings, surveying the morning shadows for chance signs of predators, or for choice bits of grass, quietly meditating on the scenery, or soaking up the solitude and the warmth of the early morning sun.

Nearly from the very beginning of her time with us, Winspiration accepted the role of matriarch. It was natural for her since she was the oldest horse on the farm; she was quietly, but absolutely, self-reliant, and felt no fear in moving about the property ahead of the others, doing as she pleased, when she pleased whether or not another horse accompanied her. If she wanted to take a bath in the pond, stand alone in the shade of the shed, or take a solitary early morning walk, she simply did it. The others could follow or watch, or ignore her, but she did exactly as she chose.

The first day we turned Winnie into the pasture with Star, Dorit and John, as I could have predicted, Dorit immediately threw herself at the new horse. There were a few minutes of running, stomping, biting as the group of three horses became four for the first time. Matriarch Winspiration was not impressed with this vulgar attempt at a pushy introduction. She rebuffed Dorit with a swift kick of her hind feet into the rude bay mare's chest. I saw the chunk of hair fly off Dorit's left pectoral muscle. I thought: "Ouch! *That* must have hurt!" I thought it was sort of like getting punched in the stomach when you offer a handshake in introduction. However, in Dorit's case, it seemed like she was trying to bear-hug a complete stranger rather than offer a polite hoof.

That straightforward rebuke did not deter Dorit's pesky attempts to get to *know* Win; she persevered amid her new matriarch's obvious lack of interest and assertive rebuffs. Dorit remained paired with John, and Winnie took up company with Star. Rod and I joked to each other that the two x-racehorses enjoyed swapping stories of the track. I also thought that Star and Wins were the two loners, and it seemed sort of natural they would occasionally seek each other's company.

That afternoon of Win's first day in the lower pasture she indulged herself the singular luxury of bathing in the pond, alone. No other horse was anywhere nearby. I was forking manure from the horse shed, and watched in amazement as Win elegantly approached the pond and entered like an ancient Egyptian queen going for her bath. Cleopatra herself could not have made more silken sighs of pleasure and satisfaction as she descended into a perfumed golden pool than did Winnie into the shallow water and mud of our pond. One would have thought the horse believed she was experiencing the height of luxury as she lowered herself into and out of the water again and again, slowly rolling over in the water, glistening with water and mud, rejoicing and reveling with contented groans of sheer enjoyment.

I watched the entire process with fascination; none of our horses had ever displayed such a love for bathing, nor exhibited a desire for such luxurious self-grooming. Ann had told us the day we met Winnie that she loved *to be* groomed, but had not mentioned this particular penchant for bathing. When I remarked about Winnie's beauty bath in an email to Ann, she responded that Winnie had been deprived of those for quite a while because they had to place her in a different pasture after the heavy rains that spring. She was not surprised; enjoying a bath was one of Winnie's greatest pleasures.

In later years, Pascal was another one of our horses who loved to get into the pond, especially on hot, sticky summer days though his pleasure in the water was much different from Winnie's, more like a swimmer practicing for a meet. By then we had put in two other deeper ponds. Pascal's favorite trick was to cross the entire pond. In the middle of the pond we could see only his head, neck and a bit of his back, until he began to exit the water on the opposite bank. Rod called him the *Loch Ness Monster* because he did look like *Nessie* in the middle of the pond and even as he ambled out the other bank all slimy and wet with water and mud! He looked even more grotesque when he went in for his swim in his full-body, knee length summer fly sheet. Then he really resembled the jousting mounts of medieval times.

Dorit and John joined in fun sometimes, but, like children, they seemed to prefer to dash their front feet in the shallow water, and make a ruckus splashing themselves. Sometimes they liked to lie down on their sides, half on the shore and half in the water to give their hair a good coating of mud. Dorit was especially adept at the mud pack. Maybe she thought it would add a lustrous sheen to her coat. The caked mud looked tight and hurtful when it dried, and she let us know we were risking her wrath if we tried to remove the mud from her coat.

Star approached the water too at times, though without the fanfare Winnie exhibited. She sometimes acted as if bathing were a duty for a lady, something to finish as quickly as possible. Star liked her bath to be a matter of slipping in and out before anyone noticed. She dipped her hooves into the water, quickly and quietly followed with her legs which she collapsed to the pond floor to bring the water flowing upon her back up to her neck. She rolled over once, then quickly returned to her feet, shook herself off and exited the water as if her allotted minutes were up and she would be charged extra for a longer soak. That was it; the task was completed. She was very matter-of-fact about it, almost business-like—a quick dip in and out, nothing more. Though it was obviously fun for her, something she enjoyed—she just did not make a big show of her pleasure. Star took her bath the same way she lived her life—she did her job, she did it well, she did it quietly without a display. What made her bathing funny was such a brief, shallow wash and rinse cycle actually made her dirtier *after* her bath than before. Since Star was grey and her coat reflected the sun, she didn't seem to need to cool off as often as the others. However, because she was grey, almost white, the mud was very noticeable. We could always tell when she had been in the pond even when she was far from the house. She glistened when she was wet, and looked dirty and unkempt when the mud dried, though they all looked dirty when they had indulged in a mud bath. Interestingly enough, many times only one side would be mud-coated. I always said our horses "obliged us" by bathing in the pond, half-jokingly, half sarcastically. Mud removal hurt. Sometimes we opted to let the rain rinse the horses off rather than fight with them to remove it with brushes.

All our horses enjoyed the pond, but it truly was, in her secluded moments, Winspiration's Royal Spa. For the others, a dip there was playful recreation or a cooling swim on a hot summer day. For the imperial Winnie, the place was a lavish retreat where she privately immersed herself and cooed with utter bliss and satisfaction. She really did remind me of a princess taking her beauty soak among the lilies and rare perfumes though there were no lilies or perfumed waters here.

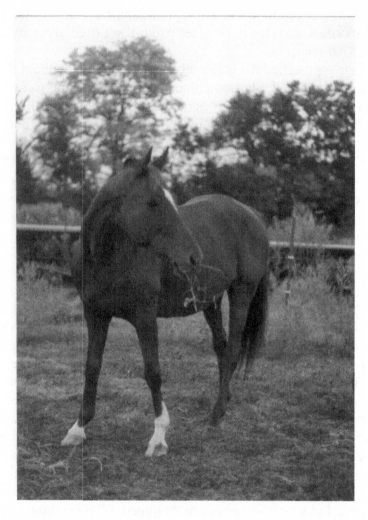

Winspiration, my Aristocrat!

Winnie (L) with John (R)

Winspiration on her early morning patrol of the premises

*(Above) Mary Barbara and Winspiration.(Below) Winnie and Star take up
one another's company.*

Winspiration sought out solitude. The fog makes an eerily beautiful picture.

Those first many months I didn't interiorize knowing *Winnie*; I just groomed her and rode her every afternoon. I didn't have to get to know her; it seemed we already knew one another. We were friends from the start. I remember those as some of the happiest days of my life. We trotted around the north pasture in every diagonal and circle we could imagine. It was really a time of borrowed freedom, a "separate peace," and an incomparable time we both looked forward to. Afterwards I fed her and lead her back to her "friends." She became my special contact to carry me into a free and simple time. It seemed we were friends since my childhood.

Once I released her, it was interesting to watch her interact with Star, John and Dorit, and see her act out her part as head mare, or matriarch, without rehearsal, and without "winning it." No one ever gave her any instruction on how to be at the top, she just knew. Her position was not disputed. Being "queen" just happened here at this time for Win; it was as though the others instinctively knew she was the oldest and entitled to unquestioned respect. Winnie had no tolerance for anyone to question her supremacy; she could turn her hind quarters and deliver a swift kick to the offender. Sometimes a simple flick of her ear quickly quelled any intention of disagreement.

Since Winnie was related to Man o' War, I began reading books about this amazing race horse. Winnie seemed to have inherited not only a similar white diamond on the head, but also some of his other character traits as related by Dorothy Ours in her book Man o' War: A Legend Like Lightning. Like Man o' War, she loved sugar cubes and sought them by touching my pocket. Even if I did not bring them for weeks, even years, she seemed to "know" when I had them, and always "asked" for them. Also like her ancestor, she was independent and had specific likes and dislikes; she was *an individual*, and like Man o' War, there was always something dignified, almost royal about my new horse. She had "that look of eagles" even though she did not inherit Man o' War's or War Admiral's racing speed. Page Cooper and Roger L. Treat began their book, Man O' War, stating in their Introduction that that Man o' War was always a horse referred to as "who" instead of "which" or "that." I liked this and afterwards always employed it in referring to *all* our horses always when talking or writing about any of them. For me it shows my love and respect for these excellent creatures God created for my enjoyment and instruction. I was of the same mind as Sheik Ilderim in the 1959 movie *Ben-Hur*: *"Do you think you can treat my horses like animals?"* All our horses were so much more to me than "just animals."

Feeding four horses now instead of three took some time to arrange and accomplish in an organized fashion. We had an orderly system for three, but our current place at the shed entrance was not adaptable for four. We now had to consider the emotions of the individual horses too—something I had not really given much thought to until Winnie came to live with us. Perhaps it was the old idiom about not being able to teach old dogs, in this case *horses*, new tricks. Perhaps Winnie just needed time to adjust to her new life just as it took me awhile to adjust to new situations. Even for a horse, it takes what it takes.

Every day we put a halter on each one, and tied each horse up for feeding and grooming. We used the time while they were eating to look for cuts or other problems, and to clean their feet, but our primary purpose was to keep them all friendly and accustomed to being caught. Well we remembered the chases we had in those first days with Star; it was worth it to us to keep them used to being caught. We caught them in descending order, from most dominant to least since we quickly learned the lower horse would become very agitated if tied while those "higher on the ladder" were loose. We wanted to keep everything calm and comfortable for everyone, ourselves included. If one horse became nervous or upset, it produced a sort of *domino effect*—the next horse in "superiority" became nervous and one-by-one made each successively lower member in the hierarchal ladder nervous. It definitely made the others uneasy, and ultimately affected Rod and me too since we were trying to keep everyone calm and accomplish feeding, grooming, and checking for potential problems or difficulties.

Ultimately, we decided we should make a feeding pen at the north end of the horse pasture: a rectangular enclosure with gates on either end, a place large enough for each horse to have his or her own space. Once we bought the gates, pipes and posts, John and Dorit "helped" Rod make the new pen. While Rod, Dorit and John worked on our newest building project, Star and Winnie, two x-racehorses with stories to share, "hung-out" together, ate and, I imagined, maybe swapped stories of their racing days.

John and Dorit help Rod start to build the new feeding pen

Rod picks up square bales with the accumulator

Chapter 11
Winter Feeding Challenges

The end of July was the first time I saw John breeding Winnie. He may have done it before since they were always in the same pasture together. I did not notice until now that Dorit was no longer "coming into heat." I suddenly realized it when John accepted Winnie's invitation to breed her, and Dorit attempted to distract or stop him. After successfully getting John away from Winnie, Dorit ran up to Winnie with body language that tried to convey a very solicitous, consoling affect as if she were saying: "Oh, my dear! Was that stallion trying to breed you? Oh, you poor thing! I'll keep him away from you!" Neither Winnie, nor John, nor Rod, nor I were fooled. Dort was jealous! She regarded John as "hers," and she did not want him breeding anyone else because *she* was in foal by him.

This whole episode of John breeding another mare was normal: the stallion ran with the mares, and bred them when they came in to season. No stallion could miss a mare in season—she was *very obvious* about it. The jealousy was surprising to us. I never thought horses were monogamous, that they partnered for life, so I was surprised by the display of possessiveness. One stallion breeding many mares was common, but unknown to Dorit. Our frantic little bay mare had been bitten by "the green-eyed monster." As persistent as she was at attempting to keep John away from Winnie, and Winnie away from John, she was still no match for their hormones.

Winnie was determined and demanding, and she was "in season." John was the young, exuberant lord of his harem thanks to the good diet we had been feeding him. Winnie's estrus cycle lasted about five or six days. She and John then had a rest for about two weeks before it returned. She asked John to breed her every single day during her estrus cycle, and John obliged her. However, she did not "settle," that is, she did not conceive that first summer.

An Indian summer is a beautiful time in Kansas. One late September afternoon when Rod and I were out with the horses, riding a little, taking pictures, and just enjoying our good horses, Rod took my picture with Winnie, and then with Star. John was hanging around, letting us pet him, just being friendly. Winnie's estrus cycle was apparently over for this season, and Star still had not cycled since her miscarriage and, therefore, had no interest in breeding. Things were very peaceful. Suddenly Dorit backed up to John and raised her tail. My heart sank into my stomach. Rod and I looked at each other sadly.

"She's lost the foal. She's not pregnant anymore; she's back in heat again. I wonder when it happened."

Rod and I were both disappointed. We were so looking forward to that foal. John seemed to be fertile; at least he *acted fertile*. He certainly seemed to be doing *his* part admirably. Winnie was not settling, and Star was not interested in even trying to conceive. Dorit had been our one hope.

Yet I realized that this was nothing compared to the ordeal we had experienced with Star's loss of the twins the previous December. Star had less than three months left of her pregnancy; Dorit's was an early natural miscarriage, just as is common with women in the first trimester. For her there was no bleeding, no noticeable discharge, though one of her udders was swollen. Our little mare was barely pregnant, two or possibly three months into an 11- month gestational period. Nevertheless, she was pregnant no longer; the baby was gone. Foals, it seemed, were not meant to happen for our horses yet. However, John had other ideas. He bred Dorit again that same September afternoon. Five months later the vet confirmed what we were suspecting by then: she was in foal.

Winter follows autumn as inevitably as day ends and night begins. Winters seem longer to me than the other seasons. The horses didn't seem to mind it at all. God, in His eternal wisdom, designed the horse to grow a warm winter coat, and He seemed to have favored Star greatest in the grace and speed department, and in the winter coat department. As wintry weather approached each year we took note of Star's thickening coat and feared we would have a horrible winter until we came to understand that she was no prophetess. She grew a substantial winter coat whether our winter was mild or hard; she was always thin, and God wanted her prepared to stay warm. Sometimes it seemed to me the horses liked winter best because there were no flies to stomp or swish away. They seemed to love running races in the snow and frigid temperatures just as much as they loved running over the grass in the spring and summer, maybe even more.

Our horses had more than their heavy hair to help them through this harsh season. We were fortunate enough to be able to give our horses plenty of hay because we grew our own. Our first few years of horse ownership we bought hay. Finding someone selling hay for a decent price was usually a job in itself. We were never sure we were buying good hay, but even if it was questionable we felt it impolite to turn around and walk away after scheduling a time to pick it up. The price could be settled on the phone, the quality could not. Getting the bales, loading them into our truck, bringing them home, and unloading all took time. Growing our own hay and buying a used hay rake and baler to harvest it was a definite advantage for us and for the horses.

In the square-bale-days of our horse ownership if Rod was at work in the early winter mornings, I walked down to break the ice on the pond, and pushed a cart loaded with two seventy-pound square hay bales to feed the horses. Later we saved money from each pay check, subtracted like a payment, and entered it in the back of the check book until we had enough to buy a small round baler. The round bales were delivered by tractor every several days instead of twice a day every day by hand-pushed cart, which definitely made our life easier. However, in those first horse-ownership years we hauled hay morning and night. I liked it best when Rod's and my tracks from a previous day remained in the snow and made a trodden path for me to follow. Mornings of glistening new snowfall were pretty, but it was more difficult to trudge through the thick frosty mass pushing the cart. Dry above freezing mornings were my favorites because there was no ice to break, no snow to plow through. The horses always spotted me, and made me feel so welcome and needed by waiting for me at the gate as they watched me approach. I was not deceived; they were mostly interested in the food I brought for them, not in me, but it always made me feel good to be welcomed so warmly. As soon as I saw their heads hanging over the fence near the gate, I began to call my greetings to each of them.

"Good morning, Star! Good morning, Dorit! Good morning, Winnie! Good morning, John! How are my good horses? How are my babies?" I always referred to them as "my babies" though none were babies. When we first bought Dorit, Veronica knowingly predicted: "Whatever we name the horse, Mom will call it 'Baby.'"

She was right; I suppose to me they are *babies* because we take care of them and they depend completely on us. I was alone a lot of the time; I had no one else to talk to, so I talked to the horses. They understood I liked them and that I was happy to see them and that was all that mattered especially because I was bringing a new supply of hay.

Before I could push the cart through the feeding pen exit gate which led directly into their pasture, all four ravenously attacked the two bales wedged in the cart and began pulling off huge mouthfuls of hay, gleefully gobbling and munching as I continued to slowly push the cart forward through the often snowy, muddy, traffic jam of horses to dispense their breakfast into the feeders. In his great eagerness to eat, John especially had a knack for being able to dislodge an entire bale from the cart. Sometimes the force he used to grab his first bites of his meal made the heavy load burst and shatter. The baling twine could not stand such abuse and broke under the force of John's eager, hungry jaw scattering flakes of hay on the ground in a flurry before I managed to get it into their feeders. I had to quickly gather up the loose squares of hay, called flakes, and carry them to the safety of the feeders before the horses trampled upon them and lost potential food. They might nibble at hay on the ground initially, but definitely preferred to grab it from the feeders. It became a game to see who could get to the hay first: would I be able serve it before they helped themselves? Every day was a frenzied, but always good natured contest.

Once their feeders were stocked, our horses were polite and all ate from one area, while I filled the remaining feeders. We had four horses, but we had at least six stations where they could eat lest one horse higher on the totem pole nudge out someone of lower caste. They also loved to scrounge hay fallings from the cart. Tasty seeds fell into the floor of the "feed wagon" and they relished those like candy.

Since I was delivering food, I was closely watched and followed; tufts of the prized hay was sometimes greedily yanked from my arms and eaten before I could deliver it to its destination. Never was I so popular! I remember laughing sometimes and asking: "Can't you wait?" *Obviously they could not!* They acted like they were starving—as if their last feed was weeks ago, instead of just the evening before. Usually, after unloading all the flakes of hay, and petting them while they began munching at their chosen places, I walked down to the pond and broke ice with the wooden handle end of the garden fork, and then pitched out the pieces of floating frozen water and threw the broken shards out on to the iced-over pond. I always made at least two, openings in the ice so one horse could not "hog" the hole, chase the others away and not allow them to drink. If one drinking hole re-froze, perhaps the other might remain open until Rod and I came in the later afternoon to give them grain, restock the hay, and re-break the ice for the night. A frequently used hole in the ice froze less rapidly than one that was not used, so we did not make more than two holes.

Sometimes Paws, one of our cats, followed me to the pond, and scurried around on top of the ice playfully batting at the scattering shattered pieces I threw on top of the frozen floor. Occasionally one of the horses quietly followed me, or walked with me to the pond to wait as I broke the ice and then gratefully took a drink. I like to watch horses drink: they seem to drink like they are drinking through a straw, or like they are sipping instead of lap, lap, lapping like a dog, or quietly licking like a cat. I was surprised the first time I observed it.

Frequently after the hay was dispersed into the feeders, the horses began playing a game that reminded me of musical chairs. This game had no music, but I called it "musical eating positions" anyway. It was a dominance game played for the choicest bits of hay and the most comfortable position—usually out of the cold north or west winter wind, or nearest the largest pile of hay. One minute every horse was happily eating, and then one, often Queen Winnie, decided *she* wanted to eat somewhere else, or thought the hay looked tastier where another horse was eating, and in the flick of an ear, the great rotation began. John was "low horse" but he was nonplused by his ladies' antics. Wherever he ended up, he ate happily. It was no big deal to him to walk around to the other side of the feeder, or even to another feeder. There was plenty of food, and that was all he cared about. Actually, the four of them got along very well. There was never any biting or kicking. Winnie simply tossed her head, gave another horse "that look," pointed her nose in another direction, or flicked her ear and the other horse moved. During Winnie's first winter with us, I frequently saw Winnie and Star together. Star practiced the same intimidation on Dorit: an almost imperceptible nod of her head sent Dorit scurrying to another place to eat. John moved if he thought Winnie or Star wanted him to eat elsewhere, but he was not as afraid of them as Dorit was. Once in a while, Dorit tried to intimidate John, but they were friends, and usually ate together. John seemed to extinguish Dorit's "nit-picky" attempts at dominance with a good natured, broad-minded male shrug that seemed to say: "Oh, forget that dumb stuff, Dorit. Let's just eat. There's ample hay for all of us."

The last two days of January that year brought a damaging ice storm. The newscasters called it "the storm of the century." Cities north of us, Kansas City and St. Joseph had heavy snow; we had ice. Power lines were down everywhere, branches were broken, roads were blocked and impassable, and every blade of grass, every tree limb, every fence wire and post looked as if it was dipped in glass. Travel was treacherous. Fortunately those two days happened to be Rod's days off from work. We did not leave the house the first day except to feed the horses. They remained in their shed to stay out of the ice and wind; they did not venture out at all the first day. All were hungry and were so glad we brought them hay and water. They definitely depended on us to provide for them.

We were without electrical power for two days; fortunately we heat our house with a wood burning stove. Not knowing when the electricity would return, the second afternoon we decided to drive into town, 25 miles away, to get bags of ice and containers to store our refrigerated and frozen foods. We barely recognized the landscape! It seemed as if we had been transported to an ice kingdom where broken trees, downed power lines, every building, fence, tree and farm glistened like diamonds from the ice coating that had poured from the sky and not missed even the smallest crevice. It truly seemed a different world, and was beautiful even in its inconvenience.

The horses seemed happy and content because they had us to provide their food and water, and a shed to protect them from the wind, ice and cold. They did not find the harsh weather an inconvenience or a disturbance, but just serenely accepted the weather as part of God's seasonal plan for which He had set their biological clocks very accurately. They were so adaptable! They accepted without protest whatever came their way. Their ready adaptability and their trust in their providers was another one of God's instructional gifts to me as I grew to accept my quiet, hidden life in the country. Our horses, to me, were an example of Christ's advice: "Therefore do not be anxious, saying, 'What shall we eat?' or 'What shall we drink?' or 'What shall we wear?' …your heavenly Father knows that you need them all." (Matthew 6: 31-32) The horses became my example to trust God to provide and teach in the hidden quiet, and in all times.

Chapter 12
Spring: Thoughts of Breeding and Birthing

The month of March in Kansas is always a disappointment. I look for spring, but it is still winter: the hard-blowing north wind is almost ever-present, and there is still the chance of single digit weather overnight, which yields frozen ponds with ice to break, and sometimes snow. However, the white stuff usually melts faster with spring approaching than it does in December, January or February and is much wetter. In March there is the real hope that warmer weather is coming. The horses seem to sense it approaching too as they begin to shed their winter coats, and hunt for tufts of green grass. They seem to have every new green blade "staked-out," and try to mow down the tender new blades the moment they stick their new arms from the earth.

As the spring began to bloom, we thought of breeding our mares, Winnie and Star, and of the coming of Dorit's foal the beginning of August. Though Star remained sterile, that is, completely out of her estrus cycle, and had no interest in John, Winnie was very interested in him. Star and Win remained friends, but Star looked away when Winnie made herself available to John. Since Winnie did not "settle" last year, this year we decided to try a different approach, one recommended for humans having difficulty conceiving. Instead of allowing John to breed her every day, which is what she wanted, and which John obligingly did, we allowed him to breed one day, then skipped the next. At the end of a breeding day, we put Win in the north pasture along with her friend, Star, where the two remained until the next breeding day, when we again turned all the horses into the same pasture.

With Star we decided to take more radical measures. A close friend told me she had a horse who miscarried at six months and that horse never came into heat again. Star had lost her twins in almost her ninth month of eleven months of pregnancy. A late-term foal loss seemed to induce sterility. I saw this reign of infertility as very possibly assaulting Star the rest of her life. The beginning of May I consulted the vet about Star's infertility. He told me the same prostaglandin he gave Dorit four years ago, at age two, to miscarry the possible foal from Pascal, could be given to Star as an intramuscular injection to induce ovulation. The shot would "jump start" Star's hormones so she would allow John to breed her. Since we had initially bought Star with the intention she would be a brood mare, Rod and I decided it was worth the attempt to get her to conceive. The vet said he knew we were adept at giving our horses their regular shots, and he had no problem selling us the prostaglandin and allowing us to inject it ourselves rather than paying for a separate visit for him to give the injection.

I drove to the veterinarian's office to pick up the "In-Synch" for Star. The vet was adamant that I not touch the medicine. I remember distinctly his instructions:

"Have your husband draw up and give this. I don't care if you have no intention of ever becoming pregnant again, have your husband handle the syringe and give the injection."

I simply answered in the affirmative, though the thought of me considering becoming a mother again at age fifty-three certainly never crossed my mind. However, I was sufficiently impressed that the prostaglandin was a heavy-duty drug, and carefully carried it home in the zip-lock plastic bag. The next day, May 3rd, Rod drew up the prostaglandin and gave Star the injection. The vet said we could expect estrus to occur in four to seven days. He was right, though results happened sooner than predicted. Star encouraged John to breed her every day beginning May 6th through May 11th. We were convinced the medicine worked: Star definitely came into estrus, and John definitely performed his role. Since Star had conceived twins in the past, the vet suggested an ultrasound to determine whether she was again carrying twins. If the timing was absolutely correct, and she had conceived twins, he could, as he put it, "pinch off" one of the developing fetal horses in an attempt to save one of the horses, and the pregnancy. He warned us there was a chance in doing this procedure that he would cause both foals to be lost. The idea of intentionally killing one of the fetuses made me scared and sad enough, but the idea that in doing so we could lose both was worse. I hoped this procedure would not be necessary.

May 24th we loaded Star into the trailer and drove to the vet. Whenever we take Star somewhere in the trailer, she reminds me of a dog who likes to go for rides in the car: she jumps right in as if she is excited to go. When we arrived at the veterinary hospital, as chance would have it, there was another horse ahead of us who was miscarrying twins in the side yard of the vet's office in front of the ultrasound shed. There was blood all over the ground, and the mare was very agitated. *This* was *not* what I needed or wanted to see at this time. I felt horrible for the poor mare in the driveway. I hoped and prayed this would not happen to Star.

Star had to be clamped into a turnstile sort of cage the vet called "stocks." She was exceptionally good during the whole procedure, even when the vet donned a long, elbow- length latex glove and did an internal exam. She just stood there like the true dignified lady she always was. We were so proud of her. The bad news was, according to the ultrasound, she was *not* pregnant! The vet asked if we were *sure* the stallion had bred Star. When I informed him John had bred Star daily for six days, he exclaimed:

"Oh! I didn't expect him to be so exuberant."

We knew John; we were not surprised. We knew he never refused a mare's invitation. What did surprise us was Star's sudden receptivity brought on by the "In-Synch." The heavy-duty medicine definitely worked.

"Sometimes it is simply too early to tell, and a second ultrasound will reveal she is indeed pregnant," the vet told us. He instructed us to watch for returning signs of estrus, and to return in two weeks for a repeat ultrasound. We paid him, and left, somewhat disheartened, but still with hope. John had certainly done his part admirably; Star just *had* to have conceived. If she had not conceived, we would try the every other day routine we had tried with Winnie.

Three days later, May 27th, John bred Winnie again. Neither Winnie nor Star ever returned to their heat cycles; both mares were in foal. We returned with Star to the vet for a second, and what we knew would be a conformational ultrasound June 5th. This time the picture revealed a single fetal foal. Thank God! We were so excited—our long-awaited baby was finally on its way two years after originally planned.

By the beginning of summer we had three mares in foal, and life in the pasture settled down. No more squealing, no more breeding. John definitely proved he could do his job as a stallion. Life was good.

The horses frequently came to the fence along the road as I jogged by in the early mornings, and I obliged them by picking through the damp grass to scratch their heads and pet their noses wet with morning dew. Usually, immediately upon my return from my run, before I changed my clothes or ate my breakfast, I gathered their fly masks, and donned my knee-high rubber boots, my "Big Boots," to wade through the tall grass to put on their fly masks. I reminded myself of a drawing of Christopher Robin discovering the North Pole in the book Winnie the Pooh of childhood memory. When Christopher Robin put on his "Big Boots," Pooh knew an "Adventure" was about to happen. Perhaps the sight of me trekking through the tall grass signaled an adventure for the horses. They always greeted me with friendly nuzzles, and checked to see if I had brought them carrots, which I often did. They appreciated their fly masks, and often lined up to receive them when they saw me approaching. One morning, however, I found only Star. I put her mask on and asked:

"Where is Dorit, Star?" As if she understood, and perhaps she really did since they all definitely knew their names, and the names of the others. Star pointed her nose to the northeast where I saw Dorit coming up over the terrace.

"Dorit! Come here to get your mask," I called. Dorit began walking toward me, but then she turned her head over her back and gave a loud nicker. Suddenly John came galumphing in his awkward, stiff half trot, half canter to join Dorit and let me put on his mask too. Winnie did not follow John. I could not find Winnie, and none of the other three gave me any hint as to her whereabouts. I called and called for her, but she was nowhere to be found. Continuing to call, I thrashed through the high, wet grass toward the shed. I usually looked in the shed for the horses on my return from my run; the shed opens to the south, and from the road one can often see horses a quarter mile away. Winnie liked to be alone in the shed's shady, cool darkness in the mornings, but I had not noticed anyone in the shed today. Maybe she was all the way in the back, hidden in the dark corner. I kept calling as I neared. Finally, as I was approaching the back of the shed, Winnie curved her head around the outside wall and gave me that "Winnie look"—that long, elegant, aristocratic, wide-eyed look of eagles--her ancestor War Admiral's special look, and hers.

"Yes? You called?" her gaze seemed to say. She seemed to have *no idea* I was calling for her, or at least she *acted* as if she had not heard me. Perhaps she was lost in her own "thoughts" and shut out my calling for her. In her quiet, independent manner, she was doing her own thing, enjoying the coolness and shade of the shed, alone, out of the reach of flies and the other horses. Winnie met me halfway, and, as Star always did, politely lowered her head for her fly mask. Mothers-to-be, I thought with a smile, are entitled to a few idiosyncrasies. However, as years went by, we noticed that Winnie's hearing was always selective—she heard what she wanted to hear, pregnant or not.

While our four horses were playing games, enjoying a life of ease, Pascal was finishing his second year with Veronica at a stable near her university. She was working on her Doctorate in English, and he was studying dressage and jumping. For this second year Veronica moved him to a different barn, one where he worked out to classical music and enjoyed daily turn-out from his stall. One of Veronica's roommates, Melissa, an accomplished horsewoman since her youth, arranged to lease Pascal, which meant she helped with his board fee, and rode him two or three days a week as did Veronica. Being ridden nearly every day, Pascal was learning a lot.

Rod and I visited Veronica and Pascal in April; I thought he really seemed to remember us. It was fun to see them both in this new environment. Pascal seemed happy: he was in a friendly place where he had other horse and people friends, was learning new things and was receiving good food plus a lot of attention. As in everything else she did, Veronica took her horse-owning responsibility seriously. Everyone at the barn loved Pascal; people who knew horses well said he "had a good mind." By then he had a new name: no one called him *Pascal*, everyone knew him as *Buddy*. He was Veronica's buddy—someone she looked forward to seeing, and who looked forward to seeing her, and a much-needed and much-appreciated break from her fellowship teaching and her doctoral studies.

That May Pascal and Veronica entered a show and won several ribbons. I considered them both our highly competent and shining scholars.

Veronica and Pascal clear a jump in a show.

Pascal's Wager

Chapter 13
Chaos: A Prophetic Name Choice

Dorit was due to foal in early August, but the vet, and my books on foaling, warned us that summer foals frequently came early. I read and re-read my two books on foaling, and we gathered the suggested supplies in preparation for the big day: clean towels, fleet enema, thermometer, bulb syringe, plastic trash bags for the placenta, and so on. We watched for signs that indicated Dorit was almost ready.

On July 13, coincidentally my Aunt Cookie's birth date, all day long Dorit kept to herself in the pasture and barely ate at all. Both of these behaviors were unusual for her and could be signs of impending delivery. She seemed to be "thinking." We also thought we noticed relaxation of the muscles over her hips and around her tail, and that her abdomen seemed more centered than lopsided, and appeared to have dropped. Her udders had been waxing, dripping, milk for two weeks. That evening at 6 PM, we left to attend the Saturday night Vigil Mass for our Sunday obligation. When we returned home about 7:30, Rod said he was going to check on the horses and take the fly masks off for the night. We noticed John, Winnie and Star standing along the west fence of the large pasture we had hayed, but we did not see Dorit. Rod went on ahead of me, and when I came out of the house, he called:

"Bring your stuff!"

I had everything assembled. I grabbed the bucket with all the equipment and ran toward the hay field. Rod was on his knees pulling the foal's front legs out and tearing the amniotic sac as the foal's legs, then head, emerged. We removed the amniotic sac leavings from the nose area and used the bulb syringe and towel to remove fluid from the nose to make sure the foal could breathe. Suddenly a new, wet, blinking eyed foal was quietly looking around. She was a chestnut, like her father, with a white blaze. She was over two weeks premature, small and thin, but she appeared healthy.

John, the nervous father on the other side of the fence, was the most agitated of the three standing there. He seemed "worried" about

Dorit as she labored hard. Dorit, still reclining, turned her head around and looked at the foal. Her eyes widened, and she stood and sort of sniffed her, but that was all. She did not lick her, or seem very interested. She began looking for her companions. She had not passed the placenta. The books I read both said the placenta was usually passed within a few minutes, at least by an hour; if it was not discharged after three hours the vet should be called. It was a Saturday night, and the last thing I wanted to do was call the vet at home to report a retained placenta, but I did. I did not want to wait until 11 PM for the initial call, so I called him at 9 PM to alert him it had been over an hour since delivery. He said we were correct in the time frame, and to call him back if she did not deliver the placenta by the end of 3 hours.

Perhaps I could have waited until the next morning; probably by then she would have delivered the placenta on her own, but this was our first foal delivery. Later I was told we could wait up to 8 hours without a problem. Rod and I were both fairly new at this. He had pulled many calves on his father's ranch, and he had been with me for the birth of each of our three children, but his father's horses delivered their foals by themselves in the hills. I had worked as a nurse helping women have babies in a hospital, but had never assisted a horse. Rod did know and had stressed to me the importance of letting the mare bond with the foal—of not getting in the way too much, not interfering with, or possibly destroying, the mare and foal's natural instincts.

By the time I had to call the vet again, his attitude had changed. Annoyed about being called out on Saturday night, he was angry by the time he arrived, and roughly, rapidly, and loudly reassembled our round pen panels into a smaller circle to enclose the mare and foal. He was mad and resentful toward Dorit for not accepting her baby, miffed about being called out late on a Saturday night, incensed about the retained placenta and the work it involved. I winced; his distemper made me feel like it was *our* fault. I could not help but remember the times I, as a nurse, was called to assist nurses with an emergency delivery, or had to answer the page of a home care patient at two in the morning for some tenuous reason. I didn't like it either, but being "on-call" goes with the medical professional's territory.

"If you can't stand the heat, get out of the kitchen. If you hate what you do, do something else," I thought to myself as he banged the round pen panels, and thrashed angrily, hastily through his supplies. This same vet had been so compassionate, so gentle to horse and owner's feelings when he treated Star's twin foal loss on a cold December Saturday morning. He seemed to have a personal grudge against Dorit—as if she were a sullen, spoiled teenager who was doing all this on purpose. Maybe he was just angry to be called away from his home and family on a weekend night. I know I would have been irritated too, but hopefully I would not take it out on the patient.

He washed her womb, gave her drugs to contract her uterus, and antibiotics to prevent infection. The flashlights and the truck headlights seemed to disturb both mare and foal, so we turned them off. It was pitch black. After midnight, just before the vet left, he said the mare would deliver the placenta by morning, and he would return to check her and examine it. In the darkness we could hear sucking, and assumed the foal was nursing. We did not turn on any more lights because lights seemed to aggravate Dorit.

At the first hint of daylight the next morning we checked on Dorit and the foal. The foal was *outside* the pen; Dorit, standing inside the enclosure, appeared hostile to the foal. How the little one managed to get out of the round pen panels we never knew.

The vet arrived early and in a more amiable frame of mind. He carefully inspected the placenta, and palpated Dorit's uterus. He was knowledgeable and capable, and an excellent doctor especially when he was in a good temper. The placenta was expelled intact, which he told us was "a good thing." Pieces of retained placenta could cause infection and hemorrhaging, just as in human mothers. In addition to providing possible physical and medical complications for the mare, he would have to anesthetize Dorit again for the removal of the tissue, and the price for resolving these problems and services would greatly increase our bill. I assumed that was what he meant by a "good thing."

The only problem we had was that Dorit had no inkling she had foaled. The anesthesia and antibiotics from the night before had left her with no memory of giving birth. Unlike human mothers, seeing the baby was not enough to trigger her recollection. She refused to allow the foal to nurse; she recognized the foal as an intruder. The sucking noise we had heard in the dark was the poor foal searching for Dorit's teats, sucking on her legs, her side, on anything she encountered hoping to find milk. The vet left, and Rod and I led Dorit and the foal to the shed and closed the gates. We hoped if Dorit and the foal were alone, she would relax and allow her to nurse.

Dorit regarded the foal as a complete stranger and snapped at her. We ultimately had to restrain the mother and make her allow her baby to suck. Dorit was very angry: she showed the whites of her eyes, and sunk her teeth into the 6x6" support post in the center of the shed. She tried to bite and kick the foal, but between the two of us, and a muzzle, we were able to get some colostrum, first milk full of important antibodies, into the new little foal. Poor little girl! We felt so sorry for her. Her mother seemed to hate her and didn't want her near. What a battle it was to help the foal to nurse and not be kicked in the process, or get kicked or bitten ourselves. With our joint persistence, the hungry unwanted new little one had a full tummy, curled up in the hay, and went to sleep.

We did not dare leave Dorit alone with the foal for fear she would kill her. We either took turns, or stayed together in the shed guarding mother and baby. Rod took two days of vacation from work, and I slept in the shed the first two nights, rising each time the foal wanted to nurse to restrain Dorit. It was a constant battle. In the pre-dawn darkness of my second morning in the shed, Rod came down and found me asleep. Dorit was lying down on the floor of the shed, baby Chaos—her name before she was born—was one her knees nursing as her mother, flat out on the floor, either slept, or, in exhaustion, had given up fighting. Our little Chaos was determined to live.

About the time Veronica got her horse, she talked of Chaos Theory and very briefly explained it to us. We thought Chaos was a good name for a thoroughbred horse, but she selected Pascal's Wager. We decided our first foal would be called *Chaos.* It was a prophetic name in a way because the main idea of chaos theory is a small change at the start of a process, or a life, may make a large change in it as time goes on. This proved to be very true for our Chaos whose life certainly began in chaos.

As Rod roused us all, we looked at Dorit's udder and noticed one side was swollen and tender to the touch. We now knew there was

111

another reason Dorit refused to allow Chaos to nurse: she had mastitis, inflammation of her teats: sucking was painful. The morning of the third day of Chaos' frail life, in desperation, we decided we had to start to get real food into her. We turned Dorit out of the shed. She immediately hurried to the south end of the pasture, near the fence and stood there looking at the shed from a safe distance. She did not return to the other horses or even look in their direction. Little Chaos walked up to the flattened hay on the shed floor where her mother had lain, sniffed it, and looked towards Dorit. The meltingly sad, questioning look in Chaos' eyes broke my heart. Chaos *knew* Dorit was her mother, and she knew her mother did not want her. This beautiful little foal, alone, rejected, discarded— nobody to comfort her, to feed her, to nurture her. From her protected distance, Dorit glared at Chaos as if she were a thing of evil: something she despised and resented. She would never go back. Her rejection of Chaos was final and complete. In a response very unlike herself and the nature we had come to know as "Dorit," she remained aloof from the herd for the rest of the day and night, choosing to stay under the trees near the south fence.

Baby Chaos, with a full tummy, nestles in the hay for a nap.

Litle Dorit's filly, Noble Chaos

Now that Dorit had separated herself permanently from the role as Chaos' mother, Rod and I set about getting food into our little baby. Though rejected by her mother, this amazingly strong-willed little filly was determined to live, to stay alive no matter what. We had a large bottle with a nipple my friend, Barbara, who raised cattle had loaned us "just in case." She used it to feed many claves; we had hoped we would not need it, but wanted to have it on hand. Thankfully, we also prepared enough to purchase powdered milk. Chaos could not figure out how to use the nipple on the bottle. We even tried smaller nipples, but she understood nothing about sucking on them. However, when we gave her a bucket of milk, she knew exactly how to plunge her mouth and nose into the bucket and rapidly guzzle the milk until the bucket was empty.

Thus began our eight-month parenting project. Rod and I fed Chaos every 2 to 3 hours. He took the 11 PM feeding when he returned from work, and I took the 2 and 5 AM feedings. Rod usually took the mid-morning feeding. When he left for work, just after 1 PM, I walked down to the shed to feed Chaos and spend at least an hour currying her, petting her, and talking to her. In the evenings after her feeding, I took a walk with her along the fence, leading her with rope and halter, letting her eat grass and explore. Later I removed the halter and rope and just let her walk beside me. I liked to watch our elongated shadows on the summer grass. She stayed right by my side though she did wander off a little bit to nibble grass and look around. These were beautiful, quiet hours, hours that radiated peace, contentment, and joy. This little foal seemed the complete embodiment of new life, trust, beauty, and wide-eyed exploration. It was exciting beyond words to watch Chaos introduce herself to the world and regard me as her security. She needed me completely. The quiet July and August evenings with Chaos walking near me as the shadows lengthened seemed almost a glimpse of heaven—our own special "separate peace." This truly felt like a childhood, or some part of my life, I had somehow missed by living in the city. The rushing world of cities, and suburban neighborhoods, all the hustle and bustle, vanished in those hours of quiet strolls together. I treasured them and was so thankful I could be part of this foal's life in these hushed hours as each day grew to a close. The words of Isaiah seemed to fit: "Can a woman forget her sucking child...Even these may forget, yet I will not forget you." (Isaiah 49:15) God had not forgotten me either, He lovingly taught me through His horses.

During those walks in the summer evening, the other four adult horses were grazing in the large pasture where Rod cut hay in May; their entry to the smaller pasture with the shed was blocked by the gate into the pen where we fed them. They had a pond at the north end of the large pasture, and had no need to enter Chaos' smaller one. Sometimes John would come up to the fence as Chaos walked by with me; Winnie and Star often looked in our direction, and sometimes moved a bit closer, but Dorit, if she even looked, dared not come near—she did not want to come near. John, I believe, knew Chaos was his daughter, and as time went on, it was John who was most considerate of her.

Dorit returned to estrus about a week after she delivered Chaos, which my books told me was normal. She was bred by John, but returned to estrus after several breeding attempts by John, so we knew she had not conceived. However, September 27th when John bred Dorit, she did not come back into heat. She was pregnant along with Star and Winnie, and would deliver in early August, or before. Chaos had been over two weeks premature; the vet and my books correctly warned summer foals often are born early. We hoped this time her baby would be full-term and Dorit would accept her baby.

It seemed Rod and I had become Chaos' father and mother, and we enjoyed it, though it definitely made demands on our time. It was almost like having another baby, even to getting up in the night to feed her. Our daughter-in-law, Kelli, had a little girl born in May that year, Maria, and we sometimes empathized about night feedings. She said she was glad she did not have to get into the car and drive a quarter mile at 2 AM to feed her daughter, but only had to walk from one room to another. A baby in the house was a far cry from a horse in a shed in the pasture, but both were responsibilities. Rod and I *had* to be home to feed Chaos, so that meant we did not venture far from home nearly that entire year. I think our family thought we were overdoing it a bit—after all, "she's *just* a horse."

For "just a horse" we were devoted "parents." In the mornings we forked the manure out of her shed, and put down fresh hay. She often followed as one or the other of us carried out the manure, and often she wandered a short distance away, exploring and nibbling grass. One morning when I returned to the shed for another forkful of manure; I did not realize that Chaos had not seen me leave. She began wildly running around and around the shed with a frightened look in her eyes, nickering loudly. At first I did not connect her alarm with my absence, but then I realized that she was unaware I was just inside. I stepped out from the shadows of the shed into the sunlight, and as soon as she saw me she came up to me and stood at my side. I pet her soft neck and reassured her. I clearly understood Rod and I were her security.

We called several places attempting to get a nanny goat so Chaos could suckle, but everyone told us they "let their nannies dry up." It was July, not April or May. Finally we found a couple who offered to loan us a yearling goat as a companion for our baby. Kindly, they said we could keep *Carrots* as long as we liked, and return her when we no longer needed her.

Chaos and the little white goat were instant friends. They were always snuggled next to each other when we came to the shed in the mornings or afternoons, though we were never quite fast enough to take their picture. Soon they went everywhere together. It was heart-warming to see those two trot into the hay pasture together to join the other horses. With the little goat as her constant companion, we soon felt much more at ease about allowing Chaos to join the "herd".

That little white goat was a blessing for Chaos. She had no real friend in our other horses. While they never bothered her, they were not attentive to her like a mother, nor were they interested in being her companion or playmate. John was the kindest, but he did not fall into the "buddy" role little Carrots naturally assumed upon her introduction to Chaos. Carrots somehow instinctively knew she was intended to take care of baby Chaos, and she did just that.

Sometimes for a weekend outing, we walked Chaos up near the house and let her inspect our yard and eat grass. Once in her wide-eyed curiosity, she even stepped up on the back porch, but then became frightened about getting off. She ended up jumping off the six-inch high cement slab as if she was taking a leap across a rapidly bubbling stream and had to fly high and wide to make the ground on the other side. Carrots always followed on these excursions and enjoyed eating weeds while always keeping an eye on Chaos. Our nimble goat liked to climb atop our car hood; if we were pushing the cart full of hay down to feed the horses, she easily jumped aboard and began eating the hay. She was as mischievous as she was darling.

We kept Carrots until the end of Chaos' third month, and then we returned her to her owners. We thought Carrots seemed as if she preferred to remain with us; it was sad to have to return her—we had grown attached to her. However, by that time, Chaos had acclimated herself to the herd, and was now accepted as a horse by the others. I do not know what Dorit's feelings toward Chaos were by this time, but the important thing was she did not try to attack or bully her rejected child; they sort of avoided each other, especially for Dorit's part. We continued to let Chaos graze with the adult horses during the day, and as fall turned to winter, we put her in the shelter of the shed at night if it was forecast to be below freezing.

We continued to feed Chaos milk until she was nearly seven months old, though we discontinued the night feedings, and were down to just two feedings a day by October. When we brought her bucket of milk, Chaos saw us and dashed across the nearly quarter mile of mowed hay field as if she were in the backstretch heading for the finish line in an important race. At the perfect moment, she braked to a stop inches from us to gulp down her milk as fast as she could. When she finished, after a few hugs and pets, she liked to dart back to the part of the field where the adult horses were. Reaching the adults, she leapt, jumped and ran around excitedly, almost clicking her four hooves together, as if trying to tell her staid seniors: "Wake up! Life is good! It's great to be alive! Yippy!" In response to this ruckus, the older horses momentarily looked up from their eating, and then settled down again to their grass, as if they thought: *"Whatever!"* or *"For crying out loud! The way youngsters act today!"* John, friendly to Chaos from the beginning, now became the one adult who did interact with her. They played together, and ate together. It was obvious that he truly cared for her. He was, after all, her father, and the youngest horse next to Chaos. It did our hearts good to see this bonding.

Chaos and goat friend, Carrots

Rod and Chaos with Carrots atop square hay bales in cart

Drawing of Chaos and Carrots snuggled in the hay.

Chapter 14
A Babysitter for Chaos and a Dog Named Joker

Since we did not put Chaos in the shed every winter night, we could never understand how our cat, *Paws,* knew the exact nights Chaos was there. Paws, though, was always waiting whenever we brought the foal in to shelter her from the cold. We kept a small coffee can with a lid on it full of cat food in the shed, and stored a bowl there behind the kick boards. On cold nights we filled the bowl with cat

food. The bowl was always empty the next morning, and I thought I saw a small nest in the hay. It was clear that Paws had assumed the role Carrots started: care-taker, adoptive mother, or night-time babysitter for little Chaos. Rod and I were still very much committed to our roles too. Almost nothing was too hard to do to ensure safety for our little filly.

The first years we owned horses we used half of the shed for hay storage. The cats had lived in the hay side of the shed, or at least were fed there, and liked to snuggle in the hay. Now that we had a large hay barn near the house, we trained, with some difficulty at first, the cats to stay in the new barn. Perhaps Paws saw me lead Chaos toward the shed on colder evenings, or perhaps she sensed the temperature was dropping and hurried down there to join her. We never understood *how* Paws knew, or why she befriended Chaos, she just did. Perhaps, unknown to us, our cats still spent their nights with the horses, and Paws perceived Chaos was missing from the pasture and the others. For some reason this wise kitty decided to fill the gap on those cold nights. We called her "the mommy kitty," or "Mommy Paws." We had both our cats spayed at a young age, so Paws never had her own kittens, but she seemed to sense it was her mission to tend our little motherless foal and she quietly, dependably fulfilled it. It seemed to us just another display of how God similarly watches over us even without our asking. He never forgets us. We were again aware of how He constantly shows us little glimpses of Himself through His animals.

It was that first winter that we had Chaos, about the time we noticed John and Chaos pairing off together, that we noticed Winnie had begun to show a preference for Dorit's company over Star's. It was unexplainable, and this new arrangement gave a strange twist to the pasture mates' hierarchy—actually their social ladder now sort of made a circle: Dorit was afraid of Star, Star now avoided Winnie. Winnie seemed dominated by Dorit though Dorit absolutely feared being separated from "her Winnie." Wins reigned over Star, John and Chaos.

I thought Dorit was a clever opportunist: she liked to eat, and if she positioned herself beside Winnie, Star would not dare bother her for fear of Winnie. Winnie still retained many qualities of the queenly matriarch: she still often went off alone to walk about the premises, eat hay or grass alone, or just stand and look off into the distance as a sort of sentry for approaching danger. However, now she was befriended by, dominated by, or stuck like glue to Dorit. We never quite figured out if Dorit was Winnie's best friend or her nemesis—maybe she was her "hair shirt!" Dorit never bit Winnie or otherwise visibly intimidated her by even putting her ears back, but it was very clear that Dorit was in control. She did frequently herd Winnie away from the drinking water, or to the shed, or to the hay when *she* wanted to eat. Winnie was dominant over Star; and Star, never one to start fights, moved out of the way if Winnie flicked her ears back or pointed her nose at her in a mean way. However, Star was superior to Dorit in the chain of command—Dorit was terrified of Star and at times I actually saw her hide behind Winnie while Winnie gave Star the intimidating mean old step-mother look. We had a circle; we had no real "head mare." Our pasture society did not jive with what the books wrote about horses' social ladders. There was no absolute leader but there were three "wanna-be's" and two, John and Chaos, who were happy just to eat and have peace. .

The one who seemed least affected by the social ladder of the pasture was John. John was the male, the protector of his harem and his daughter. He did not involve himself in the petty dominance games the ladies played. He stood out from the herd and watched for danger, and, we thought, took pride in his herd. Chaos stayed near

John and sort of managed to slip under things unnoticed; she also still had Rod and me to protect and provide for her.

The year Chaos was born, we planned to have Thanksgiving with our daughter, Catherine, her husband, and their son, Michael, in a suburb of Boston. Chaos needed to continue getting her milk and feed while we were away; turning her out alone with the larger horses might have been all right, but we were not confident about this. There was a young woman who lived about 14 miles from us from whom I had taken some riding lessons during the spring and summer. She raised horses, and took attentive care of them from the moment they were born. I knew she would board Chaos for a few days and care for her the way we wanted.

We trained Chaos to get into our stock trailer while I stood in the trailer with her bucket of milk. Chaos loved her milk; it was not difficult for Rod to coax her into the trailer from outside if she saw me inside holding her little white milk bucket as a reward. Without any deliberation, this four-month old foal effortlessly transferred her weight from her front feet to her back feet and stepped gracefully into the trailer; she was happy to stand by me and anxiously gulp down her milk. When the day before our departure to the east coast arrived, we loaded Chaos into the trailer easily with the milk bribe; she traveled quietly to her temporary lodging.

Chaos jumped out of the trailer without mishap, and seemed curious about her new surroundings, not afraid. It was late afternoon, and since we were keeping her in the shed at night, my friend decided to put her in one of her birthing stalls at night, and turn her out into a corral during the day. Chaos entered the stall without protest, but objected by vehemently kicking the stall wall after the door was closed and she remained inside. The three of us gave each other a sort of "Yikes! I-*hope*-she-will-be all right" look. We told her when and how much we fed Chaos, and left our bucket with her. We were positive she would take the best care of our baby, but also knew it would not be the same for her; she would miss her surrogate mom and dad.

We returned after dark from the airport after our trip to Boston, so we did not pick Chaos up until the next afternoon when her keeper returned from work. As we drove up, Chaos was sitting alone on the corral ground with her legs folded under her, basking in the golden, warm afternoon sun, resting her nose on the soft dirt. She looked solitary, not unhappy, just alone. I jumped from the truck and called:

"Is that my baby Chaos?"

Immediately she lifted her head, jumped to her feet and ran to meet us at the gate. She drew her head up to us, devouring our pets and caresses. She willingly, even forcefully dropped her head into the halter; eagerly pranced beside us as we held her lead rope and lead her to the trailer where she climbed in without her milk as an incentive. As we started the truck and began the turn out of the circular driveway, we noticed a young colt frantically racing around and around the corral Chaos had just left. We had not seen him until now. He was very upset, just like Chaos had been that morning she thought she had lost me.

"Poor little guy," I said.

"Yeah, he's going to miss her. He liked her a lot. They were friends. He doesn't have any other companions his size," my friend said.

I was glad to have Chaos back, but I felt so sorry for the little colt now missing her. I wished we could take him with us.

In our absence over the Thanksgiving holiday, we discovered upon our return we had acquired a dog! The poor animal was cowering behind the woodpile in our barn, shaking and low-growling, showing the whites of his eyes in very evident fear, and seeming to beg: "Please, don't beat me!"

He looked like a Black Lab puppy or Lab-mix, and appeared to be a couple of months old. We ran ads for him in the county paper and in the free advertiser, but no one claimed him. We kept him and named him *Joker*. We quickly discovered he drug away the overshoes Rod left outside the back door—Rod at first wondered if he had taken them off somewhere else. I discovered that he had carried off the blanket I had put in the barn for him to sleep upon, and taken it into the field east of the barn. Perhaps he was hiding it in case we kicked him out—already packing his things for his next eviction.

Finally he must have decided we were not going to run him off because he accepted residence in our barn. As he matured he looked ferocious, but he was actually a coward except when it came to cats, rabbits and pack rats. He never killed the cats, but he thought it was his duty to try; the pack rats and rabbits were not so lucky. Paws and

Tiger were suddenly ousted from their job as companions in our horse feeding chores. Joker now was our guide and escort, and the cats only ventured out when Joker was chained up at night, or was out of chasing range. Sometimes during the day we saw Joker in hot pursuit of one of our cats who fortunately managed to slide under the barn wall before his teeth sunk into her. Joker quickly learned that the horses were the primary care receivers, the most important, or favored, animals on the farm. If Joker indeed sensed that we favored the horses, his deduction no doubt sprung from the fact that caring for them took more time than did his care or the cats.' Though he never really acted jealous in an aggressive way, I thought he never quite accepted his position as a dog. He even tried eating grass, perhaps in hopes of tricking us into thinking he was a horse. The grass made him sick every time.

He was certainly an unforgettable character. Sometimes when the horses treated us to an unannounced horserace and galloped about the pasture just for fun, Joker ran with them. We never figured out if he was trying to be a horse, thought he was a horse, was pretending he was chasing them, or pretending they were chasing him. The horses were not the least bit afraid of him. Joker devoured the feed that fell from the horses' mouths as they ate, and even ate carrots if a piece fell. Perhaps he hoped he would become a horse if he ate horse feed. Most likely he just wanted the attention we gave the equines. He already had free choice dry dog food in the barn and occasional table scraps. Sometimes he brought home remains of road kill, or his own victims. Other times he carried home bones from animals the neighbor butchered, or bones from animals left by hunters.

When I was growing up we had two pet cocker spaniels—the first lived with us for ten years, the second for thirteen. Both Holly and Palmy lived in the house, roamed the backyard, and were taken for walks on a leash. There was "a leash law" as some of our-less-fond-of-dogs neighbors liked to remind us if our dog happened to escape out our front door and begin running and sniffing around *their* yards, or decided to cross the pavement when their cars were using the street. There is no leash law in the country.

Rod also grew up with dogs on his parents' ranch—their several dogs were chained up outside at night to prevent them running in packs or wandering away, and they *stayed* outside at all times—they were not allowed into the house, no exceptions. Therefore, Rod was of the mindset that animals belong outside, so that is where Joker stayed. We chained him up at nights so he did not roam. I grew up with dogs in the house, and was completely at home with the idea then, but the idea of a large dog staying outside in the country made sense.

City dogs may bury a bone from Sunday's dinner or even pancakes from Sunday breakfast in the backyard, but they do not drag home deer vertebrae, or a dead skunk and gleefully proceed to roll on it and toss it up in the air. It was hard for me to view these habits as anything but disgusting. We definitely gave him kindness, plenty of food and shelter. He became our dog and friend; he accompanied us every time we left the house to do chores.

The horses seemed to find his ways hard to take. While they accepted the cats and provided them protection and shade, they only tolerated Joker. He was black and had longish hair, but he never tried to lie in the horses' shadows to get out of the sun—perhaps he feared being stepped upon. None of the McKay equine seemed inclined to befriend him, and I am not quite sure they ever came to an agreement whether he was really a friend, a foe, or something in between. He was mainly an annoyance to them. Of all the horses, Star was the most unnerved by Joker. To her he never rose above the level of uninvited guest, or more aptly, intruder. She pointed her nose, flattened her ears back, and swung her hind end at him if he even came near her while she was eating. She did not want him near her in the pasture either. Joker had enough sense to stay out of her path.

One Sunday afternoon after Joker had been with us for nearly a year, two girls rode by on horseback in the grass alongside the gravel road by the front of our house. I was in the front yard, and stopped to talk with them. Our horses were all very curious, and were hanging over the fence to get a sniff of these horses from somewhere else. When the girls left, Joker left with them and followed them up the road. I thought he would come back. He did not. The next day, Rod drove two miles north to the home where we knew the girls lived, but Joker was not there though the owners' dogs were at the house. We decided Joker either left us, or didn't know the way home. The next day a pick-up drove into our driveway with Joker in the truck bed. It was the neighbor Rod visited the day before when looking for Joker. He told us he'd found him with his horses. Maybe Joker really was confused and thought he was supposed to be a horse, or maybe he just felt more comfortable around the neighbor's horses than with their dogs. He did know we were his owners; he knew we fed him and gave him a place in the barn to sleep. We accepted him, and he became our dog and friend.

Chapter 15
Chaos: a Long First Winter

In our time in Kansas, some winters were fairly mild, with little snow or cold weather, while others were bitterly cold and dumped a lot of snow and ice on us. Though it had been sunny and dry when we returned from Boston the end of November, that year we had a good share of the white stuff. The first week of December was sunny and mild, but the temperature was forecast to drop drastically, and the cold was to hit us hard the following week.

Rod and I had done some soul searching: we had three pregnant mares; when they delivered, we would have six horses, and our stallion. If we left everything as it was, the following year we would have three more foals, and the problem of the father attempting to breed any more fillies we had in addition to Chaos. We did not have a separate pen with a strong fence to keep John away from the mares. We ran ads in the Kansas City newspaper for John, and taught him to load into the trailer. We only had a few, not-very-serious calls, and no lookers. We decided the most responsible thing to do was to geld him. It made us sad to have to do this because he produced good offspring—beautiful in confirmation and temperament, as evidenced by Chaos.

We arranged for the vet to come for the procedure the second week of December, but he called and moved the date ahead a week to prevent having to have John lie anesthetized on the frozen ground during the operation. John slept through the whole operation, and had no infection. The doctor performed a very humane and clean operation, and certainly was kind to be concerned about the horse having to lie on the cold ground. This year, this particular winter, one week made a huge difference in temperature. John tolerated recovery well. We could tell he hurt, and just as with Pascal, we could tell John knew he was changed forever. Though the operation was humane and there were no unforeseen side effects of the operation, having to have the procedure was still sad for us. John also had a good memory, however, and when the vet came in the spring to give the initial West Nile Virus shot to all our horses, which was required by law that first year, John became very nervous when he saw the vet drive up in his truck. He remembered *that* truck! The vet noticed how anxious John had become, and kindly let Rod give the injection instead of giving it himself as he did for the other horses.

The week after John's gelding, our winter began in earnest. The horses all seemed to like the snow and the colder weather. Often we saw them running about the pasture, kicking up their heels, and initiating races just for the sheer fun of it. The cold did not bother them; they all had plenty of hay to eat. Pulling the cart loaded with two bales of hay down to the horses with ten inches of snow inhibiting my forward passage, however, was an ordeal many times, or just a lot of work other times. Sometimes the cart needed a few extra hard shoves, or required me to turn it around and pull it instead of push it to make it through the drifts and over the terraces between the barn and the horse pasture. As always, the horses knew when I was coming; they watched and waited at their gate for me to arrive with their hay. They did not know it was a chore getting their food to them; they were just glad I was bringing it, and anxious for it to get there.

We were still bringing milk to Chaos, and I let her into the feeding pen to guzzle her milk down first. Afterwards, as I pushed the cart through the south gate of the pen, the horses began their usual winter game of snatching clumps of hay as the cart entered their space. One day Winnie and Star positioned themselves strategically on the side of the entering cart, and between it and the open gate, slipped around the cart, through the gate, and hurriedly scrambled through the north gate, which I had unintentionally left open, and danced triumphantly and gleefully out into the heretofore empty north pasture blanketed in glistening, crystal white, silent snow, untouched except for my footprints and the cart's wheel tracks from the hay barn to their feeding pen.

They leaped and bounded like Santa's reindeer, prancing and arching their heads as if they thought they were in a winter dressage performance. Their highly carried heads, their raised tails, and their high prancing feet told me they were very proud of their escape, their adventure. They acted as if they had never before been into the north pasture and were exploring completely new territory. Such excitement! After her initial rearing, running and jumping, Winnie dropped to her knees and began happily rolling in the snow while her compatriot in crime, Star, sped lithely through the silvery, marble white frost so lightly that I would have said she floated had I not seen her footprints recorded in the snow. She glided with the speed of a bird, smoothly, exquisitely, and silently. I had never dreamed of, let alone seen, such flowing, graceful motion. She was awesome! I laughed softly to myself and my mind said: "Winnie is making snow angels, and Star is racing on the clouds!"

I had neglected to completely close the north gate because I didn't anticipate the horses slipping into the feeding pen, *and thus* into the north pasture. My mistake was their sheer enjoyment. It was not at all difficult to make them return: as soon as they saw me putting hay into the feeders, they hustled to the gate to be readmitted to their regular pasture.

Dorit was utterly chagrinned that Winnie and Star could run and play in the north field while she was imprisoned in the south pasture. She galloped at fiery, resentful, break-neck speed back and forth along the east-west dividing fence complaining in loud nickers about being left out. John, the man of the pasture, just stood quietly by watching the crazy ladies and patiently waiting for his hay.

Horses seem to have a knack for finding the holes in our best laid plans. I guess it is their natural curiosity. I do know horses teach us to be more alert to the chance things will happen.

Little Chaos' first winter was hard on her. Foals born earlier were larger by the time winter arrived, and they had their mothers for warmth and protection from the cold. Born in mid-July, Chaos was just five months old at Christmas. Even all the good food and milk we gave her could never replace a mother's love. Rod thought she looked "poor." We changed and increased her feed, continued to give her milk three times a day, treated her with Penicillin when she had a runny nose, and always put her in the shed at night so she was protected from the bitter, howling North and West winds. Giving Chaos the shed meant the adults had to stand behind cedar trees to shelter themselves from the wind, and load up on hay, both of which they did freely.

One day in early January we were warned heavy snowfall and frigid temperatures were on the way. The sun was fading and clouds were already sifting out large white flakes. We were worried about our baby Chaos who was already starting to have a bad winter—becoming thin and frequently sick. Rod called a tack store that afternoon as the flakes began to flutter down, and then drove to Kansas City in what fast became a blizzard to get Chaos a blanket to help keep her warmer. Driving into a snowstorm to buy a blanket for a little horse is true fatherly concern and devotion. As I led Chaos toward the shed the big white flakes contrasted with her chestnut head and the deep purple halter. She looked elegant, even regal. From the moment Rod left, I was praying for his safety driving north into the storm, and for Chaos' safety through the winter that was not half over and already seemed too long.

When Rod arrived home with the blanket, we both went down to the shed to put it on Chaos. We wondered if she would be afraid of this strange red garment she had never before been introduced to, and refuse to have it put on. We were in for a surprise! She trusted us so much she let us put the blanket on her right away without the slightest protest. It was as if she expected it, as if *she knew* it was for *her,* to keep her warm. Her trust brought back memories of her mother's first winter here with us: Dorit accepted Rod putting the blanket over her that morning she was covered with ice—she had inherited her mother's trust that we were there to help her. Little Chaos actually *seemed to like* her new blanket! It made us so happy we had done it for her. She was like a little girl in a new dress—so proud of herself in her new raiment.

Baby Chaos made it through her first winter with our attentive care, her new blanket, her nanny-cat, Paws, her day-time companion, John, her food—her milk, her grain, and her hay. It was a relief when spring gradually began to burst forth bringing new life and warmth to the landscape, to our now almost-yearling, and to our three pregnant mares.

Chaos in her new winter blanket with "Mommy Paws"

Chapter 16
Two Long Desired Foals

The normal length of pregnancy in horses is eleven months, or between 330 and 350 days, according to my manual. The author suggests taking the mid-point, 340 days; and simplifying the calculation by counting back 25 days from the last day of breeding, and then adding a year. That is the approximate date the mare will foal. Since John last bred Star May 12, I calculated Star's due date was about April 17 the following year.

Dorit delivered at least two weeks early, not unusual for a July delivery. Having borne three children, and having worked in maternity nursing for over five years, I knew ultimately babies come when they are ready unless labor is induced, or a caesarian section is required. Our first child was born two weeks early, our middle child was two weeks late, and our third child arrived on time, but she was induced.

To prepare for Star's delivery, a month before her due date, Rod and I decided to separate our two pregnant mares, Star and Winnie, from the other three members of the herd, and keep them together nearer the house, in our north pasture. From this location it was easier for us to observe them whether we were inside or outside the house, and be able to help them if needed. Our north pasture became the "antepartum," or *before delivery* pasture of our farm. The two mares in foal dined on blue grass and seemed to accept each other's company as equals and as if they knew why they were getting *the special treatment.*

Two weeks before Star's expected due date, Rod and I began taking turns going out to the pasture during the night with a flashlight to check on her. Having her closer to the house made this duty far easier than hunting for her in the larger, hilly south pasture among the other horses and trees. The north pasture is relatively flat and treeless. Rod checked on Star when he came home from work just before 11 PM, and then I checked on her about 1 or 2 AM, and one or the other of us—whoever woke up--checked on her again before daybreak. Sometimes when I carefully rose, and tried to slip into my jeans without making a sound, Rod would tell me he had just checked her. He was a much lighter sleeper than I, and nearly always seemed to notice if I got up no matter how quiet I tried to be.

We did not have a birthing stall, and we did not drag a sleeping bag out at night to spend the nights in the pasture, but we were watchful. Rod's family's horses bore their foals in the hills alone, and he said horses had been "having foals alone forever," so Star would most probably be all right. We both feared we interfered too much with Dorit's delivery. We thought perhaps if we stood back and left her completely alone, or had not even been home, Dorit might have accepted Chaos and passed the placenta naturally.

During the day we watched Star carefully both from the house and when we were outside. This was the long-anticipated, the long-desired, wished-for foal from the beautiful mare Rod had chosen as our broodmare. One day from our window during lunch we saw Star lying down for over a half an hour, and began to wonder if this was *the day* since lying down for an extended period can be a sign of the onset of labor. Maybe she would deliver in broad day light instead of sneaking her baby out in the darkness of night. We hoped she would. Our excitement vanished when she stood up and contentedly continued to graze. She was just resting. Star gave us no discernable signs of imminent delivery as Dorit had. She was a larger horse, and always tended toward thinness. Her belly didn't center as Dorit's had, nor did she drip milk from her udders as Dorit did, and as she did just before her miscarriage of the twin foals. Unknown to me then, "waxing" done two months early is a sign of impending loss. Star, the self-possessed loner, the quiet, aloof lady, wanted to do everything herself, and she did.

The morning of April 13th, Rod left for his morning shift at 5:15 and said later he had seen our nearest-to-delivery mare at the west corner of the north fence. He didn't know where Winnie was, but thought Star was still pregnant and "just quietly standing there." I deduced later she already delivered when Rod saw her standing as I found her about an hour later. I went out for my morning check on our expectant mare, and in the softly breaking spring sunshine I could see there was a brown bundle at Star's feet. My heart sank!

"Oh, no! Another loss! Poor Star is standing over her dead foal just as she stood over the place where her twins had lain," my mind cautioned me.

I began to prepare myself for grief. The previous miscarriage had readied my mind for just this kind of negative outcome. However, as I crept through the softly green, dewy April grass I saw the foal was breathing, and Star stood proudly over her *living* baby. I was breathlessly excited and happy. A *live* foal! My negative assumptions, thankfully, had been completely premature and incorrect. Praise God! Star had done everything by herself, perfectly, of course, because she is a wonderful horse.

"Oh, Star! Your baby is beautiful! Can I pet your little one?" I whispered softly, reverently, not wishing to frighten either one. I slowly reached forward to touch her delicate red-brown bundle.

Star, in the joy-filled pride of a new mother, made no attempt to stop me from gently petting the delicate, truly baby-soft little body she guarded. She knew I would do no harm. I tenderly stroked the sleeping foal, admiring her dark coloring, and eyelids with tiny white speckles. Her foal was so very soft, and so very beautiful! I was completely in awe. Finally managing to pry myself away from what I thought was absolutely the most beautiful sight I ever was privileged to see on our little farm, I crept slowly back to the house until I was on the backdoor step. Once inside I barged through the house into the bedroom where Veronica, who had arrived home from graduate school the night before for Easter Break, was peacefully sleeping.

"Veronica! Veronica! Star had her baby! Come see! Come see!" I called like a cheer-leader.

Veronica sat up startled. Even when awakened so rudely, she was still the calm, rational one. I am certain she thinks her mother is a bit daft, especially when it comes to horses, and this outburst, no doubt, served only to strengthen that conviction. Soon she met me at the back door with sleepy eyes and tousled hair, in rapidly donned jeans, a rumpled jacket, and untied shoes. Hurriedly ecstatic, wide-eyed and smiling from ear-to-ear, I ushered her outside. I was barely able to contain my joy or jump out the door fast enough--armed this time, with my camera.

We sifted through the dewy grass, and slipped under the fence toward where Star remained standing statuesque. Veronica looked at the foal who was just raising its head, and said:

"That's really good, Mom. I'm glad everything went all right." Then she turned and returned to the house and to bed while I remained with Star, basking in her motherly joy and pride, taking a few pictures, and observing mother and baby's interactions. The foal stood up and began to nurse; she was a filly. There was no rejection; no nipping—mother and baby knew exactly what to do. As baby nursed, Star lifted her head in proud satisfaction, pleasure and delight. I imagined I could almost see her smile.

"Now I am fulfilled," her elegantly tall stance said. She seemed so filled with joyful achievement; now she was complete.

When the foal finished nursing, Star and her newborn walked together toward the other end of the pasture side by side. It was such a portrait of peace and perfection that I could not contain my joy within myself. I cannot imagine anyone with anything good to tell keeping it to herself! I called Rod at work to share the news. We decided that the baby was probably already there when he left for work before dawn, but he had only been able to discern Star in the dark grassy northwest corner.

I found the placenta near the round pen at the southeast end of the pasture. It is very similar to a human placenta. I examined it; it was complete. Just-delivered mother and minutes-old baby traveled a long way to the pasture's northeast corner where I discovered them; no wonder the infant was sleeping. We never knew exactly when or where Star foaled, but she birthed her baby all by herself with no help from us. Star and God brought a beautiful new little horse into the world while we slept. Our chosen broodmare became one of the most perfect examples of motherhood I could ever imagine from that moment on. God bless her sweet, beautiful, big heart!

While the mother proudly and vigilantly kept her baby always by her side, the little (or rather large) filly willingly stayed there. It was beautiful to watch. As an introduction to all the many lessons this mother would impart to her child, Star began teaching her to trot her first day of life. This ever-patient dam never nipped at her fast-learning star pupil, or ever gave her even the slightest disapproving look; Star's whole being seemed in awe of, totally devoted to, and joyously completely subservient to this beautifully amazing new

little horse. Now, with Star delivered safely and a healthy foal, we could turn our attention upon the arrival of Winspiration's foal, according to my calculations, due May 2nd.

Above and Below: Star with new filly nursing

Painting of Star and her filly, Star's Suzanne

Just as we did with Star, two weeks before Winnie's May 2nd due date, Rod and I began getting up several times in the night, going out into the dark night of the north pasture, to check on her. Star delivered four days ahead of her due date; we reasoned Winnie might also deliver early. She did not. Neither she nor her baby seemed to be in any hurry to accomplish this event.

The entire day and into the evening of May 8th Winnie continued to show none of the classic visible or predictable signs of foaling— no udders waxing early milk, no belly centering, no distancing herself from the herd. About 6:30 the radio advised me we were under a "tornado warning" from 7 to 8 PM; we began getting heavy rain and strong winds. The storm was making the horses anxious to be with their friends, so I opened the gates between the fields so they could be all together during the storm. I expected them all to immediately make a mad dash for the shed; instead, all six horses, including Star and her just over three-week-old filly, remained in the north pasture with their tails to the wind, their heads to the ground, eating grass in the rain with their manes and tails blowing wildly. They were all oblivious to the approaching possible tornado. I *thought* horses could sense when a storm was eminent! Winnie, eating calmly with the others, seemed completely unaware that she was six days past her due date; she was doing nothing to indicate she was preparing for delivery. Perhaps the weather would do it for her, as is so often true with human deliveries when there was change in barometric pressure. Every labor nurse knows it is no *old wives' tale* that a deluge of rain, or any big change in the weather, can render a full delivery wing and nursery at the hospital.

I watched them until sometime after 9 o'clock when it became too dark to see. When Rod came home just before 11 PM, he checked on Winnie, and there was no sign a foal was on the way. At 2 AM Rod awoke and, just as faithfully as he had checked on our own children in the night, he went out into the pasture in the pouring rain to check on our equine mother-to-be. He came back inside, removed his wet clothes, and said:

"The foal is up. Winnie is fine, but she will not let me near her in this rain. We'll have to wait until morning."

We were up at daybreak, and immediately saw the new mother right outside our kitchen window with the foal at her side. The poor filly was trying to suckle, but Winnie would not let her. The baby looked completely healthy and normal, but her mother would not let her eat! We couldn't understand it. We were beginning to wonder if she had killed the first foal on purpose. "Doesn't she want her baby? Doesn't she know she needs to let her nurse?" we wondered. Then Winnie began to answer all the riddles for us: she dropped to her knees, leaned on to her side, and flopped on to her back and furiously began to roll in the wet grass. She stood up, shook herself vehemently, paced a few steps forward, and repeated the same process again, and once again. The poor filly stood humbly by watching her mother. Finally after all her gymnastics, Winnie expelled the placenta, or afterbirth, stood up, and ever so softly coaxed and directed her foal to her udder to suck. The baby found the teat without difficulty, readily latched on and began to suck. Winnie continued to look around at the foal; she could not take her gaze away from her. She looked very proud, satisfied and watchful. It seemed obvious to me now that Winnie had to expel the placenta *before* she could allow the foal to nurse. With human mothers we usually placed the newborn on the mother's abdomen and encouraged the infant to suckle the breast in order to hasten the mother's uterus to contract and aid in the rapid and complete expulsion of the placenta—not so with the equine species, I just learned. Nevertheless, we were blessed with a second successful delivery and mother-foal bonding. Thank God! I had also just received very helpful bonus instruction in horse birthing from my naturally wise horse.

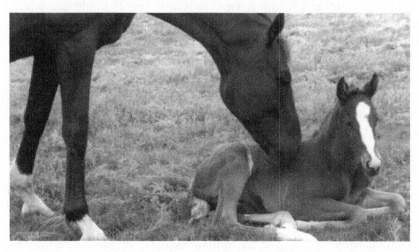

(Above and below): Winspiration and her newborn filly, Dark Stormy Night.

Chapter 17
Of Mothers and Foals

Winnie, like Star, was a completely accommodating mother. She never nipped at her baby, never corrected her, and was completely patient with every request, which was usually for milk. I soon learned that the way foals ask for milk is not to nicker, which, it seemed, would be akin to a human baby's cry, or even root toward the nipple. An equine baby asks for milk by first sidling alongside mom, and curving her neck across her mother's chest to stop her in her tracks; then completing the circle around her, and quickly finding the udder to begin nursing.

Winnie and Star never spurned their foals' request for food, but immediately stood completely still. Quietly, patiently, and, it seemed to me, lovingly they each let their baby eat whenever and wherever each wanted. Their whole lives were gladly and gratefully devoted to their foals. I believed both mares' previous losses made these babies very special indeed—at least that is what their body language seemed to tell me. Winnie, it seemed, made a particularly careful effort to be watchful of where she placed her feet, and not to ever step on her little foal.

Star had a great supply of milk; her udder was so generous she reminded me of a cow who is feeding a calf. Winnie had an excellent supply of milk too, but not as much as Star. Both babies were thriving, and completely loved. They had each other to frolic about and play with in the green spring grass, and the warm sunshine to warm them as they lay napping under the watchful gaze of their mothers. It was common to see those contented little ones lying flat in the grass, practically hidden, with their mothers grazing nearby. The foals slept a lot, just as human babies do; their mothers were reliable "markers" of where their children were when they could not be readily seen. Mother and child were never far apart. The mothers were definitely watchful, but not in a nervous way. The pair of mothers and foals had the entire north pasture to themselves; they radiated peace, comfort, happiness and security. They also exuded life; I felt very privileged to be able to observe and somewhat participate in this adventure of new life—it had a beauty and a joy that renewed my own wonder in the gift of life for all God's creatures.

We fed the mares large buckets of grain twice a day, and kept a good supply of fresh water in the tank at the north end of the pasture. Winnie and Star both had beautiful coats and bodies; both appeared healthier, fitter and more beautiful than they had before they became pregnant. Motherhood definitely agreed with both of them, and they both embraced it with devotion. They seemed good examples for human mothers.

After much deliberation, we called Star's foal *Star's Suzanne,* the reverse of her grandfather's name, which was *Suzanne's Star.* When I first saw that name for her sire on Star's pedigree, I thought it was a strange name for a stallion, but maybe the owner's wife, daughter, or a girl-friend was named Suzanne, and probably Star's sire was called *Star,* like we called *Pascal's Wager, Pascal,* and *John's Sue,* John, and *Teeter on a Star,* Star.

Win's foal, since she was born during a tornado warning, we had called *Stormy* from the day of her birth. *Tornado* seemed like too harsh a name. It might scare anyone from ever wanting to climb on her back. However, we once had a farrier who told us in his experience, horses given names like *Buttercup* tended to be hardest to handle. *Stormy* is a common name for a horse. We chose *Stormy Night,* but it was already taken. We were given our second choice, and her registered name became *Dark Stormy Night.* We called her *Stormy, Storms,* or just *Storm.* Sometimes I wished I named her *Beautiful Storm,* or *Joyful Storm* because of her happy disposition; then she could also be called "Joy" or "Beauty" or, as I often called her, "Storm."

In spite of being named for a wild weather system, she was anything but a storm. From the very beginning, just like her pasture-mate and half-sister, Suzanne, she had a sweet, gentle, joyful, laid-back disposition. The name *Stormy,* to me, denotes power and might, largeness. In this respect her given name fit her for she was large boned. Eventually she grew to be larger not only than Winnie, but also bigger than John. Rod even joked that Storm was not really *all* thoroughbred, that perhaps a Belgian workhorse had jumped the fence and courted Winnie. Of course, that was preposterous because we had seen John breed her, and there were no big, strapping workhorses in our neighborhood. We were also quite certain Winnie had not stolen away one night and found a Belgian sweetheart! She was not the type to jump fences in search of a more suitable stallion. She had willingly invited John's advances, but she was not a hussy!

Both foals were, as some call their breed, pure "fire breathing, high-strung thoroughbreds," but both were as amicable and tame as puppies from birth. Since both Winnie and Star tended to be high-strung, we could only credit John with their gentleness, or assume that the mothers' had lost their sociability and gentility through their training or experience.

The two foals were fun to watch in their play. Both could dart and tear about the field as if they were running races, or trying to set the field on fire, jump quickly and excitedly about, and rear up on to their hind legs, or kick their back legs out to the side. Their short curly tails flopping about behind them always made me laugh; and sometimes when they ran the little whisks of tails flew straight out behind them in the speeding flurry of their flight. They could also just as quickly collapse on the ground completely stretched out flat and sleep in the sunshine nearly as still as if they were tumbled statues until their stomachs told them it was time "for a little something," as Winnie the Pooh's stomach told him when he was hungry. When their tummies prompted them, first their heads would rise and beacon around for mom, who was ever standing near-by; then they would rise, sidle up to momma, and drink from her generous udders. Star and Winnie never had anything more pressing to interfere with attending to their babies' wishes; they never refused their children food or their immediate and complete affection and attention.

Everything was fun to the foals, and all they knew was sweetness and light. Each item about the pasture—flowers, the salt lick, the water tub, the hills of the terraces, the fence—everything was something new to be explored and investigated. One only has to watch any baby to know what joy is, to know what adventure is, and to see the hand of God in new life. The foals brightened our lives with laughter as we watched their sheer exuberance in being alive, and we were continually amused and awed by their undeterred curiosity. God was at work everywhere. I loved to see them poised, wide-eyed, heads triggered halfway between ground and sky, noses pointing at whatever gained their attention, legs splayed, ready to run if the need arose, but bursting to find out what the new thing was. They were so full of living! They could run as fast as baby rabbits one minute, and be as still as little fawns the next. They were both friendly and unafraid even in their first days with us. Their mothers trusted us completely, too, and seemed to very much enjoy our fuss over their beautiful babies. We were the adoring fans; they were the doting, proud mothers and they relished our attentions toward their offspring.

I found it amazing that we could never walk through the pasture without the foals coming to greet us. They actually brought themselves into our paths so we had no choice but to stop and pet their furry backs and heads. Both fillies were affectionate, but Suzanne loved to demonstrate her fondness for us by licking us—our hands, our jeans—she was just trying to say she liked us. Licking has always been thought to be a sign of affection in animals; Suzanne *loved* us, or was about to eat us. They were so curious about us: they nuzzled our hands, sniffed our pockets, and truly enjoyed our stroking their soft foal-coats. Who could not love the feel of the baby-soft foal coat? They liked to walk beside us as we went down to feed the other horses and their mothers, and, of course, usually stood by their mothers as they ate their grain. All our horses, but especially the foals, made us feel very needed and loved. No one since our own little children ever made such a fuss over us.

The foals knew their names quickly. Sometimes a reclining foal was difficult to spot in the high green grass especially if her mother had wandered a short distance away. However, if we called her name, we'd quickly see a head and neck pop up in expectation, as if to say: "Here I am! What do you want?"

One day I was preparing to feed the horses and I could not find Stormy anywhere. All the others were there at their usual places ready to eat. I should have known she was some place safe and near-by because Winnie was not at all anxious or alarmed by her absence. She must have known exactly where she was hiding.

"Where is my good baby, Stormy?" I called in an expectant, half-worried voice. A little chestnut head and neck flipped up instantly from behind a feed bunk and a pile of hay, and a big, excited nicker greeted my query. It made my day to hear her reply.

"Here *I am! Over here!"* she seemed to answer. There on the other side of the wooden feeder, behind a pile of hay, lying on the cool summer ground in the shade of enormous old walnut tree was the gone astray *Baby Stormy*. That too became one of her nick-names and stuck even when she was definitely no baby.

Later on we called Stormy and Chaos "the talking horses" because they were two most vociferous. When they saw us walking through the field to feed them, or when they saw us at the house and thought it was time for us to feed them, they nickered to us in anticipation or inquiry. "Is it time yet? Are you coming to feed and care for us now?" they seemed to be asking. I wondered what made those two horses so verbal, as Pascal was, and not the others? Some people are more out-going, more confident, and more loquacious, so perhaps horses too can have a talkative "horsenality," the term coined by Natural Horse-Man-Ship's Pat Parelli. It was a trait the two of them always kept: when they saw us approach, they nickered in greeting and anticipation. It was as if they were saying: "Hey! Hello! How are you? Do you want to come eat some hay with me, or feed me some treats?" Each horse was definitely an individual.

Horses are definitely good communicators. Several times I remember starting out to bring ours to the feeding pen and when I was halfway to the place where I usually found them, hearing them nicker at me from another part of our farm. Like owls perched up in a tree observing the ground below, they saw me though I was unaware of their observation and vantage point. They observed me on the mealtime trek, and, it seemed, wanted me to know where they were rather than have me go to the wrong place and not find them. Once they alerted me, they often came the distance to meet me and we strolled down to the feeding pen together. If Stormy or Chaos decided to stay near the shed while others were milling around near the feeding pen, I could just call them by name and immediately receive an answer in the form of a big nicker followed by either a slow amble or a frisky trot, or gallop, to join the others for their food. The opposite was also true, if one horse realized it was time to eat, he or she always communicated the news to the others with a big nicker that seemed to say: "Hey you guys, there's food up here!"

Rod had erected a large extension to the feeding pen using 2 x 4's. The foals were short enough to get under the boards, and their little feed buckets were safely inside this foal *area*, out of the reach of the adult horses. Star and Winnie were obliging mothers, but, if able, they would have eaten the foal's feed without a second thought. After all, they *were* feeding them *all* their milk. The babies clicked their teeth together when another adult horse approached too closely and made them nervous. We had seen Chaos do this a few times, sadly even in later years when Dorit approached her, but Chaos had not been with adult horses as early as Suzanne and Stormy were. It was the foals' way of saying: "I'm a baby, don't hurt me!" None of the big horses ever tried to hurt the little ones; of course, the offender would have Star or Winnie to answer to, and that in itself was enough deterrent. Both mares were fiercely protective of, and flawlessly devoted to, their foals, and John was the proud father, ever watchful of his harem and daughters. He most often could be seen standing out from the herd of females as if on the lookout for danger, as if proudly and carefully guarding his ladies and daughters. Though he was no longer a stallion, this was *his* herd, this was his nature, and this was his job.

Chapter 18
Return of Pascal

This is a sad chapter. I write this as a warning to prepare the reader because I prefer to be warned if tragedy is about to occur. Though disaster often occurs without warning in life and, with the help of God, we meet it as best we can. I admit to sometimes reading the end of a book first, and especially if I suspect the main character dies, especially if it is an animal, and then I may not read the book. This chapter and the next are both sad. I do not like sad episodes, I like them less the older I become, but I know sadness is part of every life this side of heaven. Hopefully misfortune makes us grow, helps us become stronger, better people. We can offer it to God as a sacrifice to make up for our own failings, or those of others. We can join it to Christ's suffering on the cross, offer it in reparation for our sins or those of others, and thus sanctify it. I came late in life to understand this. My life in the country taught me to understand how to apply what I often heard in grade school: "Offer it up."

The first few days of July that year we had the foals, Rod and I planned to take our truck and trailer to bring Pascal home for a while. Veronica could then more fully devote her time and energy to completing her doctoral thesis and not have to provide her horse with his needed companionship, exercise and feeding. Our plan changed when our son, Paul, thought it would be fun to make the trip with his father and his three-year old son, Matthew. It would be a "once-in-a-life-time opportunity," to make it "a guys' trip." Even the horse they were bringing back was male. It was perfect.

It was also a feat of endurance! Paul and little Matthew arrived from Oklahoma the night before, and the three men headed out in the truck, pulling the trailer, before sun-up the next morning. It is about a 600-mile, twelve hour drive. They spent a day with Veronica, then drove home the next day with Pascal and arrived about 7 PM.

I saw them pull up, and hurried to the east gate near the shed to meet them. Pascal unloaded from the trailer in his summer flysheet and shipping boots, with his perfectly groomed mane, tail, and hooves, and glistening dark bay coat. He looked regal—like a horse from King Arthur's Court or a steed returning triumphantly from the Crusades perfectly groomed for a celebratory parade. He seemed bigger than I remembered—illustrious, kingly--an aristocrat.

I expected him to remember Dorit and our pastures, and everything about the home of the first three years of his life, but only at the shed did a spark of memory seem to momentarily alight. There was a slight glint of recognition that seemed to extinguish itself like a fragment of a dream one remembers for a split second upon awakening and then loses, or a brief cloud burst on a hot afternoon whose rain specks evaporate as soon as they hit the ground. It made me sad. I thought Pascal would be happy to be home again, but this was no longer his home, or else he did not remember it as such, at least not right away. Since Pascal seemed to recognize the shed, we let him stay near it that night. The other seven horses were across the fence grazing on hay-stubble and re-growth in the nearly 30-acre pasture where we cut hay in May.

It is hard to describe how Pascal seemed that first night back home. He definitely had a presence about him. I viewed him with a sense of awe; he looked so grand and cultured, and so powerful. He moved slowly, thoughtfully, contemplatively, maybe almost sadly.

This was another lesson for me. Pascal was such a big, nice guy, and because he had been here before, I thought everything would be fine. I was wrong. Our little farm had changed very much since he had been here. Although it had been his old home, the environment now was very, very different from his customary stable mates and routine in his previous stable. When he gave his good-bye call in the early morning darkness on the day he left three years ago, only Dorit answered and she and Star were the only equines on the farm. Now there were two foals, a yearling, a new mare, and a gelding Pascal had never met—all complete strangers to him. Maybe, I thought to myself, everyone here seems like "country bumpkins" now to a sophisticated university graduate like himself. If I were able to do this all again, I never would have turned Pascal in with the herd so quickly.

The next morning as I jogged home from my run, I noticed Pascal and John just down the hill from the shed, near the old pond. They were side by side, trotting, but I thought at first maybe John was jostling Pascal, even perhaps attempting to bite at his mane. They went behind the shed, and after that they parted. I went on to the house, and didn't think any more about the encounter. From the window we saw John standing out in the recently hayed pasture in his lookout position apart from his mares and foals, and Pascal alone a long distance north in the same field, probably at least two-thirds of the length of the nearly quarter-mile pasture.

In the mid-afternoon, Rod came running into the house from outside calling me to come quickly. He dashed back outside. By the time I made it to the fence, Rod was leading John to the gate. He handed me the lead rope and told me to put John into the round pen. He told me he was going to try to find Pascal in the tree line along the north end of our property, and he hoped he had not gotten caught in the barbed wire.

"Pascal was eating grass way up here at the north end of the field, and John came after him from near the south fence, circling him, moving in for the kill, running him into the trees and the fence at the north end of the pasture," Rod hurriedly told me.

I couldn't believe it! John? Our laid-back, even-tempered, easy-going horse, John, did that? I took John to the round pen and closed the gate. I took off the halter and lead rope, and brought him water. There he would stay until we found someone to take him. We had promised Veronica she could leave Pascal with us while she finished her thesis. We had to find another home for John.

Poor Pascal! I kept thinking: "He must be wondering: '*What happened? Why was I taken away from the safety of my clean stall and posh cultured life at the stable near the university? What did I do to that other horse?*'"

He had been attacked as an enemy intruder for simply minding his own business, trying to stay away from the herd, and chiefly out of the herd guardian's way. It was inconceivably horrible to us that John had swooped down and charged Pascal totally unprovoked. This huge beautiful prince of a gelding, 17 hands high, who'd only known "sweetness and light" his whole existence, suddenly nearly killed by John who was a whole hand, four whole inches, shorter than he.

Pascal's legs were badly lacerated, but the lacerations were not so deep as to require stitches. We cleaned and put antibiotic powder on his wounds, and bandaged the worst ones. Of his own volition, Pascal relegated himself to the shed—the one familiar place in this very unfriendly environment. It broke our hearts to see this beautiful creature in self-imposed isolation—solitary confinement. How awful it is to come to a new place hoping everything will go well, giving it your best shot, and being rejected, fought, basically told you are not wanted. I think nearly everyone has been to that lonely, horrible place at least once in a lifetime—alone in a new school, unsure in a new job, wrongly rejected by the crowd for something said or done, inner despair because everything has gone wrong and God does not seem to answer prayers sent His way. At least the poor guy had Rod and me; he had no horse friends now.

That night I called a young couple I recently met who I knew wanted another horse, and asked them if they would like to have John. This young man and his father did team roping; he was a cowboy. We had promised Veronica she could keep her horse here indefinitely, and we could not have John trying to run Pascal off, or kill him. The couple said they wanted John, the wife even said it was "a blessing." They came to look at him the next day, and decided to take him.

Rod and I wanted to take John to this couple's home rather than have them come pick him up because he was accustomed to our trailer, it is larger and roomier than a normal one-horse trailer, and we wanted his departure to be as smooth and as kind as possible. One of Rod's co-workers, and his wife came over in case we needed help loading him. When we had thought of selling John we taught him to load into our trailer, but it had been awhile since he'd practiced this maneuver. However, this time, John walked right into the trailer without a single hesitation.

He gave me the look that seemed to say: "There! I did it exactly right, didn't I?" It seemed as if he almost smiled, proud he accomplished what he was asked.

It broke my heart! He tried *so* hard to please us, and we were getting rid of him. He was only doing what he thought he was supposed to do: protect his mares and foals. He had no way of knowing Pascal would not harm the other horses. It wasn't fair. Life isn't fair.

We took John to his new home, and left quickly. The startled, sad, and betrayed look on John's face when he backed out of the trailer into a strange place broke my heart again. I thought I was going to cry right there in front of everyone.

"It just is *not* fair!" my heart screamed in my head. This predicament was so deeply painful for all three of us: John, Rod and me, but especially for John. We felt sorry for him, and Rod and I felt as if we had deserted him, totally abandoned him. We hoped he would be well treated, but the new owners seemed to regard him with curiosity rather than kindness, and the first thing they did was tie him to a bent rickety twig of a post that barely reached his chest in height and looked as if the slightest tug would crack into splinters.

I thought to myself: "I thought a horse is supposed to be tied at least at the height of his withers. Don't you *horse people* know that?"

Rod said to me quietly: "Let's go before anything happens."

We politely refused going inside, we bid a quick good-bye to the new owners, and returned to our truck with the now empty trailer. John had pleased us by loading perfectly into the trailer, and we had brought him to this strange place and left him. He did what we asked, and it brought him this. The poor horse! He did not deserve it.

We were sadly quiet on the way home, occasionally looking at each other and shaking our heads. As little as I knew about horses, I knew a lot more than some people who *thought* they knew a lot, especially in the area of how to handle and treat horses. It all comes down to treating the horse as we would want to be treated. When we got home we hugged each other. I know I cried.

John stayed with these owners for probably four or six months. The young man's wife left him, and he had too many horses for one man to manage; he was also a little afraid of John because he was bigger than his other horses. He eventually gave him to another horseman who admired him. John bucked the man off once or twice. We heard John works as a bucking horse in a rodeo circuit; the young man we originally gave John to no longer lives in our vicinity. I always hope we will happen upon John somehow someday, and he will remember us. The foals our mares had from him were all gentle, even-tempered, large boned, beautiful, kind foals, and he was such a good, beautiful horse who tried to know and do the right thing.

Rod lets John sniff Matthew before putting Matthew on his back.

Matthew on John with Rod holding him.

John

Chapter 19
Little Emily

(Warning to the reader: This is a sad chapter.)

I was completely unprepared for John's departure, I was also unprepared for John's unprovoked attack on Pascal and Pascal's lacerated legs, though it could have been much worse. The things that happened with John and Pascal, and the things that followed wounded my heart. The reader may also want to skip this chapter entirely until he feels he can endure a very sad story. This chapter never becomes easier for me to read.

As a high school graduation gift, my cousin, Sandy, Candy's sister, gave me a book of the poetry of Henry Wadsworth Longfellow with pictures by the editors of Country Beautiful: America the Beautiful in the Words of Henry Wadsworth Longfellow. I liked Longfellow's poetry, and loved the photographs with the poems. One of my favorite poems was *My Lost Youth.* I loved his words "my youth comes back to me" and agreed with Longfellow that "the thoughts of youth are long, long thoughts" as a senior in high school, and have ever since. I read it over and over, memorized some of my favorite lines, and called them to mind at different times in my life just as with Tennyson's poem *Ulysses.* The following words of the poem seem to fit so well for what I now shall record, and recorded in the last chapter:

> "There are things of which I may not speak;
> There are dreams that cannot die;
> There are thoughts that make the strong heart weak,
> And bring a pallor into the cheek,
> And a mist before the eye."
>   -Henry Wadsworth Longfellow *My Lost Youth*

The day John left; we placed Dorit in the north pasture with her best friend, Winnie and her foal, Stormy. I suppose after all the commotion of Pascal's arrival, and John's departure settled down, Dorit relaxed enough and decided *NOW* she could have her foal…over three weeks premature. Dorit was in the north blue grass pasture alone when I first opened the shades that morning. I walked away from the window and came back five minutes later, and there was the tiniest foal I had ever seen standing beside her! Even from the window of the house I could see the foal near the far fence was a chestnut with a white diamond. Incredible! That fast—one minute there was just Dorit, and not five minutes later there was her tiny foal standing next to her. It was astounding especially remembering her extended ordeal with Chaos. Then I watched Dorit roll and roll on her back several times until she discharged the placenta—just as Winnie did. It was over nearly "in the blink of an eye."

I went out to look at the baby. Dorit was allowing her to nurse, and it seemed like everything was going to be all right this time. It seemed incredible. Dorit was accepting this foal! The other horses gathered at the fence, and Chaos in particular seemed to know this was *her* full sister. At that moment I saw Dorit look at Chaos differently. A light seemed to go on in her head--like she finally realized Chaos had been *her* foal. All the other horses pressed admiringly against the fence straining to see the new little one. Dorit forgot all fear of Star and nipped at her when Star sniffed too closely to *her* baby! Wonders never cease! Dorit was defending her baby. Everything was working out well, it seemed.

I brought Dorit a bucket of bran mash and continued to watch the baby nurse, and walk next to Dorit. The foal never left Dorit's side; she appeared glued to her mother. Sometimes the foal lay down, and Dorit stood guard over her. I put the other horses into the large field to the east, and opened the gate into the south pasture so Dorit and her foal could get under the trees for shade if they wanted to. I worried about the foal being exposed to the intense July sun all afternoon with no relief. The vet too had warned us that this was a problem with summer foals. Human premature infants have a hard time regulating their body temperature; the foal might need the hot sunshine. I did not know. Mother and foal may have known, and probably did know, better than I.

When Rod came home that afternoon we gave the foal the tetanus injection. Stormy sniffed noses with the new little foal; Winnie and Dorit were overseeing everything. Everything and everyone appeared peaceful. I was filled with happiness.

Early the next morning Rod set out on his morning jog. He was back before much time elapsed. I was surprised to hear him re-enter the house.

"Break your heart! Come quickly!

Our little premature foal had not made it through the night. I named her *Little Emily* after the character in Charles Dickens' <u>David Copperfield</u> who David never got to know beyond childhood because of circumstances in his and Emily's lives. Though years have passed, it is still difficult for me to even think, let alone *speak,* of Little Emily. I will always love and remember the tiny little filly with the white diamond on her forehead whose life ended before it could really begin. It seemed fitting to bury her in the vicinity of Star's twin foals.

Life is never perfect, never without trials and sadness this side of heaven. It seemed this summer had more than its fair share of unexpected disappointments and sad times. We try to get through the hard times the best we can, and ask God's help in bearing the sorrow.

Chapter 20
Joys of Young Horses

Summer continued to sear our countryside after Pascal's return, John's departure and the loss of Little Emily all within days of one another that July. Our now seven horses and our farm had to contend with drought. July and August were so dry the grass "burned up" and turned brown; we had to begin feeding the hay bales Rod had put up in May. Feeding hay was something we had been able to postpone until November in other years. Then the last day of August and the first two days of September we received a healing four inches of rain. Within a week the grass was green and lush again, and the horses returned to eating grass in the large pasture of nearly thirty acres where Rod cut the hay in the spring. It's amazing how God can transform the landscape nearly overnight with a few days of good rain. We were so grateful for this wonderful rain!

That summer Rod and I were building fences for part of the pasture division and for a riding arena using steel pipe attached to posts that we set in cement, and of course the horses were again "helping us." After it was erected, I was assigned to paint the fence that ran northward to connect to the border fence, while Rod dug postholes and cemented the arena posts firmly in place. Chaos, now a golden butterscotch brownie colored yearling, and the two nearly four-month-old foals, Stormy and Suzanne, enjoyed whetting their curiosity about what exactly I was applying with my paint brush and can, and determining if it was edible, by rubbing against the fence and streaking their beautiful coats with smears of black paint.

Chaos, though nearly a year older, was no less the prankster than her two younger half-siblings. She brought her nose right down to the paint can, and, of course, soon had black paint on her nose as well as her sides. If I had a rag or an extra paintbrush in my back pocket, all three of these "babies" were quite skilled at picking my pockets. They thought it was great fun. It was no use to get mad about it or try to scold the perpetrators, one could only laugh. It was then we noticed that many of Chaos' mannerisms would have given it away to a total stranger that she was Dorit's daughter. The way she cocked her head and sniffed new things, the way she liked to paw the ground to investigate things, and the way she wedged herself into tight areas—all these were so obviously "Dorit traits" to us. Rod predicted rightly that one day in the future Chaos and Dorit would graze together and be friends simply because they were mother and daughter, blood related them.

Suzanne and Stormy were always friendly, but it was Suzanne who most loved to come and put her face up to our faces, and who especially sought us out to pet her and to have us keep her company and give her our attention. Rod always got a very noticeable lump in his throat, a wobbly voice and held back tears whenever he talked of this sweetest of all horses, this "special little girl" who no one could help but love. Suzanne was the only horse I ever knew who forever loved to lick us every time she saw us—not just our hands like Dorit liked to do, but our arms, our pant legs, she would even have licked our faces if we let her. Her licking was a sign of affection and trust. It was as if she were telling us: *"I love you! I love you! I love you!"* We loved her!

Rod and I both agreed we would probably never see this lovable, this charming a horse ever again. We wondered why Suzanne was so demonstrably affectionate. Star, her dam, was not at all demonstrative, though we did not know what her training and experience had been for the eight years before we owned her. She was a lady, always polite, but she rarely showed signs of warmth to people—once we saw her put her nose up to Veronica's shoulder after Veronica rode her. Perhaps she would have been friendly given the opportunity. It seemed almost as if she had been punished for seeking friendship with humans. We sometimes wondered if she were rescued from a mean situation and that was the reason the people we purchased her from requested they be allowed to buy her back if we ever sold her. According to her papers, she had been bought and sold many times before she came to us. We could not tell what her background had been. John, Suzanne's sire, was sociable, pleasant, and of a gentle temperament—he wanted to be friendly, and he was always grateful. Whatever the secret ingredients of Suzanne's "horsenality," the end result was a winning and wonderful recipe. We doubted a sweeter horse had ever, or would ever, live.

Both of our little girls were as curious as kittens or small children, but Stormy's curiosities lead her to inquire and inspect things *before* getting into them, and, unlike Suzanne, she normally liked to inspect with her head and keep her feet planted on the ground. Her grey half-sister seemed to instead enjoy marching feet-first into the unknown and thinking later. This barge-right-in, or step-right-over attribute of Suzanne's we blamed for several nasty cuts—two which required washing and bandaging for many weeks, and one escape. Suzanne was fearless! Before Stormy was even born, when she was less than a month old, Suzanne one evening slipped over the smooth-wire fence and into our unfenced front yard. I was there with her, but I was alone. She never panicked because she never realized she was outside the fenced pasture where her mother was. Star was not far away, grazing, and never suspected her baby was outside the home pasture. Fortunately, I was able to coax Suzanne back into her pasture by holding up the smooth wire fence before separation anxiety alarms went off in her head, or in Star's.

Stormy had no such tendency to roam yet, but she was very curious. She had that inquisitive, bright-faced, could-be-annoying question-asking curiosity that wanted to know *what* everything was. She loved to snoop. We had a large plastic bin with a lid near the feeding pen in which we kept the tack box with brushes, combs, hoof picks and the halters. If we left it open, Stormy loved to sneak over to it and carefully begin pulling out the halters and lead ropes one at a time and letting them fall on the ground. Sometimes I thought she must be very orderly, and want to re-organize everything to make it tidy. Other times I thought maybe she just wanted to see how big a mess she could make. I had to shake my head and laugh. She made me remember myself as a little girl going through my mother's sewing box as she sat busily at her sewing machine, or as she sat mending on the couch next to me.

"Oh, Mommy! What is this? What did this button go on? What is this for? Can I have this?" I would ask. Stormy seemed to be doing the same thing, and I could almost hear her asking: "What is this, Mom?"

Stormy was never upset about us laying things over her back, and later accepted both bareback pad and saddle pad and saddle with little acclimation and little protest. One day she worked to get Rod's jacket off the fence until it hung over her ears and neck. She seemed

159

totally unconcerned about what was on her head, and continued to inspect her surroundings even with her funny headdress on. Another horse would have snorted and backed or reared, but not Stormy. She was content and curious; very little rattled or upset her. From our first attempt, she naturally flexed her head around to the side if we pulled on her lead rope. She learned quickly, and there seemed to be that "orderly" streak about her—she even repositioned her feed bucket before we put food in it, and waited until we put the food in before she stuck her head in—unlike some of the others who wanted to begin eating before we could get the food into the bucket. She also was our "picky eater:" each new feed underwent her sniffing scrutiny and maybe rejection.

Both foals were completely comfortable with us touching them though we had not rubbed them all over with our hands during the first few hours they were newborns—a technique called "Imprinting" which is renowned to desensitize foals and make them amenable to human touch. Like Suzanne and John, Stormy showed a laid-back and gentle disposition but she was particularly possessive of her mother. When I rode Winnie I let Stormy stay in the same pasture with her mother to prevent separation anxiety in either mother or infant. She liked to observe us for a while, then when we slowed or stopped Stormy would charge toward us at a full gallop and come to a perfectly timed halt at her mother's side. Winnie was undisturbed by her daughter's antics; she stood still until Stormy took a drink of milk if she wanted one, and then walked on when Storm wandered off to eat grass.

From the beginning, it seemed to me there was a danger Stormy would take second place to "the Beautiful Suzanne." Suzanne *was* a looker; in comparison, Stormy was just cute. Lest Stormy be left out, feel inferior, or ever be even the slightest bit neglected, I took her on as my special friend and charge, and she soon looked to me for security if anything frightened her. Once I was walking her along the driveway; Rod forgot we were there and started his chainsaw. Stormy startled in place and started to jump away, but then returned to stand beside me. Another time during her first autumn with us, Joker had chased a rabbit inside a long pipe and began running from end to end jumping and barking. Stormy gave a loud nicker and a quick look to find me. She showed her affection by putting her nose on my cheek, and breathing out slowly. I considered these "horse kisses" and blew gently into her nose. We repeated this several times in a row each time. I loved to walk beside her when returning her to her pasture, sometimes she just stayed next to me without a lead rope. As we traveled, I liked to tell her stories about her ancestry. I bragged to her that someday my grandchildren and great grandchildren might ask me to tell them the story of *Dark Stormy Night*. I told her I would say: "Yes! It's one of my favorite stories! Stormy was descended from the most famous race horses—*Man O' War* and *War Admiral*, on her mother's side, and *Bold Ruler* and *Citation* on her father's side." I always smiled and laughed a little as I recited these lines to her. I liked to imagine it was one of her favorite stories too. I knew that talking to her in this adoring, gentle way could only serve to make her more comfortable around me. I remembered a song from my time at Girl Scout camp the summer before 6th grade and liked to sing it quietly only to her. The only two verses I learned ended with the words: *"Now I know that God has made this world for me."* With these magnificent creatures at my side, I could only believe God truly *made this world for me.*

Our beautiful Suzanne, as we so frequently called her, began to shed her "foal coat" the end of June and into July. It was very obvious in her case more than in the two chestnuts, Stormy and Chaos. Suzanne had been a deep red-brown and shed out into a deep beautiful grey. We realized that Star had once had color like her daughter, even a white blaze and one white foot that now were indistinct because she was so pale, and eventually Suzanne's coat would lighten as Star's had. Star's registration papers called her a "roan filly." I learned from the *Thoroughbred Champions--Genetics of Color in the Thoroughbred* web page that a grey horse is born a base color and lightens as he ages; the grey gene instructs the base color to change. Star looked white from a distance, but she only had all-white markings: a white blaze and a white sock on her right hind foot which could only be detected upon close-up inspection. The rest of her body was grey, actually grey and brown dots on a grey-white coat; her mane and tail were darker; all of her would whiten as she aged— like people.

Suzanne begins to shed her foal coat.

Rod digging holes for setting posts for the arena fence with "horse help."

Chapter 21
Winter Perils

As October and November approached and the fillies passed the sixth month since their births, I wondered if Winnie and Star would begin "disciplining" their foals—nipping at them when they wanted them to do something differently, when they wanted to teach them good horse manners, or wanted to discourage suckling. Neither of the mares endeavored to discipline her offspring, nor attempted to dissuade her now very large foal from nursing. I was amazed that the mares did not undertake this chore of leading their daughters toward maturity, and that Suzanne and Stormy still wanted to drink their mothers' milk. It was rather comical to see such large foals nursing, but the mothers encouraged it. As long as we continued to feed the mares twice a day, they maintained their weight and seemed quite content to have their babies with them and to feed them. In fact, like some human mothers, Winnie and Star seemed totally enamored with the joys and responsibilities of motherhood, and seemed very reluctant to ever relinquish babyhood demands and allow their children to grow up. Rod and I decided not to force the weaning matter with winter approaching, but to allow the foals to continue with their mothers' milk over the winter if they wanted to. They wanted to, and did.

Though Winnie kept her matriarchal role, Pascal gently assumed leadership of the herd. He bowed to no one, but he was never even the least bit mean or pushy about establishing his authority. He was always kind, his manner always gentle. Sometimes when I was alone in the afternoons, I liked to just walk out into the horse pasture and pet and visit the horses. I often brought along a currycomb or mane and tail comb, and began currying any horse who happened to walk up to me. If Pascal decided *he* wanted to be curried while another horse was getting the beauty treatment, he would smoothly make an almost imperceptible exchange with the other horse. Suddenly I had his mane or side in front of me and the other horse had willingly moved to his side and seemed content to remain there next to him while he received the grooming instead. There was never any fear or meanness associated with the substitution; no biting, lunging, or ear pinning. He was the gentle giant. He didn't fight anyone. He was simply a commanding presence—huge, dark, regal, quiet, and beautiful. His coat shone, and he shone with it. He went anywhere he wanted to go, did anything he wanted to do, and enforced his will simply by his magnificent size and kingly carriage. The mares kept playing their own silly, very petty dominance games, but Pascal never participated; he did not have to. No one ever questioned that he was *the boss*. The others patiently waited their turns, and approached one by one after Pascal had his fill of being groomed. Each expected her turn!

Though older now, Pascal retained the love for teasing he had displayed as a youngster and sometimes liked to pretend he did not want to be caught to be fed or to have his fly mask or fly sheet removed at night. Veronica bought him a fly sheet because he still had the baby-soft hair and sensitive skin he had the first day we met him as a four-month-old. We used it for him since he had it; he was the *only one* to get such a singular privilege. Sometimes as we approached he would playfully give a small squeal and jump to the opposite side of our approach—never at us. Once in a while he would add a small kick to the side away from us. He never was trying to hurt us; he was making a benign protest—simply letting us know he teasingly disapproved. I did not become too upset by his jerky behavior, but I did nothing to encourage it either. I simply told him it was all right, if he did not want to eat, or did not want to have his mask removed, he did not have to. Then I proceeded to lead everyone else in to eat, and once everyone else was secured and ready to be, or being, fed there stood Pascal at the gate hanging his head over the fence and looking very dejected. He seemed to be saying: "Poor me! Can I please eat too?" Of course, at this point he would let me place the halter on him and lead him in to his bucket. It was the same with the fly mask and fly sheet, by the time I removed everyone else's, and he came to me to have his removed for the night too. I don't think Pascal ever really realized how big he was—17 hands high is a *big* horse. Had he known how truly enormous he loomed, and had even the slightest mean streak, he could have been a monster. Thankfully he did not have a mean bone in his body. He was never rough, never bossy, just the gentle, friendly teaser and undisputed "king of the heap."

I was beginning to know our horses and to accept and understand living in the country at least somewhat. I began to understand that God wanted me to be here now. He wanted me to live a very quiet, simple life because *this* was what was good for me now, and *this* was where HE wanted me to most perfectly learn to love Him. I finally accepted that this was who I was, and I would be grateful. I came to believe I was privileged to be able to live on this sort of permanent retreat, this "separate peace," this charmed life among these magnificent horses and this husband who loved me, who built a house for me, and wanted me to have this quiet, safe life. In spite of some of the annoying drawbacks of country life like dry, smoky, sultry gravel roads that covered everything with a fine layer of dirty dust every time a car or truck drove by in the hot dry summers, and when wet, threw what sounded like thousands of bullets of gravelly mud into the car wheel-wells as we traversed them. Our cars are always dirty; some people look down on country people as less intelligent, unkempt. The long distances required traveling for any necessity or enjoyment is also an annoying disadvantage. In spite of probably always missing a lot of the convenient benefits of a city, I began to adapt to, and began to interiorize meaning in a different kind of existence, an authentic life, made more satisfying by these magnificent, very peaceful good horses who accepted their life and made the most of it just as it was.

The first winter Pascal was back with us was wet and very cold. We broke ice on the pond twice a day so the horses could drink, and we fed them plenty of hay—two large square bales in the morning and two more in the late afternoon. I always did one of the feedings alone while Rod was at work. Eight to ten inches of snow made pulling, or pushing two seventy-pound bales in our wooden cart with the large bicycle tires nearly impossible for me. To make my job easier, Rod used the tractor bucket to carry the hay to the feeding pen for me, and set two bales on pallets near the pen where we brought hay through for the horses. I trudged through the snow pulling the empty cart, carefully using the tractor ruts as a path to make my passage easier. Once inside the pen, I loaded the bales into the cart to distribute it into feeders. Just as in previous years, the horses saw me coming and waited expectantly for me at the gate, like little children crowding around an ice cream truck, jostling for first position. They made me feel needed and appreciated, and even made the chore pleasant just because of their eagerness and delight in my approach. However, this tedious twice daily task was about to change abruptly.

One early evening when Rod and I were feeding together, as we tied the horses up in the feeding pen to give them their nightly grain and place hay into the feeders while they ate, we noticed the hair on Stormy's hind legs and rump appeared to have been wet and to have dried. We also noticed manure and hoof prints on the ice on the pond, and an obvious broken area in the pond. The snow covered the ice on the water and gave it the guise of land; underneath the snow, the ice was weak in some places. It should not have been surprising that the foals had been walking on the pond, maybe thinking there was earth beneath the snow, but I truly thought they would naturally remember where the land ended and the pond began because they lived there and used it every day. Walking on ice certainly was not a hobby or talent we wanted them to even consider cultivating. Since the problem already surfaced, and we were fortunate this first time, we decided that rather than risk a sick or dead foal, we would move all seven horses into the north pasture and lock the gates to the south pasture. I had heard stories of owners losing precious foals in ponds in winter, and did not want that sort of disaster happening here. A warning was sufficient; all the horses would go to the north pasture until the snow melted. The only drawback was there was no shed to shelter the horses from the elements there, but our house, garage, large hay barn and some trees along the north fence now provided a far better windbreak than Little Dorit had her first winter with us. We decided our horses could bunch together, turn their tails to the wind, and eat hay to keep warm far better than we could deal with losing one of them in the frigid water. Stormy had tried Suzanne's stepping method of investigation and learned it was dangerous; I doubted she would ever try it again.

We filled a galvanized water tank and placed a large heating element inside to keep their drinking water from freezing, and began distributing the hay for them to eat out on the ground in the new area. This arrangement was very satisfactory for the horses because they were excited to be in a "new and different" place, albeit the pasture adjacent to their own which they had been in many times before. They had a great time inspecting it and acted as if they were never before in it. This temporary scheme for winter was very satisfactory for us too because we did not have to haul hay very far, nor break ice on the pond. It was also a special treat for us to look out the house windows and have our equine friends less than twenty-five feet from us. It was almost as if they had moved in with us; we found we were more often going out to pet them and visit them now that they were so close. As the snow eventually began to melt, the north pasture inhabitants enjoyed sunning themselves as they lay on the islands of brown grass with iceberg-type patches of snow about them. When the snow melted completely and the pond again became visible as a pond instead of as part of the snow-covered pasture, we returned the horses to the lower field. They were not really far away, but I missed them whenever I passed the windows in the south side of the house or stepped outside and the wonderful horses were no longer there to greet me.

Pastel portrait of Suzanne

Chaos silhouetted against snow and winter sky

Four horses nibbling the grass peeking up through snow

Chaos and Pascal sunning themselves; Suzanne and Dorit in background

170

Painting of Star

With a new pasture arrangement, everyone survived the winter. Finally the snow melted, and the horses returned to the lower pasture to eagerly devour the greening new grass as soon as it poked up through the earth. April and May brought the one-year anniversaries of the births of Suzanne and Stormy. Much to our amazement, both fillies were *still* drinking their mother's milk, and both mothers were still obliging their darlings' demands. We could not believe it. Star and Winnie *had* to be the most willing mothers in horse history. As soon as Rod cut the hay, baled and stored the hay in the large barn, we placed the adult horses in the former hay field, and placed the two yearling fillies in the north pasture, with Chaos as a link to the older horses, and sort of a "babysitter" for her two younger half-sisters.

Chaos seemed to understand her new role, and take it seriously. She indeed did prevent Stormy and Suzanne from stressing about their mothers' absence. Of course, they could see Star and Winnie in the large hay field, and could go to the fence to watch them eating grass. They did not seem to mind even when the adults crossed to the far side of the large field; they did not nicker or call after their mothers, nor did they run anxiously back and forth along the fence.

Of the two mares, Winnie accepted the separation more willingly. She approached the fence, but remained at least one length away from it, and greeted Storm from this distance. Star, however, was quite different. In her devotion to Suzanne, she came to the fence and turned to her side so her beloved daughter could reach between the smooth fence wires and nurse! Suzanne was indeed nursing less, but she was *still* nursing.

We saw an ad in one of our horse magazines for a device that outfitted the mare with a soft blanket-type material to cover the udders, and elastic straps sewn to the sides of the blanket which stretched up and fastened upon the mare's rump with hooks. It was well made, and seemed like the perfect solution to our problem. Star, however, was not willing to relinquish her maternal role, and Suzanne was not to be confused or disturbed by a piece of fuzzy material. Within a single day this determined yearling had devised a way to wiggle her nose and mouth between the fleece and her mother's skin, and attain the teat for her mother's milk. Star still did her daughter the favor of standing beside the fence so Suzanne could easily slip her head between the smooth wires. For a few days we thought perhaps it was working and this overgrown baby was nursing less frequently, so we left the device in place. However, the hooks rubbed the hair off Star's rump, and began to make a sore. In desperation, we gave up. When I relayed the information to the seller in giving the requested feedback, he said it was the first time he ever had the problem, and, while it was not what he wanted to hear, he kindly refunded our money.

For everyone's welfare we put the seven horses together in the large hay-stubble field, and decided the mothers would wean their babies when *they* were ready. Actually, Winnie had, in the time Stormy had been across the fence, almost completely weaned her though she did occasionally allow her a few little drinks. Eventually, around sixteen to eighteen months, Suzanne stopped nursing too, but even after weaning mother and daughter were nearly always together.

As said before, since the births of these two foals, I never saw their mothers nip at them; they would have given their lives for their babies—as the future would prove. Star, the loner, finally had a best friend in her daughter. Winnie, too, was nearly always with her Stormy. I did feel somewhat sorry for Dorit at this time; she was certainly taking a back seat to these two mares who were reveling in their motherhood.

I remember one rainy, windy night we were coming home in the dark on the gravel road. As we made the turn at our corner, our car's headlights flashed into the shed and we saw Star and Suzanne, and Winnie and Stormy lined up across the shed entrance—mothers and daughters looking out at the rain together. We both had the thought that many human mothers and daughters never have the joy of being as close friends as those two mares and fillies always were.

Rod between his friends, Suzanne and Chaos

Horses grazing on tender spring grass. (Right to left) Pascal, Stormy and Chaos

Suzanne visiting the pond ducks

Rod bringing in round bales to the barn.

Rod puts round bales into barn.

Round baler expels bale.

Chapter 22

A Dangerous Business Stepping Out Your Door

One of the last days of August was drawing toward nightfall. Our seven horses were where they had been all day: in the twenty-eight acre brome field grazing on the return growth after we cut and baled hay that summer. Instead of grazing near the center of the field, in the evening they liked to gather near the trees on the east side as day closed. In the mornings and evenings it was cool there along the east tree line; the trees give them some shade and some privacy. Our horses are nocturnal nomads who roam the pasture as much as, or even more at night than in the day. They all had excellent night vision too. The few times we entered the pasture at night to find them, they found us first. This evening as I left the house they had just begun their nightly wandering, and were enjoying the cool, dampening lush grass. Our house is on the far west side of our 40 acres, so to find them and remove their fly masks for the night usually meant a good walk across our property.

I look forward to the evening walk across the field to find each horse. I like to pet each one and make sure no one has a cut or seems "out of sorts." It is a peaceful time; I like the evening coolness and the chance to visit with my horses as day ends. This particular night I neglected to remember darkness comes sooner in late August

The adult horses met me, and I pet and talked to them individually as I removed each fly mask. Stormy and Suzanne, the two "babies," now 15 and 16 months old, were actually under the trees along the fence in the maze of tangled new and old trees, exploring and nibbling at leaves. Chaos, now two years old, was at the entrance of this tunnel of trees looking as if she'd like to join the younger horses' exploration, but knew better. The adults were content to eat the lush green grass further away from the trees.

I ducked my head to enter the tree lined passageway, and Stormy and Suzanne met me and allowed me remove their masks as I did every night. They did not come out, however, but returned to their hide and seek places under the tree branches of their playhouse.

"Just like little kids playing in a fort," I thought as I watched them wander back.

Suzanne, who at sixteen months was taller than many adult horses, though still an "unweaned infant," was poised next to the barbed wire fence that divided our property from the neighbor's farm. The previous owner, Edmund, may he rest in peace, probably erected this fence over sixty years ago, and never inspected or touched it afterwards. The new owner never touched the fence either. Now the fence was in very poor repair: the barbed wire was rusty; many of the posts were bent on forty-five degree angles and weakened by weather and time, and nearly the entire fence-line was overgrown with unpruned, gnarled trees and branches that actually pushed parts of the wire to within ten inches of the ground. Truthfully, until the foals decided to play in their fort along the fence I never inspected the fence. I was completely surprised by its disrepair. I noticed Suzanne was standing at one of these low points in the fence. A fence of ten inches was nothing compared to her height and the length of her legs.

Looking at her in this spot, I thought: "She could step right over that fence, and bound off into the 120 acre pasture!"

As if Suzanne read my mind, she immediately agilely stepped over the low-lying barrier and, with a brief glance back over her shoulder, trotted out through the trees on the other side of the fence into the adjoining pasture. She seemed very proud of herself, and almost seemed to laugh: "Catch me if you can!" or "Why not come with me?"

For a split second I felt intensely relieved. "Thankfully, she did not catch her foot on the barbed wire!" I thought to myself

In the next second, though, I realized I was *now* too late to stop her. As if that were not enough, I knew I would never dare try to lead her back the dangerous way she entered.

Stormy, Suzanne's companion, playmate, and best friend since her first day of life, a month after Suzanne's birth, looked at me as if *she knew* Suzanne had done something *very, very bad*! Her look seemed to say: "*Uh-oh! She shouldn't have done that!*" Thankfully, Storm showed *no* inclination to follow Suzanne, but I did not, could not expect what happened next!

Suzanne's mother, Star, was grazing nearby, no more than thirty feet away, but well outside the tree-line. She suddenly raised her head as if she internally sensed something amiss! Whistles, screaming alarms seemed to go off in her head—maternal radar! Faster than a racehorse who hears the starting bell and sees the gates open, Star instantly dove through the tangled, gnarled mass of unpruned tress, brush and barbed wire fence, which was NOT downed where she was. She raised her feet and long legs like a trained jumper, and in a perfect jump, cleared the fence and landed closer to her baby than I could have ever thought possible. The object of her devotion seemed to be expecting her arrival. Mother and baby acknowledged each other by gently touching noses, and the two of them happily trotted off a short distance into the neighbor's pasture. For a moment I simply stood there astounded.

"Now what?" I sighed in exasperation. I thought to myself: "Naturally, I am *home alone, again,* when there is a horse crisis that needs a horse person's expertise. The horse person is not here. I am alone. Me, the city girl! The rest of the herd will follow before the night is over, if not in the next few minutes!"

My imagination ran with possible scenarios. I envisioned one of them cut or caught in the barbed wire after the mass crossing. "Maybe they will decide they want to come *back* into our pasture, and then surely one or more will get caught or cut on that dangerous return. There is no way for me to secure the fence without going to get more wire and tools, which I know nothing about using, and it is growing more toward darkness by the minute."

Thankfully, for the moment, none of the other horses showed any interest in following Suzanne and Star, but I knew I must somehow get the two escapees back and the entire group to safety. Leaving the herd the way it was for the night was not an option. I needed to do something right away, and could only hope that the other horses would stay put in our field until I did.

On the way back to the house, I gathered Star's and Suzanne's halters. Once inside, I called Jesse, our new neighbor from Los Angeles, who bought old Edmund's place just a year ago. Jesse is a businessman with rental properties in Kansas City and Los Angeles who decided to move to the country and enjoy a quieter life. He had been an over-the-road truck driver. He moved to California with his family from Mexico at age 16, he worked hard and did well. Now he is sort of "a country gentleman." He is always a courteous, kind, friendly neighbor, who loves to invite us for parties with great

Mexican food and music, but who knows little about horses or fixing fences. However, this night I needed help, and I knew he would do all he could to help me. As I picked up the phone and dialed his house, I feared the line would be busy, or maybe he would not be home at all. This night, thankfully, the line was not busy. Jesse was home, and answered his phone.

"Jesse," I said quickly, "this is Barbara." He always calls me Barbara, and that is fine with me—anything but *Mary!*

"Ah! Senorita Barbara! Good evening! How are you?" Jesse always calls me *Senorita*, even though I know he was well aware I have not been a senorita for years. He is a kind, happy, friendly man with the "gift of gab," and the gift of a love for people. He loves to visit, loves to laugh, to have a good time, loves to make others feel at ease, and loves to help whenever needed. Being a good neighbor is something he took seriously from the first day he moved in.

"I am well, Jesse, thank you. Tonight, however, I have a *big* problem! Two of my horses, a mother and a daughter, went over the fence and are in your pasture. Can you help me get them back to my place?"

"Sure, Senorita Barbara, I will be glad to help you! It is best if we go through my pasture up here. My pick-up truck has a flat tire, but we can go in my van. I will pick you up in a few minutes."

Within minutes, Jesse was in my driveway in his conversion van, not the best vehicle for traversing the rough terrain of his pasture, but we had to find the two escapees, and get them back into their own pasture if we could tonight before it became really dark.

We drove a quarter mile north back to his driveway and then continued through the gates near his barn into his pasture. As we bumped and lurched over formerly hidden potholes and mounds, I imagined Star and Suzanne would be long gone, enjoying their freedom somewhere in this huge unexplored field of new grass. It was beginning to get dark, and I was getting concerned about finding them in such a large area.

Jesse's van was not made for this rough terrain, but it continued to forge ahead jolting and bumping across the pasture. He asked me where they went through the fence, and I directed him to the spot in the tree line where I thought Suzanne crossed the barbed wire. When we arrived at the spot, I saw no horses in sight. I turned and looked to the north and east from within the van. There was nothing out in the pasture to the east, and nothing along the tree line. I thought maybe they might be further south, so we drove on slowly. Suddenly I saw open space in the tree line, and a perfectly intact, upright fence. Against the gray sky and lengthening shadows, I saw Star and Suzanne standing on Jesse's side of the fence, the east side, and our other five horses crowded as close as they could get against the fence on the west side. The herd! All seven horses crowded together as closely as possible. Star has very strong herd instincts—I learned that the hard way long ago. She had no desire to leave her friends behind. Thankfully the other five had not followed her over the fence.

"There they are!" I told Jesse. I thought to myself: "*Now, if* they'll let us catch them."

Jesse said he would park his van right there, and we could walk to his gate after we caught the horses; he kindly offered to return later to get his van. Jesse followed me from a distance as I walked toward Star and Suzanne. I expected to see Star bleeding and scratched from her jump through the trees, but as I drew closer I saw not a scratch. What a miracle! I was mentally prepared for Star and Suzanne to *buzz me,* silently laughing their horse laughs at escaping me, running off into Jesse's 120-acre pasture rather than be caught. I was wrong again. Star stood still as stone next to the fence; Suzanne, also seemingly chiseled in stone beside her mother; she showed no desire to dart off alone this time. I advanced slowly toward Star; pet her and talked to her. She remained totally motionless, to my utter amazement. She seemed to sense I was there to help her.

"Hi, Star! Hi, Beautiful! Good Star. Good lady." I rubbed the halter on her head, pet her neck, secured the halter, and brought her to Jesse. She followed without the slightest protest.

I instructed Jesse: "Let me get Suzanne. Once I have Suzanne, lead Star toward your southeast gate along the road. I know Suzanne will follow her mother." I just hoped Star would not give Jesse a hassle and keep turning around to look back at the herd of five across the fence, or try to return to the fence and her friends. I just had to hope Jesse would know how to make Star keep moving forward if she wanted to go in the opposite direction. I gave him Star because I thought she'd be easier for him the handle than Suzanne. Like Star, Suzanne did not resist haltering, and within minutes I was walking through the dampness of the August night tall grass following Jesse leading Star.

The quarter mile hike eastward led us to his south gate that opens on to the well-traveled gravel road. Although it seemed like a long walk through the grass; the horses did not mind the walk, and gave us no resistance. Finally we reached the gate to the gravel road. I hoped we would not encounter much traffic this time of night—cars do whiz up and down this road during the day, and sometimes at night; some drivers seem to have no respect at all for people, bikers or dogs, let alone for even less frequently seen horses. I think some drivers never stop to consider their car could scare a horse. Fortunately, this night we encountered not a single car.

With every step I half expected Star to jerk away from Jesse and head back toward the fence and her friends, or take off down the gravel road either ahead or back the way we came, but she did neither. She walked alongside Jesse as if this was her nightly routine, and Jesse too looked completely relaxed holding the lead rope casually in his hand as he sauntered west toward our property. From the back, he even looked happy. Sometimes he even appeared to be talking to Star as her head and his turned in toward each other momentarily as they walked down the road. Suzanne trustingly followed her mother's lead down the middle of the gravel road; she did not pull back or try to go ahead of me, but walked peacefully by my side. This was her first time ever on a gravel road, her first time ever out of her own pasture, and she was totally calm. They were both perfect ladies. What good horses! I knew God was watching over us--helping us lead the horses, providing a quiet road and telling them to quietly trust us.

The other five herd-mates were waiting as we approached our property and their fenced pasture; they walked in a group alongside us from within their fence. Our south gate into the hay field, the closest, was locked, so we returned to the road and walked the extra eighth of a mile and turned the corner to our west gate, which we always use and never lock. Jesse and Star still looked like buddies who took this sort of walk every night. Suzanne followed trustingly, perfectly at ease. I was so proud of her, proud of both of them. They knew we were bringing them home.

We finally arrived at the west gate, and brought Star and Suzanne inside. They both stood quietly until we removed both their halters and stepped back from them. Once released, the two vaulted like summer lightning in the greatest haste across the lower hilly pasture toward the gate which opens into the hay pasture to rejoin their friends in the now settling darkness.

In J. R.R. Tolkien's <u>The Fellowship of the Ring</u>, Bilbo warns Frodo it is "a dangerous business going out of your door" and cautioned if he didn't "keep" his feet, there was no telling where he "might be swept off to." Suzanne never met Bilbo or Frodo, and never read the book, so she never got the warning. She thought it an exciting adventure to go out her door and to be swept off to someplace new, but she did seem willing and grateful to come home. She always was a horse to explore, to "step into the road." She was always curious about what might be over the next fence.

Star reaffirmed once again the perfect mother she always was. Her only concern was for her child, now a huge almost eighteen-month-old "baby" who was nearly taller than she was. Star's radar beeped the minute Suzanne stepped over that sagging barbwire fence, and she leapt into action to save her from unknown danger no matter what the consequences were for her. Our wonderful Star was forever a beautiful example of motherhood. She would have given her life for her Suzanne.

Jesse walked back to get his van, and I walked back to the house. A few days later Jesse told Rod he had never led a horse before, and said, actually, he is sort of afraid of horses. I could not believe it. He certainly had risen to the occasion. I told him he handled the whole thing perfectly. I'd never have guessed he had any fear of horses. I suspect after this incident he was a lot less afraid.

I certainly was glad he was home that evening, and so willing to help me. He was a good neighbor, always thinking of others. It was the grace of God that allowed this misadventure to end so well. Jesse was such a generous help, and the horses all reacted perfectly to our efforts. No one could ask for a more "neighborly" neighbor, or for better horses.

Ink drawing of Star jumping fence to find Suzanne

Chapter 23
Fence Repair, Wood Cutting; an Injury and a Loss

After Suzanne and Star's athletic, curiosity-driven near escape, Rod and I knew we had to quickly repair the damaged fence areas before we left for Massachusetts in a few weeks to visit our daughter and her family. We knew Jesse did not know how to fix it; he was definitely not a fence repairman. Fence building and repair, I learned since living in the country, is an art one learns carefully over time, almost as an apprentice. Since watching Rod construct fences, I had a great respect for people who built straight, sturdy ones. Fencing was no easy craft; a "fence master" had to be carefully taught. Rod's father had instructed him well in this largely lost art. Some "old timers" say in their younger days there was *always* something to do on a farm, "fix fence if nothing else." We had no further to look than our own property to see that fences needed to be maintained, though our neighbors throughout our county and all connecting counties also exhibited both phenomena: fences that needed great repair, and few people who knew how to build, or had the time to build a strong, straight fence. Rod's fences were strong and straight, it was the ones he did not build that needed repair.

We walked the fence lines together and spotted places where the wires and post were as seriously falling down as where Suzanne escaped. Rod put up new metal posts, and fresh smooth wire wherever it was needed. We did not use barbed wire; it is too easy for a horse to get hurt in it.

It was early fall: beautiful, dry, warm weather—a wonderful time to be outside. In some places we had to cut away some of the trees that had grown into the fence, or had limbs that actually pushed the entire fence posts, and/or the wires down. Since we heat our house with wood, we decided this would be a good time to also cut some wood to put aside for the next winter. Rod used his chain saw to fell some of the older trees, and then cut them into chunks to fit in our outdoor wood-burning stove. When we first arrived in Kansas he found an old gravity wagon at an auction, and later refurbished its running gear with used lumber to make a very useful farm wagon since we no longer needed the grain box to hold our harvested soy beans. Rod pulled the wagon with his small Ford tractor, and I enjoyed not only loading the wagon with wood, but also sitting on the wagon bed as we bumped back to the house. Doing these fun, simple things, it seemed almost as if I were again a child.

Whenever we worked outdoors, the horses liked to come see what we were doing, and keep us company. Sometimes they nibbled the bark on the logs, once in a while one of them decided to pull a particularly interesting piece of wood off the wagon. It thudded to the ground, spooking the culprit and others momentarily. I had an instant of alarm, too, as I saw the startled window shoppers snort and spread their legs as if they might take off, but quickly everyone relaxed and went back to eating grass and swiftly resumed sniffing and examining the wagon contents.

As we cut wood in the large mowed hay pasture, and in the horses' lower pasture, and then piled the logs on the wagon bed even our adopted dog, Joker, joined us. He had longish, thick black hair, and liked to rest in the shade under the wagon, but he really liked to hunt pack rats that built homes at the base of some of the trees. The first time I saw them, I thought pack rat homes looked like miniature misplaced beaver dams minus the water. A mound of sticks at the base of the tree signaled a pack rat home, and Joker went right to work digging out the poor unsuspecting pack rat, and carrying off his squeaking victim to devour him *alive. UGH!* The poor pack rat! I turned my head and never watched its untimely, violent end.

To say that we had more help than we needed is an understatement. Suzanne, it seemed, was forever at one of our elbows, licking us, sniffing us, putting her head on our shoulders or chests. She had to be right where we were, just like Dorit and Chaos. Dorit was still inching herself right in beside Rod, wanting to be in the middle of what he was doing—helping him or supervising him. Chaos must have inherited the coziness trait, because she was right in the middle of the work too; her "facial expressions" and body language again just like Dorit's. It was strange and sad to me Dorit did not acknowledge her as her daughter. Chaos always knew Dorit was her mother. These equine curiosity seekers would at first jump back when Rod started the chain saw, but as soon as it stopped they picked their way back over branches to be with us and sometimes to undo our work—moving logs on the ground or pulling them off the wagon after we carefully stacked them. Suzanne stepped back and forth over the wagon tongue that hinged the wagon to the tractor entirely without coaxing. She *loved* to step over things, as her fence antics had already taught us, and would teach us again and again. How many times had we tried to get another horse to go over a plastic pipe on the ground and been refused with snorts and planted feet? To Suzanne this game of stepping over things was as natural as breathing, eating, or licking us. Her instinctive affection for people was just as natural. She was by far the most demonstrative and sociable horse we ever had the privilege of having on our farm, and the most inquisitive, and the most acrobatic too.

Suzanne did not have the only corner on inquisitiveness, however. Rod recently bought a new seat cushion for the old Ford tractor because the other was broken-down, was missing stuffing, and was very uncomfortable. We bought the tractor, many times "second hand," for more than it was worth several years ago. It probably saw at least seven or eight owners before us; parts of it were from other models and had been thrown on in a hurry in order to make a sale. We were stupid to purchase it, but we needed a smaller tractor right away. It was a desperation purchase; a bad investment. As much as was wrong with that little old Ford, it was a good size for much of our work, and ran reasonably well mainly because Rod was a very good mechanic. He could fix nearly anything, and very often had to do just that. The new seat had not been cheap, but it was a tremendous improvement in both the visual and comfort departments.

This particular day we were cutting wood was only the second time Rod had used his new tractor seat, and he liked it a lot. As chance would have it, Pascal took a bite out of the new cushion while Rod was cutting wood and the herd was nosing around the tractor and wagon. After the initial: "Oh, no!" we just sighed, shook our heads, and finally even laughed. It was annoying, but we had to admit it was only a material thing, and Pascal had no idea what he did. No one was hurt; it had been a good day for us and for the horses. The tractor seat retained the missing right front corner for many years. However, we soon had a more serious problem than a mutilated tractor cushion.

Within a month after Star's dive over the barbed wire fence through the tangled trees to rescue Suzanne we noticed she was limping and her hind foot was swollen and hot. We were leaving in two days for our four-day trip to Massachusetts for our yearly visit with our daughter, Catherine, and her family. We had non-refundable tickets, and we had no neighbor who knew anything about horses. Star, more than any of the other horses, needed her herd. We noticed she moved more slowly, but she still managed to go where the other horses went, even traveling the quarter mile across the large pasture twice a day, morning and evening, to be near the shade of the trees along the east fence. We hoped the walks increased the circulation to the affected area, and would promote healing. We soaked her foot in Epsom salts three times a day, but did not begin a Penicillin regimen because we knew we would not be home to complete it. We prayed for her while we were home, and we prayed while we were away, and hoped for God's mercy. I left my statue of St. Francis of Assisi in the kitchen window and prayed he would intercede to God for Star's healing, and he and the Lord would watch over her in our absence.

The afternoon we returned home we were relieved to see Star still standing along with the other horses. We immediately gave the antibiotic injection. What happened over the next couple hours was amazing. So Star could finally stay off her injured foot instead of traversing nearly thirty acres of pasture several times a day and night with the herd, we were preparing to put her, with Suzanne, the same shed where we kept Chaos those cold winter nights. We brought in fresh hay, and readied the shed for the pair. By the time we had everything the way we wanted it, it was dark. We were leading Star and Suzanne toward the shed, and encountering great resistance. Star had made a surprising leap toward recovery in the two hours since we had given the first Penicillin shot, and she was showing us in no uncertain terms she *did not want* to be quarantined in the shed even with Suzanne. In the deepening darkness, Rod and I stopped in the middle of the pasture with injured mother and daughter on lead ropes to discuss whether we should just "let her be, and take what comes" or force the issue and make Star, with Suzanne, get into the shed. We thought rest was probably the best remedy for her abscessed foot, but she had made it this long walking on it.

Our discussion was abruptly interrupted when we saw a car drive into our driveway. He left his headlights on, and we saw the driver get out and walk to our door. When nobody answered the doorbell, he returned to his car, and left the driveway. I blinked my flashlight off and on so he would know we were in the pasture below the house, and I walked toward the fence that bordered the road.

A very upset, apologetic man got out of his car and ran to the fence.

"Ma'am, I'm terribly sorry, but I killed your dog!" he stammered in a worried, repentant voice. "He was in the ditch and jumped out into the road! It is a dark night. I never had a chance to see him or stop the car! I am so sorry!"

The poor man was beside himself. He seemed like he almost expected we might pull out a gun and shoot him, or call the police. Rod said: "Don't worry about it. You couldn't help it. He was a black dog and it is a black night. We are sorry he was in the way. Thank you very much for telling us."

I think the gentleman was relieved we were not screaming at him. He apologized again, returned to his car, and drove away. It was all too much for me to process on that night: Star's recovery and her refusal to stay in the shed, now Joker's death, all this after a long day of flying from the east coast, and over an hour driving home from the airport. After his departure, Rod and I decided the miracle of Penicillin had "cured" Star and we could let her remain with the other horses. We left the shed as we had prepared it, and returned to the house. We could not hunt for Joker in the darkness. The next morning Rod brought poor Joker home to rest in our own field.

It didn't really sink in until the next few days that *Joker was gone*. He had been with us nearly two years. He had been a pest to the horses: he ate the food they dribbled on the ground, and any pieces of carrots they dropped; he ran with them when they ran, pretending either to be a horse himself, or to be chasing them. He accompanied Rod on his morning jogs, but sometimes slipped under fences and chased cows, and had recently taken up chasing cars. He utterly resisted getting *in* cars, but *he lived to chase them!* He did not come when we tried to call him back from either of those practices—a crazed mob-like mindset seemed to take hold of him in his chasing. Due to the probable trauma of his earlier life, Joker never really trusted us, though I believe he trusted us more than he ever trusted anyone else, and I believe he was happier on our little farm than he had ever been. Our grandchildren loved him, especially our little granddaughter, Maria, and he faithfully accompanied us in our chores. He was a good dog and friend to us.

I remember the Easter before her second birthday when she wanted to cover Joker with kisses and hug his big furry coat; Joker would have none of it and ran away as Maria approached. His early months of mistreatment and rejection had permanently made him distrustful of *all* humans. He did not even completely trust Rod and me, and he always followed our hands with his eyes to make sure we were not going to hit him instead of pet him. Finally, to please little Maria, and to teach Joker people could be friendly, Rod held Joker by the collar while Maria hugged and kissed him. Joker trembled and looked with a wary eye as Maria covered his long hair with wet kisses and big hugs. After that Joker reluctantly began to let the children hug him, pet him, snuggle him. It was good for him, and good for them. I know the grandchildren missed him most of all.

I was certain the horses did not miss him chasing them, pretending to be one of them and, or eating the food that dropped from their buckets. As the days passed, Rod and I felt his loss more. Even with his undesirable traits, Joker was a loyal dog, and a fierce-looking watchdog. Most likely, a burglar would take one look at his large size, one listen to his deep, loud, curt bark, and decide to find another house to burglarize. He liked to lean against my leg as I waved good-bye to Rod driving out the driveway to work—sort of a hug. Joker always jumped up from his favorite place in the shade of the north corner of our back porch to accompany me the moment I stepped out the back door. He accepted the place we gave him to sleep in our barn, and gratefully ate the dry dog food we gave him and any leftovers we happened to have.

He loved it when we had guests because he was the designated leftovers eater. He supplemented his dry dog food diet with occasional rabbits, pack rats, and moles. He loved to dig up the moles and then throw them up in the air and catch them in his mouth; sometimes he liked to roll on them. It was comical to watch his rump and plumed tail waving in the air while the front half of his body was underground scouting out the poor mole. However, he did provide a good service! The poor rabbits he just tore up and ate, thankfully he never tossed them around. Rod sometimes called him

"Gollum," the villain in J. R. R. Tolkien's <u>Lord of the Rings Trilogy,</u> who also ate his food *raw*; he teased me, in Gollum-like language: *"He likesis his rabbitsis."*

One time I made cookies and burned the whole tray on the bottom shelf of the oven when I forgot to switch the cookie sheets at half the allotted baking time. Joker ate the burned cookies and loved them. To me Joker was an uninvited pet, who did a lot of things I did not expect, but he taught me about learning to trust and about being a companion and friend—he just did it. I did grow to love him. I did miss him.

A young couple whom we met the month before Joker died, were sad to learn of his passing. The man told us he worked with a woman who had a Weimaraner who had just had eleven puppies fathered by a male Black Labrador. She was *giving* them away! Thus, when these puppies were ready to leave their mother, we came to have another dog. Rod was reading Charles Dickens' <u>Hard Times.</u> A *"fancy"* was something children loved, but adults discouraged as *a waste of time.* It was the perfect name for our new puppy. We lived a simple life, but, with the addition of *Fancy*, we told ourselves we had *fancy* thoroughbred horses, and a *fancy* dog.

The horses quickly made it quite clear to our new pup that they would tolerate *none of Joker's antics* from her. The day I brought Fancy down to introduce her to the equines, Star picked our new puppy up by the scruff of the neck and tossed her on the ground. I thought it would be good to acquaint her with the horses right away, but I never expected this response! However, Fancy was a very smart dog from the very beginning; after that she kept her distance from the horses. She accompanied us to feed them, but she smartly remained outside the pen until we finished. Star set the tone, and Fancy respected the horses' wishes.

Another animal on the farm who refused to be subject to any further terrorism from a dog was our dear mommy cat, Paws. She immediately set Fancy straight that *she* was not to be chased, or in any way bothered in any dog-hate-cat manner. Fancy and Paws became respectable friends—they peacefully co-existed--and sometimes were even seen lying close to one other in the shade of the barn or near the house on hot summer afternoons. Once in a while Fancy would attempt a chase, but she was quickly reminded of the no-attack alliance with a brisk swipe of the paw, an angry spitting hiss, and Paws' arched back—all of which said: "Don't even *think* of messing with me!"

Two year old Maria, in her Easter finery, kisses a wary Joker, held by Grandpa.

Maria hugging Joker

Mommy Paws

Chapter 24
Good Horses, Good People

Some children do not like horses, but many do and are excited for the opportunity to be around them. I hoped our farm would draw not only our own children and grandchildren, but also their friends, our friends and even friends of friends because of our friendly, peaceful horses, farm and home. I wanted our home to become a sort of haven for those who did not have these gifts and who could not repay us to enjoy the animals and the serene beauty we found and built here. "Invite the poor...you will be blessed, because they cannot repay you....'Go out to the highways and hedges...that my house may be filled.'"(Luke 14:12-24) My dream has not materialized yet. Our own children do not live close-by and do not visit often, and the few attempts we have made to foster a love of being with, caring for and riding our horses with those not in our family has, so far, not come about as I hoped, although there have been a few non-family who indeed loved and enjoyed our horses.

Paul's and Kelli's first child, Matthew, our first grandchild, was introduced to horses before he could walk, just as his grandfather was. Paul wisely initiated each of his children to our horses at his first opportunity in an effort to dispel any fear, and to show them that new and different things were opportunities for fun rather than something to fear. Paul, living closest to us, but still nearly 250 miles away, visited fairly often especially when the children were small. Matthew, with Paul holding him aboard, rode Little Dorit, John, Winnie and Star, and later Dorit and Winnie alone.

Little Maria was barely two when she was lifted atop Star for one of her first horseback rides. The tiny little girl was a little wary at first, but nothing frightening happened to her, and later she came to love the big grey as her favorite horse, and Winnie as her second favorite. When we went out to ride, she always wanted to ride Star. At five years old, Maria could not contain her happiness and anticipation: "Oh! I am so excited I get to ride Star!" Star obligingly trotted or walked, whatever she was asked, and Maria balanced expertly upon her boney back. They both loved it. Our good strong Star also obligingly carried both Matthew and Maria together on her willing back with great gentleness; she seemed to realize they were children and deserved special handling. The children loved her; and she was our only horse ever to be ridden "double."

Early one autumn Saturday morning, then four year old Matthew accompanied his grandfather on an exciting, important mission: to feed the horses. As Rod walked into the hay field to catch Pascal and lead him, with the other horses following right behind, into the pen to be fed, Matthew began joyfully dashing about in the wide open space of our hay pasture. What child could resist running through a beautiful field of grass and horses on a gorgeous fall morning? Rod had just haltered Pascal to bring him to the feeding pen. Knowing that our horses were unaccustomed to seeing a small child sprinting around in front of them, and concerned they might decide to run with him, Rod quickly scooped up his grandson and set him on our dear buddy's large, wide, and very high back. Matthew, who at age 3, when he first met Pascal asked warily if he would "eat him," calmly rode his huge dark steed back to the feeding pen. All the others followed as Rod brought their leader through the gate and tied him to receive his morning grain. Matthew certainly looked noble astride his kingly mount, and Pascal carried him with kindly and kingly confidence.

I was then proud of our horses even more, if that was possible! Accomplished, cultured, blue ribbon-winning Pascal gladly carried little Matthew safely across the pasture, and gave rides to everyone who wanted to be lifted high upon his back. Star, the fastest horse on our farm always seemed glad to give the little children a ride and was even happy to follow and run beside them as they carried her lead rope and jumped over a plastic pipe set out on the ground as an obstacle. If the child leaped high over the pipe, Star tried to also jump high. She did not consider herself "above such child's play." She truly seemed to enjoy it.

One summer afternoon when Star had given rides to both Matthew and Maria off and on for over an hour, the other horses meandered down to the lower pasture to find hay and grass near the shed. Star, who usually tended to be very herd-bound, was the last one "up north." We helped Matthew off Star, removed her bridle and led her out the round pen gate. Tradition has it at the McKay farm that *after* being ridden, the horse gets a few treats—several pieces of carrot, maybe an additional cookie or sugar cube—whatever we have on hand. Star took her treats in a lady-like fashion and chewed them gratefully, enjoying every last bite. She knew she was free to return to the herd. In a very polite manner, she slowly walked several steps southward, away from the round pen. It seemed as if she did not want to hurt our feelings by leaving in a hurry. She did not want to "eat and run," nor did she want us to think she preferred horse company to human company. When she was satisfied she had been sufficiently gracious, she instantaneously effortlessly accelerated into high gear and flew across the north pasture as if she had been shot from a cannon, in her exquisitely graceful floating canter. As so often before, we could barely see her hooves touch the ground, but the air resounded with the thundering sound of her feet pounding against the earth. She looked like lightning on wings, and almost before anyone of us standing there could blink she was at the shed with her friends. She was magnificent!

Matthew looked at us with his eyes and his mouth wide open. *"Awwwe-some!"* he exclaimed. I don't think he ever saw a horse, or anything, move so fast.

"She is our Shadowfax," I said proudly.

"Even Shadowfax can't catch *her!*" Rod responded.

I had to agree. Even Tolkien's Shadowfax, *The Lord of All Horses,* might have met his match in our fast, beautiful lady. Star was never too proud to gently and patiently carry little children, never too self-important to accept hugs, pets and treats from little hands. Always a lady, almost as if she considered our feelings, she never hurried to finish what must have seemed simply, childish games, yet within seconds after the play was ended she could nearly launch herself into space like a rocket, like summer lightning, or like a falling star.

Winnie, also a favorite mount for the grandchildren and the few other children who occasionally visited us, reliably and steadily gave the rides, and seemed to enjoy the attention they lavished upon her. I suspect, though, that she was largely motivated by the happy thought of those delicious edible after-rewards. Winnie was older than Star and did not usually leave with such haste, though the few times she did decide she *was* in a hurry to re-join her friends she was not at all the "ladylike Star" in her departure. She could, and sometimes did, thunder off to join her mates kicking up dust behind her as if the starting bell sounded and she was back at the race track eager to be the first horse to cross the finish line. She seemed to be telling us she was glad to be finished with being a merry-go-round pony. She enjoyed, or at least she tolerated well, those rides while they lasted, but when the quarter ran out, when the music and treats ended, her time at the carousel was finished and she was quickly *out of there* and back to being a horse with her friends.

Dorit assented to being ridden by the grandchildren, but she really loved them to lead her around by her lead rope after they had finished their rides. She followed like an obedient, curious little puppy always at a safe distance, never pulling away, never getting too close, never nipping, and never running ahead. She liked to keep her head to the ground as if she were trying to pick up a scent. Her daughter, Chaos, was also very curious about the little children and very gentle with them. Our entire group of ride-providing horses seemed to instinctively know when a child was on board, and thus behave in a completely trustworthy manner.

One August evening when Veronica and all of Paul's family were here, we were out at the round pen letting the children take turns riding different horses. Stormy was not one of them, but must have felt the relaxed, happy atmosphere of the family time together. The horses who were not being ridden milled around outside the round pen, watching the riders and their mounts, and letting us pet them. Stormy moaned a contented moan that reminded me of her mother's comfortable sighs during her baths. Then she lay down on the grass and began to roll over in a pleased fashion. At first some of us wondered if maybe something was wrong, but she quickly reassured us everything was fine, and she was just contented and completely relaxed. She truly was a *joyful* horse! After a few rolls, she stood up, first placing her front bent legs forward and then rumbling up her hind end, shook herself, and blew air out her nose and mouth. This huge youngest horse was simply trying to tell us she was happy to be here with this comfortable bunch of horses and people, and was pleased to be included in the activities. Our horses feel comfortable around us; we know them, and they know us. We enjoy one another's company every day, but particularly this day. Once I told our vet we had nice animals, and he remarked: "Nice people have nice animals." I was complimented, but I have concluded that perhaps it is also true that good animals make people good, and good people make animals good. God certainly knew what he was doing when he gave us the animals for support and companionship. "And God saw everything that he had made, and behold, it was very good."(Genesis 1:31)

Chaos receives thank you pets and treats from Maria after a ride as Grandpa and Dad look on.

Star carries Matthew and Maria double as Grandpa leads.

Matthew on his kingly steed, Pascal, led by Grandpa.

Paul rewards Winnie with treats after her time as a "carousel horse."

Michael rides Winnie.

Nate rides Winnie as Grandpa runs alongside.

201

Chapter 25
No Stomach for Selling Horses

Rod repeatedly told me we had *too many horses*—we had seven. We advertised two of our horses, Suzanne and Chaos, for sale in the newspaper and on the internet. Intellectually I *knew* we had too many horses for two older people to train and care for adequately. Rod, was nearly 60, and worked full time, but he was still <u>an expert</u> with the horses. I was two years younger, a transplanted city dweller with little knowledge of training horses, though I was beginning to learn, and loved and helped care for them quite well. I did not want someone to neglect, mistreat, or to train our horses roughly. I have seen horses treated as "which" or "that," not <u>"who."</u> Horses definitely have real feelings and emotions, "horsenalities," they are each individuals; they are *always who* to me. Our horses trust us, and that trust is too precious to risk being destroyed by ignorant or mean handling. If we trained them, they would know us, and we would know them and they would always *bring us home*, that is, always be there for us even in a pinch. That was important to me. I could not see what was wrong with keeping *all* our horses as friends.

Our original intention in buying a stallion had been to sell the foals, but our attempts yielded few prospects and no money. I was not keen on selling any of our horses, and I had become very attached to all our foals. The horses were beautiful to look at; they were friendly, entertaining, and even therapeutic for us to interact with and care for, especially for me. We joked that they were "pasture ornaments" and our weakness. When the children of a friend of mine told me they pretended they rode our horses when they played outside, Rod said "pretend to ride our horse is just about what we do too." We spent so much time caring for them that with our other chores around our farm and Rod's work; we rarely had time to ride them. Sunday afternoons were often horse riding times, and, of course, when our grandchildren did come, they always wanted to help feed, and then ride, the horses.

Since I had bonded with Stormy, Winnie's filly, Rod said I could keep her and he would try to sell Suzanne and Chaos. I knew how much Rod loved Suzanne—how much we both loved Suzanne. She was the long-awaited horse, our *Princess Shadowfax*, from our Star, *the Lady of all Horses*. We thought Suzanne had to be the friendliest, most affectionate, beautiful and special horse anyone could imagine. She loved and trusted us. We waited through nearly two gestation periods, a broken arm, and a long period of Star's infertility for her arrival and she did not disappoint us. We believed she was God's special gift to us, and admitted to each other that she had taught us so much about the unconditional love, gratitude, and trust God gives us, and expects from us in return. Suzanne will always exemplify the humility, innocence, and openness of a child who climbs into her loving father's lap just happy to be there. We could never talk about her without Rod getting a lump in his throat and saying: "Suzanne! What a wonderful horse!"

Chaos was "our special baby." All our horses were *our babies*, but we had been mother and father to Chaos for over six months. We took turns getting up in the night to feed her, took her for walks, found a babysitter for her when we left town, rented a goat to keep her company in her first months with no mother to nurture her. We bought her a blanket to shield her from the winter's cold. We gave her the most loving care people knew how to give a horse. We would always be her adoptive "parents," and she would always be a part of us.

I did feel guilty about not offering to sell Stormy in place of Suzanne or Chaos, but not guilty enough to relinquish her. I believe Rod, in his love for me, understood I loved and *needed* Stormy. He also knew Winnie was old and would not be around many more years. In his kindness, and in his love for me loving our horses, he never once made an issue of my keeping Stormy. He gave up what he loved for the one he loved. That was a gift I will never forget.

Before any prospective buyers arrived, we had a lot of inquiries from long distances—Florida, New York, California, Texas. But we had only three actual, physical lookers. One woman who called from a long distance was very annoyed that we refused to sell Suzanne sight unseen, and have her shipped halfway across the country. She told us she was an excellent trainer, and wanted a young horse to "bring along." However, we had to tell her we had been burned—we related the story of our first potential buyer.

This had been a woman who called from less than one hundred miles away. She had seen Suzanne's pictures on the internet, knew of the article about Star in Equus Magazine, and nearly wanted to buy her over the phone. We insisted she come to look at Suzanne. When she did arrive, as we walked down to the pen where we had brought the horse for her to see, she admitted to me that everything she owned was *gray*. Her dog was a Weimaraner, and she even had a gray car. *Suzanne would coordinate well with her color scheme.* When this young woman actually saw Suzanne and realized she was just a yearling and would require extensive training, she told us she chose "not to pursue the matter further," turned on her heel and left. I never knew whether our home and our horse facility was not fancy enough, or whether she thought Suzanne should be a fully-trained horse at one year, or whether she thought our dear horse was not the right shade of gray. It was not meant to be. We were satisfied that this was for the best for all concerned.

The next potential buyer called after a friend of ours told her we had some horses we wanted to sell. This woman arranged the time over the phone, but she and her husband arrived over four hours late; they never called to alert us they had changed their plans and decided to look at another horse first. This discourtesy was the first dim intimation that this showing would be less than satisfactory. The woman I had spoken to on the phone, was the first one out of their new, very expensive car. As she closed the passenger door, she assumed an authoritative stance: legs apart, hands on hips. I was immediately struck by her "take charge" aura: she radiated a commanding and demanding presence. She was tall, lean, and muscular—she *looked like* an athlete, but not a happy or friendly one--she did not smile. On first impression, she did not seem like someone who liked horses, but rather someone who *used horses* to her advantage. She reminded me of a general in charge of a cavalry in an old western movie, or a sheriff leading a posse after some cattle rustlers. She was *all-business* as she looked about rather disdainfully at our simple home and out buildings, perhaps wondering where the horses were kept since she saw no up-scale barns and perfect stalls.

Her husband introduced himself and his wife to Rod and me, and opened the back door of his vehicle to release their dog. I wondered if they were so absolutely certain their dog would do nothing, especially in an unknown environment, to frighten our horses and ruin a sale. I could not believe they felt completely comfortable in bringing him and letting him out without even asking us--completely unannounced, uninvited and unleashed. The dog frisked and sniffed around a bit, but appeared to be obedient enough to follow when called by the man. Then the four of us, and their dog, walked down to the horse pen.

We brought all seven of our horses, one at a time, into the pen to feed them so this couple could observe them in their normal environment, interacting with each other and with us. We felt this would give them an opportunity to look at Chaos and Suzanne without making it obvious to the horses that anything different was taking place. During our walk they told us that a recent storm had taken the lives of their two horses who were struck by lightning!

Instantly I felt sadness for them. "Oh! That is horrible! I am so sorry! That would be like losing a family member," I offered sympathetically. They made no reply, nothing, not even a thank you, but I thought perhaps I detected a slight nod of the head from the man. Maybe it was *not* like losing a family member, I thought to myself. I felt as if my sympathies had been inappropriate, mistaken, or misunderstood.

Most people who see our horses comment immediately how beautiful they are, how well they get along with us and with each other, how easy they are to catch, and ask their names. Realistically, it is only good business manners to compliment people on their horses especially if one has intention to buy one. This couple had nothing good to say about any of our horses; and our horses seemed to have no curiosity about *these* visitors, which was very unusual. The woman walked critically around Suzanne and pointed out a swelling just above her hind left hock and asked how long it had been there. We told her it must have just happened because neither of us had noticed it earlier that day, and Suzanne showed no signs of lameness as she approached and walked into the pen.

The woman looked at me as if she did not believe Suzanne had just acquired the swelling. As curious as Suzanne was, and as eager as she was to investigate things, a bump or swelling was not surprising to us. She certainly did not evidence any lameness, nor had she ever. I perfectly understood that they wanted a sound horse and wanted to take no chances that she was anything less than perfect. The swelling seemed to at least temporarily eliminate Suzanne from the possible purchase line-up. Judging from what little I had observed of this woman's personality, I was glad Suzanne was, at least temporarily, no longer under consideration. The woman said she would call us in a few days to learn if the edema was still present.

The lady in charge next decided to take Chaos into the arena where she wanted Rod to demonstrate riding her, since he had been training her and she was accustomed to him being on her back. She roughly grabbed the lead rope to lead Chaos to Rod, but just then they noticed their dog was doing something he should not. As the woman turned her back to scold him, Chaos opened her mouth in a slow, wide alligator-like bite gesture. I stifled a laugh. Rod headed off catastrophe as he took the lead rope from "the woman in charge" thus allowing her to tend to her dog. Her husband thoughtfully grabbed a spare lead rope and put it on the canine-offender to keep him out of mischief. I thought their dog would be romping about with Joker and thus not disturb the horse showing, but we had not seen Joker since they arrived. (This sequence of events happened about two months before we lost Joker.)

With their unruly canine secured, Rod rode Chaos for them. Predictably, they said *nothing.* I assumed they were unimpressed. We released Chaos and the others, and the couple followed us into the house. We offered them ice water, and showed them the registration papers, and discussed our price. We talked briefly about thoroughbreds, and about Laura Hillenbrand's book *Seabiscuit: An American Legend,* which I alone had read, and the recently released movie, which we all had seen—the one thing we had in common. At one point the woman, standing at our kitchen counter, kept looking at our floor. Finally, she set her glass down and bent down and touched the floor. She gasped, and commented in a surprised fashion as she rose that it *really was* ceramic tile! To me, this seemed to be the final insult—what did tile have to do with buying horses? I had a very uneasy feeling about selling *any* of our horses to these people who seemed to be reproachful and even mocking of everything on our simple farm, our open sincerity, our truthfulness, and our good horses. Rod sometimes quoted his father saying "you can learn something from everyone, even if it *is how not to be*." To me, these people definitely taught me *how not to be* when viewing a horse. The only other positive thing I could think about this encounter was, from their actions here, *these* people most probably would not buy our horses. Christ told us to be humble and to turn the other cheek (Matthew 5:39). We were quiet, and tried to be accommodating; if it was not good enough, so be it.

Finally they said they needed to leave, and that they would call us in a few days to learn about Suzanne's leg, and give us their decision about Chaos. Rod and I returned to the house quietly after seeing them to their car. For a while we said nothing. We were both thinking about the people who had just come and gone; they seemed so abrasive. We did not want our horses going to them under *any* circumstances. Apparently Joker instinctively distrusted them because we later learned from Jesse that Joker hid at his house the whole time they were here. Rod's father said, "You can't fool dogs…" and it seemed he was exactly right. This particular horse-hunting couple did not agree with us, with Chaos, *or* our dog; none of us were fooled. We did not want to have what they were seeking, nor did we want them to have any of our horses.

"I don't think I have the stomach for selling horses," Rod finally said.

"I *know* I don't either," I replied.

"If they call back, let's just tell them we have decided not to sell them."

"That's fine with me. I didn't want to sell them anyway," I answered.

We resigned ourselves to having and keeping our seven good horses, *our* wonderful *magnificent seven,* and decided we would manage to care for them the best we could and train them as we were able. We discontinued the ads completely. Then, about a month later, we received a call asking if we *still had horses for sale?*

Initially my response was that we had not sold the horses, and had decided not to sell them. However, this wonderfully happy, kind-sounding woman on the other end of the phone line kept asking about them, telling me she was impressed with their pedigrees, and telling me that she had ridden dressage and jumped horses as a younger woman. She explained she had seen the internet ad when they lived back east, and had printed it out and saved it until they moved to Kansas. As she talked I learned more and more about her. She was the same religion as we, she home schooled her children, just as we did. She told me she and her husband had each been widowed with two daughters, and now they had three sons together. She and her children wanted to take a road trip to come meet our horses and us, if it was all right. She was very convincing; she had a vitality that was captivating, *and did not let me say* "No." I remember saying: "Well, *you seem like a nice person*--that was our issue with the other potential buyers—we feared they would not be good to our horses." That first conversation lasted nearly forty-five minutes, and ended with us arranging a time for them to come meet our horses. Her name was Sherry.

They arrived with a large van that seemed to overflow with children from infant to near adult: the oldest girl was a going to be a freshman in college, and the youngest boy was just four months old. They poured out of their van laughing and smiling; they seemed happy to be here. They all came to the horse pen and pet and talked to each one of the horses. They marveled at Pascal's beauty, size, and gentle nature, and admired Star and Suzanne and all the horses. The oldest girl went to Stormy and declared: "I think this horse is the best of all!"

"I have to agree with you," I said happily. "She is my baby! I am totally bonded to her."

This was the kind of response we expected to our horses! We returned to the house and had pizza and talked about horses, then we went back to look at the horses again. The woman asked if Pascal also was for sale, and we referred her to Veronica. She said she was also very interested in Chaos since she had the most training; now that she had seven children she would not have the time she had in her younger years to devote to horse training. There was still some uncertainty, but she definitely thought she wanted Chaos, and maybe Pascal, if Veronica was willing to sell him.

We liked this woman a lot, and we thought Chaos would be the perfect horse for her growing children. Ultimately, we told her we would trailer Chaos to her home, and if she didn't work out for her we would come again and take her back home and give her money back rather than have her sell Chaos to someone unknown, and perhaps have Chaos end up being sold over and over again. We thought this way she could not lose; we thought surely they would all love Chaos as much as we did. We made her an offer she could not refuse.

Rod continued to ride Chaos every day, and we taught her to load into the trailer again. In October we took her to her new home. Chaos accepted her new surroundings without protest, happy to eat the grass in the new pasture. As we left to return home, I saw Chaos watch us drive away from behind a beautiful white fence with a huge home behind her. I told Rod Chaos had a beautiful new home. He agreed. We thought she would adjust well. There was another chestnut thoroughbred gelding, about the size of Pascal, though older, and a pony in the next pasture who Sherry planned to put with Chaos in a day or so. In the meantime, they could visit across the fence.

That evening when we returned home, we fed the horses, and went to bed. The next morning when we came out to feed the horses they were all scattered toward the east side of the large pasture. They were much more spread out than they usually were, and we noticed Pascal furthest off, completely alone, with his head hanging down. He was not eating—just standing there. He looked completely forsaken—as if he had lost his best friend. Rod and I looked at each other.

"He misses Chaos," I said almost in tears. "Poor Buddy!"

Rod took the halter, and walked across the large pasture returning with Buddy who still walked with his head down.

"Maybe this afternoon you can come out and give this good guy some attention because he is very, very sad," Rod choked. I recognized that broken, wobbly sound of his voice from the days of reading Charles Dickens' *A Christmas Carol* to our children, and at times when he was very moved by the words and what was happening, and when he spoke of Suzanne. We both felt terribly sorry for our good Pascal-- we both were near tears. He had lost his best friend the day before. I did indeed spend time with him that afternoon, currying him, petting him—letting him know we cared about him, and that we understood he was sad.

Then in December we received a call from the same woman. She said she was sorry, but Chaos was just not working out and we had to come get her. She said Chaos barred her teeth when anyone entered the stall, tried to attack her eleven-year-old daughter when she fed her, and would not stand still to have her feet trimmed.

None of this sounded like *our Chaos!* We could not believe it was the same horse. We had promised, and we made good on our promise. It was nearly a three hour drive, and when we pulled in the driveway, we saw Chaos in the pasture. She raised her head and gave us a look of recognition. She *knew* our truck, and she knew *we* were inside. She *knew* she was going home. We visited with the family for a while before going out to the pasture to get Chaos. We wondered whether we would have to attempt trailer loading more than once, but Chaos knew why *her* trailer was there again, and *where* she was going. She glided across the dry, dusty December ground like a proud, sleekly dressed fashion model on the catwalk in an important show. At the over-eighteen inch gap from the ground to trailer floor, at which she before frequently balked, she delicately transferred her weight to her back feet and confidently walked right into the trailer without breaking stride. There was no protest when we closed the door—no foot stomping, no nickering. Their old chestnut gelding, George, however, nickered a good-bye, or maybe an objection, as Chaos boarded. He liked her. Chaos did not answer. She was going *home*, and she was glad. We were glad too.

"George is sorry to be losing his hot new girlfriend," Sherry said.

"I am really sorry she didn't work out. I could not believe she would act the way you said she did. It seems so completely out-of-character for her," I apologized.

"I think she just missed you guys too much," were Sherry's last words to me as we departed.

The three of us had a quiet trip home; we all knew where we were going, and knew it was the right place. After we parked in the driveway near the house, Rod led Chaos from the trailer, through the north pasture to the field where the other six horses were waiting for her. I remained near the house watching from a distance with tears in my eyes. We wanted to make the transition as smooth as possible without arousing a lot of excitement, reorganizing the hierarchy, or spiking the need to investigate a "new" member. Our horses can make themselves so excited upon entering a pasture they have not been in for a few weeks. Dorit especially can act like she has not seen her Winnie in a year or longer when I have simply had Winnie in the north pasture or in the arena to ride. Rod says *they love to get excited*; it is something fun to do. Today, however, there was no big commotion as Rod brought Chaos back into the herd. They did not crowd the fence, they did not rush her or hassle her; she was just back, and they were just glad. They were a whole again. I think they knew as soon as the trailer left the house that morning that is was going to get Chaos. When they saw the trailer pull into the driveway, they perhaps could smell that their Chaos had returned. The other six welcomed her quietly with gentle sniffs. She fit right back into their midst, as if she never left. They all ambled southward together toward the shed and their supply of hay. They were serene and peaceful. The next morning they were in their normal groups but closer together than they had been in her absence. Chaos, our little bucket-fed reject whose mother never wanted her, kept the herd together. They needed her, and she needed and wanted them. This was her home. We were her family—Rod and me and the other horses. She needed to stay with us; we needed her to stay with us.

The following spring I spent three weeks of the month of May in Massachusetts with our daughter, Catherine, when she delivered twins. My own mother helped me immensely when Catherine and Veronica were born, and I always looked forward to helping my daughters when they had children as much as my mother helped me. I felt honored to be there, and was grateful I could be. However, I did miss Rod and our horses, and looked forward to coming home to them. I could not wait to see them, touch them, and be with them all again.

My first morning back I had to hurry down to the shed just after day-break and let them know I was home. It was a wonderful reunion. Each horse had to come up and sniff me and greet me, and I in turn, scratched under each one's chin and neck, gently pet their necks, scratched their heads, rubbed their soft muzzles with my hands and even rubbed my face against their soft necks and noses. I said: "Hey! I am back! I am so glad to see you guys! You are so big and so beautiful! I really missed you." I imagined they felt the same.

The end of May and the early days of June are usually beautiful in our part of Kansas. The grass and trees are a lush green, the birds sing, the air is soft and new, and the stately irises are in full bloom. One of my first mornings home I was so delighted to be back with my horse friends, that I took my camera and set out on a photographic expedition. In high school I had a friend who had her own darkroom. Karen called our jaunts out to take pictures "photographic expeditions," and later we developed our own pictures in her basement darkroom. I have never lost this early love for using my camera and never tire of photographic expeditions even now.

Photography is artistic expression, just as painting is for me. I had a wonderful time snapping pictures of the horses as they enjoyed our south pond. Dorit and Winnie were not among the photogenic pond bank models that day. I suspect they were in the quiet shade of their shed; Winnie always seemed to love that shelter more than any of the others. However, I did get some very picturesque shots of five of our beautiful horses along the edge of the pond. Star even decided to take a quick "bath." It was a peaceful, delightful, and pictorially rewarding expedition that filled me with joy and gratitude for God's stunning spring world and for these gorgeous gentle giants, these beautiful beasts, these good horses who were my friends and who let me share their life.

Star taking a quick "dip" in the pond.

Five horses on pond bank.

Painting of five horses on pond bank

Painting of Star eating delicious spring grass

Chapter 26
Accused of Cruelty to Horses

Old Dale, may he rest in peace, was the father of our neighbor, John, who lives on the farm north of Jesse's, about a half mile from us. Dale and his wife lived "around the block," probably a little over a mile away. Dale could be rather "crotchety" according to some people, but he was always nice to us. He said what he thought, and he didn't care if the other person didn't want to hear it. When Rod was planting Austrian Pines as windbreaks along our north and west fence lines, Dale bluntly scolded him: "You *shoulda* planted cedars! Cedars grow best here."

Rod *knew* cedars grew well here, but he also knew cedars caught fire easily, and he didn't want a fire hazard near the house, even at the "windbreak distance" the Forest Service required for receiving the discounted price for the young trees.

Sometimes in the afternoons when we were feeding our horses, Dale and his wife drove by and they always waved to us though they barely knew us. They knew their son and his family were our neighbors who lived two farms north, and that was enough reason to be friendly. That is one of the first things I noticed about country people, they always wave. Whether they know me or not, they wave. I don't, or didn't. I suspect people think I am stuck up, blind, unobserving, or a grouch. I am none of these, just a transplanted city person who has not quite yet fully acquired this country habit. City people don't wave to one another from their cars unless they see friends or family. I hoped these kind country people would excuse my ignorance of country ways, and be somewhat forgiving. I am learning to wave now, and I tell my neighbors to be sure to check their rearview mirrors because sometimes I remember my country manners *after* they pass me.

Rod told me one time Dale stopped and told him when he died he hoped he'd "be reincarnated as one of our horses." Dale was not the only passer-by who commented on our expert care of our horses, even to calling it *spoiling* them. That was all right with us.

Imagine my shock when late one July afternoon the backdoor bell rang and I found a County Police officer standing on my back porch telling me she had an anonymous report against us for cruelty to animals, specifically horses! My jaw nearly dropped.

The woman police officer asked me to step outside with her, and repeated the charges against me: *cruelty to animals, specifically horses*. She said she had been told the horses were being starved, and were muzzled. I told the police officer I was just going down to remove their fly masks for the night, and invited her to come with me to see them. She said she had thirteen horses herself, and would like to accompany me. I was relieved to learn she was a horse owner too. I knew it would make her more understanding of our horses "plight," or lack thereof.

Fancy, our dog replacement for Joker, accompanied us. I noticed the officer thoughtfully eyeing our dog; ultimately she asked me where we got her, and what kind of dog she was. It further served to "break the ice" when I explained that Fancy's mother was a Weimaraner and her father was a Black Lab. As it turned out, *she* was the owner of Fancy's mother though I never met her when we picked out our new puppy that dark December night.

As we walked through our north pasture toward the smaller south pasture, I was thinking that the passerby who reported us was probably upset about our seven horses being in a smallish five acre enclosure, and may have thought the horses were being starved because there was not enough grass, though we did keep the hay feeder full with free-choice hay at all times. It had just rained and we closed our horses in this smaller pasture until the ground dried enough that their hooves would not leave deep hoof prints in large field where we let them graze after we cut the hay in the spring. As I opened the gate into the south pasture, explaining to the officer why the horses were there, Winnie, walked up to me; Dorit followed a short distance behind.

Winnie nuzzled my hand checking to see if I brought carrots, and let me remove her fly mask. I pet her and told her, as I always did when I greeted her, that she was beautiful. I said to the policewoman, "This is Winspiration. I call her *Wins,* or *Winnie.* They are all my 'babies.' I know that probably sounds dumb. Wins was a racehorse. She is twenty years old."

The officer exclaimed: "She does *NOT* look twenty years old!"

"Thank you!" I said. I was very pleased *this* woman at least knew a pretty horse when she saw one.

"My husband would disagree with you. He calls her "an old nag," but I think she is beautiful!" I said. "She is my aristocrat. She is a descendant of Man o' War and War Admiral, I bragged. "She tends to be our thinnest horse. As you can see, her back is a little swayed, but she definitely is not, in the least, underfed!"

The officer agreed. She looked southward at the other horses beginning to walk toward us and asked: "Are these *all* the horses?"

For a split-second I thought of trying to make some smart-alecky, joke-type remark, but I quickly put that temptation behind me. However, I thought to myself: "Of course these are *all* the horses, what other horses could people driving by possibly see?" Did she think I had several others in a barn, in another pasture, or hidden behind some trees on the east side?

I simply replied politely, and explained once again: "Yes, these are our only horses, and this is all our land. That large pasture area to the east as far as the tree line is where they normally graze after we cut and bale hay, but due to the heavy rain yesterday, we have them in this little pasture so their hooves won't pock-mark the hay field."

Dorit was fast approaching, and as I walked up to her, I pet her, and spoke to her too: "Hi, Little Dorit! How are you, good baby?" Then I turned to the police officer and said: "This horse, in fact, *does have* a muzzle. She is usually the only one who does, though we did have a muzzle on the large dark bay horse in the early spring because we were concerned he was getting too fat. If you notice, *this* horse is definitely what people politely call an 'easy keeper.' She gets fat just eating what all the other horses eat. We are worried about her foundering; notice the fat crest on her neck. She also tends to be tender- footed quite often. We keep a grazing muzzle on her most of the year, though we do take it off once a week for a day to wash it, and allow her to lick the salt blocks. We remove it whenever we feel she has slimmed down somewhat." I showed her Dorit's thickened neck under her mane.

In turn our other five horses filed up to me, letting me pet and greet each one, and remove his or her fly mask. With each removal, I told the officer: "This one is definitely not underfed." She agreed. She could see for herself that no one except Dorit had a muzzle, and none of the horses were underweight, and none were abused, neglected or underfed. The report was obviously wrong; the person who made it was obviously mistaken. Thankfully, the officer was satisfied.

As we walked back toward the house, she said: "I think I know now what happened. The person who reported you didn't know the difference between a fly mask and a muzzle. She said she was not from around here, just happened to be driving by. It was an anonymous tip."

At this point I told the officer old Dale's comment about wanting to be reincarnated as one of our horses, and added: "If anything, people around here say we spoil our horses. That is why I was so shocked when you said we were being investigated for *cruelty* to them!"

Her parting words to me were: "No, heck, these are the best looking horses in the County!" I naturally thought she was a very astute judge of horses to recognize the quality of our equines.

There are many stories of people being arrested and accused of doing things they did not do, instances of the truth being misinterpreted, or misunderstood. I certainly was grateful I had not been carried off to jail for muzzling and starving our horses by someone who knew nothing of horse-keeping. I am very glad the officer sent on this "mission" had her own horses, knew the difference between a muzzle and a fly mask, could differentiate between a fat and a thin horse, and was willing to listen to my side of our horses' story. I had to admit that it also made me happily satisfied she could recognize and appreciate their exceptional beauty too.

Chapter 27
Their Lives Thenceforth Have Separate Ends

Our niece, Rena, who worked two years at Calumet Farms in Kentucky, expressed interest in Star's foal, *Star's Suzanne*. Rod told her if she came to get her, she could have her. Though I knew we had too many horses, I did not like the idea of any of them leaving our farm, particularly Suzanne, whom I knew Rod loved more than any horse in the world. I did not worry much about it because our niece lived in eastern Oregon, and that is a long way from Kansas.

One day in October, I received a phone call from Rod's youngest sister, Kate, saying she had been emailing Veronica and they had agreed on a selling price for Pascal! I was shocked, but I consoled myself with the reality of the distance and the fact that a lot of people *say* they are going to do things, but they never end up *doing* them. Our niece talked about wanting to come get Suzanne for two years, and nothing came of it. Rod talked about meeting them somewhere halfway between Oregon and Kansas, but, thankfully, his work and very meager vacation allotment prohibited it. I vehemently opposed this idea. My opinion was: if someone wanted one of our horses, she could definitely come get him or her. I gasped in disbelief when Kate added with certainty that she, her children, Rod's sister, Dorothy, and her daughter, Rena, would be at our house the second week in November to trailer Pascal and Suzanne to Oregon. They were attending our nephew's wedding in Idaho, and intended to drive to Kansas immediately after the wedding.

I was in an uneasy state of disbelief. The date was less than a month away. None of Rod's relatives *ever* visited us. Half of me still didn't really believe it would happen; the other half already mourned the loss of Pascal and Suzanne. Two stanzas of another favorite Longfellow poem from the book my cousin Sandy gave me perfectly fit with my thoughts:

And all that fills the hearts of friends,
When first they feel, with secret pain,
Their lives thenceforth have separate ends,
And never can be one again;

The first slight swerving of the heart,
That words are powerless to express,
And leave it still unsaid in part,
Or say it in too great excess.
--Henry Wadsworth Longfellow, *The Fire of Driftwood*

Our horses were our friends. Since I could not, would not believe, Suzanne and Pascal were really leaving, I did not let myself think about it very much. It was "the first slight swerving of the heart, that words are powerless to express, and leave it still unsaid in part..." My heart was numb; I said nothing. As I do when unpleasant things approach me I simply put it out of my mind for a time until I *had* to face it. I knew I would face it when it came, *if it came*. God would help me deal with it then. We had been given less than a month notice. I thought it could not happen so fast—they would not come.

Rod began teaching Suzanne to load into the trailer, and refreshed Pascal's trailer loading capabilities. I watched from a distance, but mostly did not participate except for taking a few pictures of our horses practice loading into our trailer. It was too painful to participate, but, I knew, it would be more painful if the horses were not prepared when the time came and were fearful.

Pascal was, and had always been, Veronica's horse, but I had hoped he would always stay here with us. He had been with us a total of six years; we had known him since he was four months old. Suzanne was Rod's *Princess Shadofax*—the long-awaited, beautiful, perfect foal of Star, his beautiful *Lady Shadowfax*: "The Lady of All Horses." Star was his favored horse who ran like the wind, and whom he loved from the first day he saw her. The horse he had picked from many others. I think Rod cherished Star's baby, Suzanne, in a special way more than any of our other horses, and I know she loved him even a little more than she loved me—though she dearly loved us both, and seemed to love everyone who met her. He did the most work with her especially after she grew to be so big, and he was the nurse who carefully washed, bandaged and tended her wounded pastern for months when she cut it deeply probably, we assumed, by getting too close to the neighbor's barbed wire fence. She was so curious and unafraid, so willing and eager to attempt to step over any barriers. She was always ready to *step out of her door* and into the road even when it was *"a dangerous business."*

It was awareness of Rod's love for Suzanne that led me to adopt Stormy as *my* special project for training since I feared she would be slighted if all the attention was lavished on *the beautiful Suzanne*. I thought Suzanne would remain with us forever, and one day Rod and I would ride Suzanne and Storm down the road together—an aging couple on two aging horses we had raised from foals. It was not to be.

Rod's sisters did come that November. We had not seen Dot, or her daughter, Rena, since Rod's father's funeral over ten years earlier; we had not seen his youngest sister, Kate and her two children for almost the same amount of time. It was a wonderful reunion in every respect except that we were losing two very beautiful, very much loved horses. The visit of Rod's sisters progressed so smoothly both inside and outside the house, that I barely knew I had houseguests. Normally having five extra people in a rather small house for three nights presents some hassles or inconveniences, but not in this case. I think God knew how hard it was for us to part with Pascal and Suzanne, and so He made the entertaining, the repair and securing of the trailer, the issuing and receiving of the travel papers, and everything even remotely associated with this situation proceed without a single complication.

The day before Rod's sisters arrived, the vet came and issued travel papers and withdrew blood on the two horses. The morning the five were to leave I almost secretly hoped either both horses, or at least one, would refuse to load, and could stay right here. Though Kate's trailer was much shorter than ours, both horses had practiced loading into it without balking, and they repeated this excellent performance the day of departure. Stoically resigned, sad but dry-eyed, we watched the trailer with our two beautiful thoroughbreds head off down the gravel road with its precious cargo, as they made the long, long trip to Oregon to new homes.

Star must have been ready to say good-bye to her baby. She had been a loner until she had Suzanne. After the birth, mother and daughter were inseparable; they were *always* together. I thought Star would be depressed and desolate in Suzanne's absence, hanging her head and refusing to eat as Pascal did after Chaos left. She did not; she accepted Suzanne's departure without obvious anxiety: she adapted immediately. She was always a lady. Chaos had been very close to Pascal; in his absence she turned to Star for companionship, and Star accepted her. I was happy to see this new friendship.

The one horse that reacted unexpectedly was Little Dorit. An hour or so after the trailer left, Rod and I fed the horses in the pen where we always did. Since we now only needed to accommodate five horses, instead of seven, we moved Star into Suzanne's former place, and before we could do anything else with Pascal's old place Little Dorit, completely on her own, walked deliberately through the gate, into the pen, and with the utmost sense of purpose, determination, and certainty put herself at Pascal's bucket! I understood her to be telling us: *"This* is now *my place."* There was no moving her. Without words, she conveyed her intent and purpose. It was final!

In that moment I realized Little Dorit felt *excluded* all this time, held apart from the other six horses, treated as a step child. In truth, she had been just that. Tending to be fat, we fed her the small amount of food we gave her outside the pen while the others were tied inside the pen to receive their food. Pascal didn't get much extra food either, but he had always been inside, and the gate closed so Dorit could not intimidate and steal food from the others. Little Dorit was the only horse outside the pen at feeding time. She had become *the forgotten horse* because we had to devote time to feeding and training the foals, and to riding the others.

Dorit had once received all the attention, even the riding, but after the terrible ordeals with her foals, and the births of Suzanne and Stormy, there just were not enough of us to properly give attention to all the horses. We *did* have too many and for only that simple reason, it was for the best of the others that Suzanne and Pascal left. Five horses were still too many for "two old people," but the smaller number made a real difference. The relief showed visibly on Rod's face and posture that first afternoon; it was as if a load had been lifted from his shoulders. I had to admit feeding was easier. Rod reasoned it was good for Suzanne and Pascal to be used and enjoyed, to have a good, active life, instead of being *pasture ornaments* with us.

Since she was such a large horse, Rena decided to have a young man train Suzanne under saddle for her. He was known as a kind trainer. She sent pictures of herself in a saddle on Suzanne's back with a friend who was also on horseback; a herd of cows could be seen behind the two of them and their horses. Later she took Suzanne to her brother's registered Quarter Horse stallion; and anxiously awaited the birth of Suzanne's foal.

Pascal stayed awhile in eastern Oregon at Rod's brother's ranch. Everyone regarded him as a "huge, powerful horse" though to us he had been "a teddy bear." Kate hoped that Rod's brother, Joe, and his six children who were all excellent with horses, would "tame" Pascal for her and her two children's use. Eventually Pascal did make it to Kate's home along the Oregon coast. However, Kate decided Pascal was too much of a horse for her to responsibly keep at age fifty with a husband and two growing children. Eventually she sold him to Veronica's former graduate school roommate, Melissa, who had discarded the study of philosophy for law and now practiced in California. Melissa's family lived in Washington State, so arranging time to see and buy Pascal was quite simple. The sale went through without a hitch, and Pascal moved to California with Melissa whom he knew from his time with Veronica at graduate school.

Pascal now lives the life of pedigree and privilege, though retired. At first Melissa taught him dressage and jumping, and even gave longe line lessons to a ten-year-old daughter of one of the partners in the law firm. He has everything he could ever desire, including a woman who is an expert horsewoman to love and dote on him all his life.

224

Chaos with Pascal just before Pascal's departure

Pascal, Suzanne and Star

Rod teaching Suzanne to load into our trailer

Suzanne gives Rod a horse kiss

Drawing of Melissa and Pascal

Above: Melissa teaches Pascal Dressage. Below: Melissa gives Pascal a friendly kiss.

Pastel portrait of Pascal

Above & Below: Rena on Suzanne

Chapter 28
Heavy Snow Ushers in, "Winter of Our Discontent"

The last night of the November Pascal and Suzanne left we had a snowstorm that began about 1:30 p.m., about the time Rod left for the afternoon shift. As the evening progressed it became a heavy blizzard. Roads were covered so completely with snow that the men coming in to relieve the afternoon shift could not see where the road ended and a farmers' field began as they tried to commute to work. Men in their trucks were finding themselves driving off the road into ditches, and stuck in snowbanks. Rod called me from work to tell me he would spend the night at the plant. I was glad he was not risking a dangerous 20-mile drive home.

As soon as it was light the next morning, I layered myself in my warmest winter clothing including my cozy bomber hat and boots, that were guaranteed to keep feet warm down to twenty-five degrees below zero. It was not that cold, but my feet are hard to keep warm and I appreciate them. I grabbed my camera and headed out to find and feed our horses, and enjoy a photographic expedition. I was grateful I had nowhere else I *had* to go. I love to be the first to breathe in the quiet morning air right after a snow. The silent, pure white glistening blanket of diamonds as sun begins to reflect on the snowdrifts no one has yet disturbed with footprints always awes me. I invited our dog, Fancy, and we went in search of the horses.

I had to wade through the field immediately south of the house to get to the horse pasture, walking took double the normal amount of time due to the huge drifts left by the blowing snow of this winter storm. The snow itself, where it was not drifted, reached my knees, and in the areas where the wind had piled the snow was nearly to my hips and I am no midget. I could already see the horses making their way through the snow undeterred by its depth, sometimes running past one another, seeming to play and enjoy the quiet, sparkling morning air and changed scenery as much as I. Snow makes everything seem so pure white, almost heavenly. I fed them, broke ice on the pond so they could drink, and trudged through the snowy, hilly terrain to inspect their hay supply. I was snapping pictures and petting the horses when they came up to me to see what I was doing. I was inexplicably happy in this quiet, gorgeous winter landscape with my beautiful, friendly animals. Everywhere I turned there was another beautiful picture waiting to be taken! I was so engrossed in my adventure, I never noticed Rod had been driven home by a co-worker who owned a four-wheel drive truck. His little car could not maneuver the as-yet-unplowed gravel roads. He was in the house eating his breakfast when I happily returned to the house after nearly two hours of an enjoyable and profitable photographic expedition.

About 18 inches of snow the morning of December 1st

Painting of our five horses in the heavy December snow fall

Fancy checking out the ice on the pond

Above: Painting of Winnie and daughter, Stormy. Below: Chaos poses in snow.

Star almost camouflaged in the snowy landscape.

Stormy walks alone along the pond

The snowstorm of November 30 into December 1 was just a dim intimation of what awaited us in the bitterly cruel month of January. In the twelve years we lived here, we never experienced this oppressive, this unkind a winter. In Act I, scene I, of Shakespeare's *Tragedy of King Richard III*, the Duke of Gloucester coined the words that became my label of this particular winter. It became the first "winter of our discontent," and was a phenomenon we would see several times, and would make us grateful for the mild winters of earlier years. Older people I saw when I worked in Home Health, told stories of brutal winters in Kansas and Missouri during their own younger years: snow drifts completely covered fences and roads, of iced ponds and lakes that remained solidly iced for months allowing for months of ice skating. Horses pulled sleighs over the snow-covered roads, and once a road grader came through high drifts to take our neighbor, Edmund, to his father's funeral because the snow and wind made drifts so high and deep it was impossible for him to leave his home to go to the funeral in April! Edmund had a photographic memory complete with dates; he could vividly recall the exact scenes as well as the particular years the winters had been especially harsh. He died in his mid-eighties over six years before this storm; it would have been one more for him to add to his extreme winter memory book.

We had an ice storm before the end of the second week of January. It remained cold the entire week afterward, so the ice could not melt. Saturday afternoon it began to snow, and then temperatures dropped below freezing, so we had ice on top of the snow and ice below it. These icy layers sandwiching about eight inches of snow acted as insulation keeping it in place for over six weeks. Our pasture resembled a skating pond; walking across it was surprisingly easy in one respect because it was like walking on a freshly shoveled sidewalk, or, more appropriately, an ice arena. Instead having to slowly, tediously trudge through several inches of snow, a chore almost as tiring and unpleasant as slopping through deep mud or sand, we all, even the horses, literally "sailed" across the surface of the ice in the flat areas. It had been a long, long time since I recalled being light enough to walk "on top of" the snow. I remembered as a child, finding areas where some of the snow began to melt, and then the temperature dropped overnight and the snow re-froze. It felt, then, and now, as if I were performing a magic trick, like walking on water or, I imagined, as if I were weightless, like an astronaut in space. Birds flit around on top of the snow often; but horses and people trot around on top of it almost never. The horses did not know quite what to think of the ice; I did notice they seemed to walk a bit more slowly as they forged their nearly unprinted paths over the frozen field.

The first morning of "Iceland," Rod came into the garage after breaking the pond's ice so the horses had drinking water. I was finishing my morning walk on the treadmill. His face was scarlet from the cold, and frosty smoke still puffed from his mouth as he spoke; he looked and sounded very annoyed.

"We have a juvenile delinquent!" he said exasperatedly.

At first, I could not imagine what, or who, on earth he meant! "Juvenile? Who was juvenile around here?" I wondered. It gradually dawned on me he meant our younger horses. I thought it must relate to the pond, and must be Stormy since we knew she once before walked on the ice and probably fell through. However, this time it was not Storms.

"It's Chaos!" Rod said in an irritated tone. "The name says it all! She thinks it is great fun to prance proudly around on the top of the ice on the pond. She has *no fear!* And yes, now I *do believe* you about Stormy giving you 'that look' you said seemed to say: 'Uh-oh! She shouldn't be doing that!' *She gave it to me* when we both saw what Chaos was doing!"

Until now Rod had always laughed and said I had a "vivid imagination" when I told him Stormy gave me that "uh-oh look" when Suzanne delicately stepped over the downed fence into Jesse's pasture that summer evening. Now he had seen *the look* himself and knew I was not imagining.

"How stupid of her! She should have learned from Stormy's fall!" I said.

I could only imagine Chaos proudly prancing about on the iced-over pond as if she were a ballerina practicing pirouettes and thinking it a fine exhibition! "Can't she tell where the pond is after living down there all these years? Doesn't she *know* she doesn't walk on the water in spring, summer, and in fall?"

Rod replied: "I guess not!"

Neither of us wanted to risk losing a horse for any reason, but even the passing thought of a horse falling through the ice into the frigid water of the January pond and drowning was something neither of us wanted to imagine. Fortunately we already had a heating element and a large galvanized tank for water. Just as we had done when Stormy fell into the pond her first winter, we immediately moved our entire herd into the north pasture and closed the gates. We began feeding hay and giving water, it once again seemed our horses were almost right outside the back door because the fence to the north pasture was only about fifty feet from the house.

This I liked! Every time I went to the kitchen, dining room or living room window, and nearly every time I stepped out the back door, there was a horse standing there to greet me. Again, it was the closest thing to having them *in the house* with us.

Before we ever entered or left the house, whoever was at the fence received our verbal greeting and usually a few pets and scratches, maybe even a carrot or two if she happened to be very lucky. Winnie and Star in particular liked to take turns peeking in the garage window as I took my treadmill walks. Sometimes we stepped out the back door on to the porch and were greeted with a friendly nicker which probably meant either "come feed me" or "come pet me," but we always took it as a sign that they loved us and were genuinely glad to see us.

I felt we got to know and appreciate our horses even better that winter. They truly became our good friends even more; we all depended on each other and were there to help get each other through the awful cold—"the winter of our discontent." Even the dog seemed to like having the horses near the house and hay barn. When I went out to take a picture of the round bale Rod had set out for the horses, Fancy playfully leaped on top it and posed for her picture. I told her she was pretending to be "queen of all she surveyed." We bought her a sweater because we worried about her being out in the cold; she was a short haired dog, and very thin. Just as baby Chaos had been proud of her new blanket, Fancy seemed very proud of her new sweater. I was beginning to think that even the animals can be somewhat "materialistic;" they knew when something was *new* and was *bought just for them*. It was *new, theirs*, and they were proud of it.

Though the horses were in the north pasture, we still fed them in the pen which separated the north and south pastures. I remember

239

setting out slowly one particularly icy morning, I was walking rather cautiously and at a near snail's pace on top of that glare of ice which more resembled the pond Chaos had been practicing her pirouettes on than our north pasture. The snow had started to melt so tufts of grass showed through, but it had frozen overnight and the horses and I walked on top of a new layer of ice. Memories of many winter slips and falls on my *derrière* on the slick grade school parking lot playground lingered too vividly in my mind. I had no desire to repeat those descents into pain and embarrassment though I was not wearing a uniform jumper with only socks, boots and bare legs beneath my winter coat.

The horses nearly always saw me, and followed me to the pen to be tied up and fed. Today, however, Chaos was closest to me as I began my trip southward to the feeding pen, and she fell in behind me as if she had been assigned to give me an escort. I had all kinds of qualms and apprehensions about *her* performing this seeming favor. Chaos sometimes liked to tease us, and could playfully throw her head as she would do to another horse in invitation to run. I dreaded the possibility of slipping or being knocked down on the ice even though I was well padded with layers of warm clothing. I feared not only hitting my backside, but also the possibility of a broken bone. No thanks! Children fall much more easily and recover much faster than adults.

However, to my astonishment, Chaos must have sensed my fear by my slowed pace—maybe she was even afraid of it herself? This good horse put her nose at my right elbow and copied exactly my snail's pace. It was as if she was helping me; as if she was telepathically signaling me, telling me: *"It's okay, Mom. I am right here with you. We're going to make it. Don't worry! I've got your back!"*

Rod and I were always her "Mom and Dad"—she never forgot this. Once we reached the pen she waited while I opened the gate, and then went in and stood by the post with her feed bucket, and waited. This was not unusual for her to do. In fact, of all our horses, Chaos is the most polite at feeding time: she just comes in and stands by her bucket, waits for us to halter her, tie her lead rope to the post, and feed her. When we release the horses after feeding, she predictably waits for us after all the others have moseyed off, nuzzles us and lets us scratch her head.

Today the other four horses followed our lead, and let me tie them and bring them into the pen. When all finished eating and I began to release each one, however, these gentle giants, so sure-footed on ice and snow, were *afraid* of the slight hill that they had to maneuver to leave the feeding pen! The brief incline did not bother them coming in. I doubt that until we had this ice, they had ever found the descent any consequence. Today, however, they did. Each mare paused at the gate and refused to walk out on her own, or to be led out on a loose lead rope; each one of them wanted me right beside her head to bring her slowly down the small icy slope, back into the north pasture. I willingly obliged each dear lady.

Fancy atop hay bale in her new sweater

Beautiful Star against a snowy background

Winnie looking regal in the snow

Painting of Little Dorit in melting snow

Chapter 29
Adaptable Horses Make Sweet Uses of Adversity

The snow and cold persisted for days, and then we were hit again by another heavy wet snow that began one afternoon, and continued late into the night. I was worried about the horses being in the north pasture where there was no shed to protect them from the wind and blowing snow. When Rod called that evening from work, I asked him if he thought I should let the horses return to the south pasture for the night; I was worried they might not immediately go to the shed. Would they stay away from the pond? We decided to give it a try, and hoped they would remember they had water in the heated tank up in the north pasture. The quarter-mile walk from the south pasture to the north to get water was no trouble for them even in the heavy snow.

I bundled myself up and took a snow shovel in case I had to dig into a snow bank to open the west gate that led to the lower pasture. It was only half past eight, but it was as black as midnight. The white snow reflected enough light for me to see where I was going as my eyes grew accustomed to the darkness. I first plodded through the snow to the horses and found all five gathered around the round bale eating hay, their snow-covered tails facing the wind from the east, and every one of their coats white with thick, wet snow, the hair barely visible beneath. I called to them, but they ignored me and continued to eat.

I trudged through the snow over an eighth of a mile to the south gate and began to pull it open—at least it was less slippery with the new cover of white flakes. When the gate stuck in the snow, I shoveled until I could push it open further. Fortunately, the snow was very fluffy and light. With the gate finally all the way open, I traipsed back through the cold wet blizzard to the horses and called their names again. Reluctantly, Winnie stopped eating and must have decided **maybe** *this crazy persistent woman* had *a better idea.* She began to follow me, and, as the others saw her leave, they began to follow at a trot and passed her as if they were having one of their horse races—in a snowstorm! Undeterred, I continued my journey southwest toward the open gate. I had no fear they would run over me. I knew them, and they knew me.

I knew very well from past experiences with them at night that they could see me perfectly, and knew exactly where I was. Whenever I called them to come so I could remove their fly masks in the dark summer nights they always found me with ease, and I suspected they always knew precisely where I was and where the others were. The frigid air and blowing snow did not hamper their night vision. Matriarch Winnie followed me like a shadow.

As we neared the gate all five of them suddenly understood that I intended them to head for their shed. They all took off at a run through the darkness in the blizzard as easily as they loped through a spring pasture of grass--with sure footing enviable any time of the year in the day time, let alone at night in a whiteout pocked with ice, holes and snowdrifts. Not only was there a familiar shelter where they were going, but also two round bales of hay for late night munching and several cedar trees for added protection from the wind.

I hoped they let all five of each other assemble peaceably in the shed and forget their hierarchy for this single snowy night. Sometimes we drove by the shed and saw two horses hogging the interior while the other three stood in the wide doorway or nearby just outside; sometimes the others were some distance away, backed up to cedar trees for protection. Winnie and Dorit were frequently the two Grand Poohbahs barring the entrance; sometimes they allowed Stormy, Winnie's daughter, into their safe haven. However, we noticed that when the weather was particularly horrible all five horses sometimes were lined up together at the entrance of the shed looking out at the harsh world. That had been the case very occasionally even when there were seven horses. I hoped tonight would be one of the nights when the dominant duo were in a generous spirit, or that those lower on the totem pole would successfully demand the others move over because they were coming in, like it or not!

The next morning I wanted to get to the lower pasture early to check on the pond for footprints. It was sleeting and blowing from the south; walking into the wind was miserable. The bitter wind shot its tiny cold arrows of frosty, prickly mist into my face and neck like sharp needles. The nasty sleet seemed to be able to find a way to slip into even the smallest uncovered crevices in my hat and gloves. I thought it was too ugly a morning to ask the horses to come to the feed pen for breakfast, so I decided to fork out their shed, check their hay situation, visit them a bit, return to the house, and feed them when the weather settled down.

Forking out manure from the shed is never an unpleasant task for me. I am privileged to own horses, and the responsibility of removing manure is an obligation accompanying it. I like to give my horses a cleaner shed. Cleaning a shed is more fun than vacuuming and mopping the house because I see results faster, and I am doing it for those who cannot do it themselves.

Inside the shed, the world was suddenly comfortable again. It was dry and it was warm because the sun filtered in, undisturbed by the sleet. As I worked at clearing the shed, the horses munched hay in the wide doorway just a few feet from me. While I worked the sleet stopped. Finished with my cleaning, I said "good-bye" to my ladies for a little while. I walked away through the silent white pasture toward the house. As I neared the pen where we feed them, my five friends decided that *now* was a perfect time to thank me with an entertaining horse race.

Twice around the five acre pasture they ran, breathing hard, each one straining every muscle to obtain the lead. Star ran, as always with her head high, seeming to float just above the snowy ground; Stormy seemed to be imitating Star because she was demonstrating a beautiful floating canter I had never before seen from her. Sometimes Winnie would charge ahead, and Chaos arched to the outside in an effort to pass. Star remained in the lead but second place would have been a toss-up—one of those photograph finishes. Sometimes Dorit bucked and kicked wildly out to the side, her trade-mark galloping stunt. Chaos showed she was her mother's daughter by managing several good sideways kicks herself as she sped across the snowy terrain. Star and Stormy had to kick up their heels too lest I think they were of inferior running agility on a winter landscape. At the end of the second lap they collectively applied their brakes and, amid flying snow, stopped in front of me and the gate to the feed pen. Breathing hard after their exercise, these splendid athletes gave me a look that asked: "Hey, Mom! When do we eat?"

Certainly they had worked up an appetite, and had given me an exciting performance! They deserved some food. The sun was shining, the wind and sleet had stopped; it was now a pleasant winter morn. Actually, I was thankful for the opportunity to do this inside the pen, and lock the gate into their pasture from which we all just arrived. *Again* there were foot prints on the now snow-covered pond, and slushy areas where they had been trying to get a drink. Would they ever learn? I realized they could not be trusted to stay off the dangerous ice—or at least *one of them could not be trusted*. I suspected Chaos was the footprints-on-the-ice culprit. We kept the horses in the north pasture until the snow melted enough that the pond could not be mistaken.

We were glad we could provide this extra margin of safety when necessary. Friends help each other. We came to love our good horses for their companionship, their trust, their love; they depended on us to provide for them especially *this* winter.

I considered my writing, painting and drawing "therapeutic," but our horses became a kind of therapy too. They were my recreation; they opened my ears and eyes to understand God's purpose for me on this earth. Our horses adjust to their situation and are grateful for what we, and nature, give them. They do exactly what they are created to do, and in that, give glory to God. Our horses became my joy and let me grow to accept and begin to love the simple, quiet, hidden life in the country--life so different from anything I imagined for myself. In the quiet God could begin to teach me what He wanted me to know just as He had done for Elijah the Prophet who learned that God was not in the great and strong wind that tore the mountains and broke the rocks in pieces, nor was God in the earthquake, nor the fire after the earthquake, but in the simple, quiet whisper, a "still small voice." (1 Kings 19:11-12) God often can best be heard not in the loud or grandiose, but in the quiet. In my later years, I finally began to learn to listen for Him as I lived in the country.

The good horses helped us through this "winter of our discontent" perhaps even more than we helped them for they accepted it without protest, with simple even joyful resignation, as part of life—just as they accept everything. They actually did more than just endure this winter; they actually seemed to make the most of the adversity. On a higher plane, St. Paul tells us our sufferings are evidence of God's love for us, that He disciplines those He loves. (Hebrews 12:2-6) I do not think the horses always "suffered" through winter because so often they definitely gave me the impression they actually liked to cavort and dance playfully through the snow. In winter there were no pesky flies and hot sun. However, I did not have to be an animal psychologist to deduce that even my very adaptable horses did indeed suffer the freezing wet blizzards and ice we were subjected to *this* winter. I did not have to contend with a continually wet coat and ice ringlets on my tail and pasterns, and slippery snowballs in my hooves. I did not have to remain outside and turn my back to the chill north wind and try to eat enough hay to keep myself warm over the snowy winter nights and days. Even though I had a warm house, plenty of food, and dry clothing to wear outside, *this* winter seemed to be one that would *never end.* I believe it truly was a lengthy, rigid discipline for all of us.

I remember at different times in my life feeling that a certain block of time *would never end*: a school year with a particularly disagreeable teacher, the four years needed to graduate from high school or college, the nine months of pregnancy, the night before Christmas as a child, but everything on this earth comes to an end. "To everything there is a season and a time to every purpose under heaven." (Ecclesiastes 3:1) That purpose, that season, that end, is determined by God. All things, in this life, end; finally this seemingly endless cold winter came to a close and, praise God, the earth finally awakened to another spring.

Previous page: Rod stoking our outdoor wood-burning stove to heat our home.
Above: Chaos and Stormy wait for Rod's attention.

Faraway horses in a snowy winter landscape.

Chapter 30
Monsoon-like Rains

After such a harsh winter, spring dawned slowly but gloriously. We were indeed grateful! Rain is necessary for a good hay crop, but getting the grass cut between rains in Kansas is always a game of "cat and mouse." We keep close tabs on the forecast and try to give ourselves enough time to cut the hay, let it dry, bale it and get it into the barn. This year the weather did not cooperate at all; some of the hay never did make it into the barn.

Rod cut the hay June 9, and the following morning we had four inches of rain in three hours while the hay was still lying in the field. When it dried, Rod baled it and we decided to wait two weeks before putting it in the barn; by that time it would be completely dry and would not heat up and cause a fire. Three days before our deadline, we were deluged with fourteen and a half inches of rain. It was unbelievable! I began to wonder if the rain would ever end. Last summer in August we had no rain, now we had too much. I began to identify with Noah and his family in the arc! I had never seen so much water. People in the surrounding area received even more rain than we did, some homes were lost, and others were flooded up to the eaves. Roads were closed; whole ends of towns were under water. Rod had to take different roads to get to work because the usual highway was flooded and impassable for over a week.

The horses' pasture reminded us of a swamp. Thank God for the hills in that pasture, otherwise the horses would have had to stand all day in the mud and water. On the first clear morning I looked out the window and saw Star standing on a mound looking out over the lake covering what had been her pasture. The hay we cut was ruined. Because the bales had been so saturated, we never did trust they would be dry enough to be safely stored in the barn without fermenting. The mold and heat this would generate might cause the bales to spontaneously combust; a fire could easily destroy hay and barn. The next winter Rod had to peel off twelve to fourteen inches of rotten hay so the horses could eat from the "edible" centers of the bales.

Our custom was to allow the horses into the hay field to graze on the stubble and re-growth after we cut hay in May or June. This year we did not finish cutting hay until the end of July. Since part of our hay crop was ruined, Rod placed a temporary fence with electrical tape down the center before we let the horses into the mowed hay field. We hoped to perhaps get enough re-growth on the saved side for a second cutting of hay, and thus have more feed for the horses during the winter. July and August here are usually hot, dry months, but we knew we were in a weird weather cycle and hoped that the rain might continue and give us a second cutting. We actually did get over eight inches of rain in July, but August gave us less than one, so we did not get a second cutting.

Life for the horses following the seasons continued pretty much as usual. They always seem so happy when we first let them into the large field after we finished haying. The "new" pasture, however, always was something to investigate and make sure nothing dangerous lurked anywhere. As soon as we let the herd into the "big field" the snorting and galloping begins. They run from one end to the other in a pack, inspecting it as if it is totally new territory, scrutinizing every inch of it for possible lurking foes or surprises. Once they are satisfied it is "safe," they begin to kick up their heels, rear and buck, kick out to the side and race each other in large circles around the perimeter of their "new pasture." It is bigger, so there is more room to run; they love it. There is a little competition in the fun too, they like to see who is the fastest, who can jump the highest or kick out to the side most frequently in one pass over the playing field. It is always so beautiful to watch their manes and tails flowing out behind them, to hear their breaths coming hard and listen to the reverberation of their hooves against the earth. They look so free and happy. They splash the "new" pond as if for the first time, and seem to pretend to bat at each other with their front legs as they rear on their back legs in sheer exuberance. They seem like children released to a playground after spending hours in a stuffy classroom taking a long exam. They look as if they are saying: "This is great fun! We love this place?" Finally they drop and roll in the grass; once they return to their feet, they drop their heads and eat, and remain in that stance for hours and hours of grateful, peaceful grazing.

Star trotting in new summer pasture.

Star in foreground in a beautiful gallop. Winnie, Stormy and Chaos in background

Each summer we begin the use of fly masks again. I know it is because of my own long-standing aversion to flies, but I hate to see a poor horse with his face black with them. Each morning I gather the masks over one arm and tramp through the dewy grass to put them on for the day. The horses are grateful for the cover, and the masks really seem to protect their faces not only from the flies, but also from the sun. Rod and I liken them to sunglasses; we each need and appreciate our sunglasses, so we assume the horses like their fly masks.

One morning in early July I intended to feed the horses right after the masks were in place, because the face flies seemed to be particularly plentiful and nasty. I had Winnie's halter over one arm too. Everyone will follow Winnie, and I put her halter on and tie the matriarch up first. The others follow her into the pen for their feed like sheep following a shepherd.

I met Stormy in the field first; the others were grazing fairly near. Storm lifted her head for me to put her mask on, and then lowered it again to continue to graze. I leaned down to close the Velcro tab at her throat latch, but just then Stormy dove toward a fly on her side and her head collided with my jaw. Ouch!

Just a few days before, I bragged to Rod that I *finally* learned to keep my head out of range of a horse's downed head. Dorit and I often collided this way those first years we owned her, but never this sharply.

Stormy had no idea she bashed into my jaw. The collision seemed not to faze her. I, however, was not so fortunate! My jaw hurt and burned so fiercely I wondered if I had put my two front teeth through my lower lip. The thought of driving twenty-five miles to the nearest Emergency Room to have my lip stitched flashed through my mind. Here I was, *alone again*.

I gingerly touched the area just below my lower lip, and then glanced down at my hand. I expected to draw back fingertips bright red with blood, but they were clean and dry.

"Praise God," I thought. "*Thank You*, God!" I said. I was never in my life so glad to see nothing.

But it hurt so badly! I thought I would explode into tears and sobs with the pain. I wanted to cry. I started to cry, and Star noticed. Her head turned toward me, then, from about ten feet away, she came over close to me and let me put my head into the side of her neck.

"Oh, Star, it hurts so badly!" I sobbed.

This big wonderful grey horse wrapped her head around me, pressed it in and held it there. It was absolutely the sweetest, kindest, most caring thing I ever had a horse, or any animal, do to me. She understood I was hurting and she wanted to comfort me. She was indeed my friend!

After Star's hug, I pet her neck and side and rubbed my head against her sleek white hair with the tiny black and brown spots. Her hair always smelled like fresh air and was so soft—smooth like glass in the summer, and furry-soft like cat's or rabbit's hair in the winter.

I reciprocated her kindness by scratching her udder, which I knew she loved, and resting my head on her rump for several minutes, all the while cooing to her and telling her she was such a good, wonderful horse, and my best-ever equine friend. Another new alliance seemed to be born between us that day; Star had given me a horse's special and rare gift of friendship. I had the inkling that this was one of those *once in a life time* partnerships; probably no other horse would ever be my friend quite like Star.

"My good, good, good Star" I repeated to this amazing horse. "I love you so much!"

My lip was sore for a couple of days, and a dark blue bruise showed up on and under my lower lip two days later. When I told Rod about what had happened, he said:

"God was hugging you through Star, telling you He was sorry you were hurt." Even now as I read it, I choke back tears.

I told Rod: "*You have never lived* until you have been hugged by a horse!"

A short time later Star hugged me again. One morning I put her fly mask on her, and she walked by me stopping with her flank area right in front of me, which I knew meant: "*Please scratch my udder.*" This was a request Star started making of me shortly after Suzanne stopped nursing. The udders of a mare collect dirt which becomes greasy and thick between the two teats. It must feel good to have it cleaned out. I rested my head on her sleek rump and talked softly to her as I obligingly rubbed between her udders with my gloved hand, releasing sticky crumbles of blackish mud-type debris. The way she bobbed her head and pointed her nose, I *knew* it *felt good*. She almost seemed to purr like a contented cat. She had more "horsenality" than all the other horses—even more than Stormy and Chaos, our "talking horses." Star was so demonstrative with her likes and dislikes. This time she thanked me by once again encompassing my upper body with her head and neck and pulling me close to her. I felt as if I momentarily almost flew to heaven. Our courteous, sedate, offish horse was slowly losing her fear of showing affection. Since her daughter Suzanne was so affectionate, I often thought Star was likely naturally affectionate too until strict training frightened it out of her. No doubt our horsenality-plus Suzanne inherited the quality from her mom, or properly, "her dam."

Rod's reply for the second hug was similar to his first response: "God is hugging you through His horses, Mary Barb. He wants you to know He loves you."

God has given us these magnificent horses and continues to reveal Himself to us through our lives with them. He teaches us about Himself, His world and His purpose in creation through our horses and even our dogs and cats. We come to believe more surely day by day that God teaches us how He wants us to act and to live through our animals' humility, trust, acceptance and unconditional love. We thank Him every day for all our animals, especially for the horses. I believe God has drawn me closer to Him through living in the country. I always hoped our home would be a haven for young people and old, a second home, a place where anyone and everyone feels safe, comfortable, and welcome. I know He has entrusted us with this home and these horses for a reason. As we continue to work with and care for our horses, and learn about them and ourselves, perhaps that will be in His plan.

Pencil drawing of Star

Painting of Star

Chapter 31
A Rendezvous with Death

(A warning again for the reader, this is a very sad chapter.)

Intellectually, I knew one day one of our horses would die, and eventually they would all meet death, as had Star's twins, Little Emily and Joker. I knew one day Rod or I would die, and one of us would be here alone—unless we happened to die at the same time, which is unusual. I knew no one lives on this earth forever, and I never wanted to. For a long time I have interiorly accepted, as the poem by Alan Seeger is titled: "I Have a Rendezvous with Death."

> I have a rendezvous with Death
> At some disputed barricade,
> When Spring comes back with rustling shade
> And apple-blossoms fill the air—
> I have a rendezvous with Death
> When Spring brings back blue days and fair.

I read President John F. Kennedy often thought of death and repeated the lines of that poem. In junior high and high school I idolized JFK. I memorized the lines. I always *thought* I lived in the presence of death. Death is a reality I often contemplate. However, death has finality that we do not really grasp until it "grasps" us— until someone we love dies. I live in the presence of my own death with more ready acceptance than anyone else's. As a child, I remember telling my father I would rather die myself than have him die. He told me that I just did not want to live through the loss of one I loved. I knew he was right. He lost his own father when he was only nine years old. He knew death from an early age. He said people patted him on the head and said he did not understand, but he told me he understood perfectly.

When my father died unexpectedly of a massive heart attack at age 69 my sorrow shadowed me for years. It lodged at the very core of my heart long after people finished offering condolences and sending cards, long after the so-called "average person," if there is such a being, has laid grief to rest. Yet death of a loved one is personal for each one. It is not something I *ever get over*. My father's death changed me forever. People close to me told me I had to let go of the sorrow. Out of compassion, they said I *could not go on grieving*; that my father *would not want me to mourn so long*, that he *would want me to be happy*. While I knew my father always wanted me to be happy, I resented being told what I *could* or *could not* do with my personal resolution of this loss. After all, he was *my* father, and this was *my* grief. I alone knew what I could and would do, and what I needed to do to finally, at least somewhat lay my father to rest in my heart and mind even if it was neither what others would do, nor within their timeframe. Time would dull the pain somewhat, but it would remain with me the rest of my life. I knew the sayings: "it takes what it takes;" and "time heals all wounds," but that healing time is different for each one of us.

With my father's death, truly, part of me died and was buried with him. There are some wounds that even time cannot completely heal this side of heaven where "He will wipe away every tear from their eyes, and death shall be no more, neither shall there be mourning nor crying nor pain any more, for the former things have passed away." (Revelation 21:4)

Thankfully, my father gave me a strong religious faith. It was his prized possession. Through my faith, I believed my father was in a better place, or at least on his way there. I knew he would have no more pain of any kind once he reached heaven. I also knew that everything I did in my whole life, I did slowly; and it would be no different with my grief. My father left *before I finished* my business of loving him, of knowing him, and learning from him, of spending time with him. He left before I really let him know I loved him deeply, let him know it was *he* who always held our family together, and it was *he* I most admired and identified with of anyone in our family. I hope God has told him for me. I think when we lose someone when there is "business left to do," as Reba McEntire sang in her song *The Greatest Man I Never Knew*, it takes longer to accept the emptiness which never really "heals." There is not only sadness in the loss, but also remorse one did not make better use of the time while the other was alive--that one waited *too long* to make use of the time, and let the other know the love felt. In the same song, Reba McEntire sings the words: "The man I thought could never die…" I sensed a similar loss of my time with my father and with my time with Star, and somehow some part of me thought neither of them would really ever die, or they would die somewhere in the very distant future—beyond my thinking.

For the two preceding winters we had talked of the possibility and sort of mentally prepared ourselves for Winnie's death. She was over twenty years old; she looked "poor" because she was always thin. She was a picky eater, and that was especially true in the winter; she preferred grass to hay, and there was not much edible grass in the winter. In her twenty-first year we attempted to have her teeth floated so she would have every chance to be able to chew her food and keep her weight up. When the vet we had used almost exclusively since we moved here, told our neighbor, Jesse, he "did not come out that far anymore" we assumed we too had to find another doctor for our animals. The new vet examined her teeth but said she really needed nothing done; he finally did try to adjust them a little, but without anesthesia. It was a very uncomfortable experience for Winnie, and she reared, fell and skinned her legs badly. After the work on her teeth, we saw no difference in the amount of food she spilled at feeding time, nor in her appetite or her weight. The following year we bought a blanket for her to wear during the coldest times, when temps were 10 degrees F or less, to help her stay warmer and perhaps help keep her weight. Winnie never grew as heavy a winter coat as Star did, and the other three horses were fat—"easy keepers," every one of them.

We were mentally somewhat prepared for Winnie to perhaps fail to make it through the winter; we were not prepared to lose our completely healthy Star—the horse we thought was the strongest and soundest of all. Star was six years younger than Winnie.

Death, like life, is not fair. Death comes, as the Bible tells us, "like a thief in the night"--when we least expect it. (1 Thessalonians 5:2). One morning in the middle of February Star ran up to the feeding pen one morning with the other horses, almost snorting as if she were in pain. To me it was as if she was trying to tell me: "Look, Mom! I hurt!"

The inner part of her eye was red and appeared thickened and enlarged. Her temperature and her appetite were normal; nothing else seemed unusual. Given our last vet episode, we thought we should just watch her for a while. We observed the eye closely for two weeks. Some days we thought the redness was receding, other days her eye looked the same, but Star did not seem really herself though she continued to eat normally. Sometimes after she ate she would stretch her forelegs out in front of her and then repeat the same only with her back legs. We wondered if she was beginning to colic or if she had an ulcer; over her years with us, she had occasionally done this after she ate too much. We fed her smaller amounts several times a day so she could receive the same amount of feed, and watched her carefully. After these post-eating stretching episodes, I always walked her for a long time, even in the very cold fourteen degree weather we had on some of those days. Finally, at the end of two weeks, we called the vet we had seen for Winnie's teeth and made an appointment.

The day of the appointment, Star surprised us by being afraid to load in the trailer for the first time since we had owned her. Today she was not like the family dog who loves to go for rides—she definitely *did not* want to get into the trailer. We had not allowed a lot of extra time, nor had we thought to practice the day before because she was so predictably an "easy load." Much later the thought came to my mind that perhaps she thought we were taking her to her death that day. After nearly an hour, we were beginning to think we would have to call and cancel the appointment, but she finally entered the trailer and we closed the door and drove to the vet.

The vet anesthetized her, and showed us the third eyelid, explaining that there had probably been some trauma to the eyelid, maybe a piece of grain had gotten under it, or maybe she had bumped her head against something, but nothing was there now. He placed some ointment into the lower lid and said it would get better. He did not look into her eye with a light, nor did he check her nose for a clogged naso-lacrimal duct. I knew about that from our first year with Dorit when we had her checked for a "runny eye" and had to medicate her three times a day until that healed. Star's eye problem was something entirely different—different in color, different in the amount of fluid coming from the eye. I never thought to ask for an ultrasound or an x-ray of her head, or even how soon to expect improvement, or when to return. The vet was sort of in a hurry; he had another patient, a bovine, waiting. We felt almost as if we had wasted his time and ours, and that Star had been given a perfunctory examination. I would always wonder if things would have resolved differently had the initial treatment been different, had we taken her in the first day the redness showed up, or had we used a different vet.

Thus began the three month agony of slowly losing Star. We searched everywhere around our farm for clues as to what had caused the trauma to her eye. We examined her feed bucket and changed to one without eyelets to hold the handle; we changed her feed. We had a fresh tube of the ointment the vet had placed in her eye after the examination, so we continued that treatment for three days, and discontinued it as the instructions directed when we saw no improvement. I wish we had been in the position to then get a second and even third opinion, but we were not. However, since Star certainly seemed to be no better after her visit to the vet, we were somewhat hesitant to have her seen again.

My life entered a sort of holding pattern. I was distressed. I talked of nothing but Star to any and every listener, especially Rod. He understood my concern, but my verbal repetition of my anxiety and frustration annoyed him. I wanted an exact diagnosis and wanted her to be getting better. I had never been faced with a protracted illness of anyone close to me—my parents had, providentially, both died without a long period of suffering. I had never had to deal with the day-to-day uncertainty, the deterioration, and the questions to which no answers were forth-coming. Some days we really *thought* the eye looked better, but it was always just wishful thinking.

One morning we heard the rain begin as we awoke; from the kitchen window we saw poor Star standing in the downpour outside the shed with no other horses in sight. Rod went down to help her; he did not come back for over an hour. I knew something was not right; he later explained that he stood beside Star and kept the other horses away so she could eat. Finally I saw him leading her through the field to our new barn at the north end of the horse pasture. I joined him there, and we took turns staying with her, petting her, drying her off, and letting her eat hay until the rain ended. After that we kept Star in the north pasture by herself to eat the blue grass; we only put her with the other horses when we tied them up in the feeding pen to feed them their daily grain ration. For a time we tried putting Winnie in the north pasture with her, but when Winnie threatened to kick her we removed Winnie for good. We wanted to place Star's best friend, Chaos, there, but the north pasture grass was too lush; she would gorge herself and no longer remain sound. Chaos, like her mother, tended to gain weight easily. Sometimes Star stood expectantly at the gate into the lower horse pasture, indicating to us she wanted to return to the other horses, but we did not feel we should allow this yet because they had demonstrated they could not be kind to her.

We began placing her fly mask on during the day to shield the eye from the sun's rays even though it was March and there were no flies. She did not resist it. Most afternoons, just to spend time with her, I walked her into the hay field and let her graze on the new brome and lespedeza that would be cut for this year's hay crop. I curried her as I talked to her, and said prayers for her. Our huge white livestock guard dog, Shaggy, a Komondor-Anatolian cross, who we acquired the previous August as a puppy, often accompanied us. He seemed to know Star needed companionship. Often we saw him with Star as we looked out the kitchen window in the early spring evenings—the big white horse and the big white dog, heads down together as if they were talking and listening to each other. Shaggy stood near and watched as Star ate grass. She chased him out of that pasture as a puppy the summer before, now he was pleased to keep her company—almost as if it was his designated task. He was by nature a guard for herd-type animals though we employed him mostly as our protector and friend. Though Star had never had time or patience for *any* of our dogs, I think she really appreciated his companionship. Generally herd-bound, Star had always liked to be with the other horses; now she accepted Shaggy in their place.

Rod said: "Star is accepting this illness just as she has accepted everything else in her life: like a lady."

It was true. I prayed for her healing every day—for a miracle. I asked my friends and some of their children who had liked to ride and play with her to pray for her, but through this trial I learned that sometimes God does not answer the way we want and hope.

We arranged for the same vet to examine Star again. This time we attempted to practice loading her into the trailer the day before the appointment. We learned that she was unable to raise her foot to get in, so we arranged for him to come to our home. By this time Star was walking in circles to the right. It seemed to us she did this because she could not see out of her left eye; the swelling behind the right one was putting pressure on her optic nerve. Over the phone, when we told him she was walking in circles, the vet said it sounded to him like she might have Equine Protozoal Myeloencephalitis (*EPM*), a disease horses can catch from ingesting the clear droppings of the opossum, but when he saw her bulging right eye he told us it was likely she had cancer. He treated her for EPM with an antibiotic and a steroidal anti-inflammatory drug for a month. He also drew her blood, but her blood work was all normal.

For a while after that we really thought she was getting better—she showed none of the emaciation or lack of appetite that one typically associates with cancer victims, and the anti-inflammatory drug probably helped her. I think Star really *tried* to get better, but she did not heal.

Finally we decided to get a second opinion. Star was not losing weight as one would expect an animal with cancer to do, and her appetite remained good though she seemed to be blind. We called the vet who had taken care of Star when she lost her twins and asked him to come give us a second opinion. Unfortunately, he was busy until the end of the week, and Friday we were leaving for Connecticut to spend four days with our daughter, Catherine, and her family for our grandson, Michael's, First Communion. We set the examination for the Tuesday after our return.

While we were away my dear eighty-eight year old friend, Lavon, whom I had taken care of when I was a Home Care Nurse eleven years before and remained friends with until her death three years later, insisted she be allowed to feed Star twice daily and give her the medicines. She was the *only* one we trusted to faithfully care for Star in our absence. She afterwards told me she actually looked forward to driving the five miles each way twice daily to take care of her, and would sometimes arrive early and sit in the porch swing and watch Star. She later told me sometimes Shaggy would accompany her if she climbed through the pipe pasture fence to walk up to check on, pet and talk to Star. We specifically told her *not* to enter the pasture for her own safety. Star's feed bucket hung on the fence, so entering the pasture was not necessary. Lavon's reply was simply: "I am an old farm girl, you know!" We did not have to worry about her accidentally leaving the gate open or even getting hurt. Even at eighty-eight she was "an old farm girl"—she knew how to climb through the fence, she knew how to act around animals—she was not afraid, she took her charge seriously and lovingly.

The night we arrived home from the airport, Rod went down to feed the other four horses, and I stayed near the house to feed Star. The eye looked no better, but she was still eating well and had not lost weight. As the other four horses galloped up to the feeding pen, Star's head rose and she stood in full-alert-pose. She heard them; maybe she even could see them a little. Now that kind of running must have seemed to her something she too had done in another life. She made no move to imitate or join them; she listened and then went back to eating. In happier times she would have made haste to join them and been first, but not now. It was like an omen to me, yet I continued to pray for a last minute miracle.

Our former vet came at the appointed time the day after we arrived home to give us that second opinion. He was never one with a friendly or tactful bedside manner, never one of comforting words—he was intelligent, but abrupt, and sharply matter-of-fact.

"That eye has to come out!" he said immediately with his first look at her.

When we asked if he could perform the operation, he said that he could not and that if he did find someone who could, the procedure would be extremely expensive and dangerous. He also thought she was beyond the operating stage now.

It was almost as if Star's body understood his assessment. She began to deteriorate over the next two days. She seemed to have trouble eating, sometimes bunching the food into one side of her mouth like a hamster or guinea pig. Other times she plunged her face into the water tank nearly up to her eyes and swished her head back and forth as if she were trying to sooth her poor head. Sometimes she walked a path around the upper pasture in great haste—I later learned this too meant she was in pain. She began to lose weight, and sometimes ground her teeth, which I sensed meant she was frustrated with the pain. Thursday we called the vet who had just seen her and asked him to come the following day and put her to sleep. I suppose it would have been proper etiquette to call the earlier vet, but we felt like we knew this one somewhat more, and he had just seen her. Familiarity is important to me in time of tragedy—

one looks for someone who "knows and understands," even just a little bit just for some slight comfort. However, in retrospect I wish I had called the other vet for Star's sake—she had not "seen him" in a while and might have been less afraid.

The doctor arranged to come take care of the task at 4:30 the next afternoon. We called a neighbor who had a backhoe to come at 1:30 and dig a hole in which to bury Star.

On the surface, that Friday morning started out like all the other spring mornings. After we had given all the horses their "breakfasts" I was doing some household chores. I happened to glance out the kitchen window and saw our beautiful Star wearing Suzanne's extra-large red fly mask which I had put on earlier when I fed her. Star's bulging right eye made her own mask tight and uncomfortable, so in these last weeks we had been putting Suzanne's extra-large mask on her.

Looking at her now, I thought to myself: "Everything else can wait. This is the last day I have to spend with Star. I am going to spend every minute with her."

For a few minutes after I went outside, I just sat on the edge of the porch with a book, planning to sit there and read while Star ate grass. However, my good friend left her area of grass and came over and stood at the fence to be near me. At this sign of recognition and affection, I climbed through the fence and began talking to her and petting her. I leaned my body slightly against hers. I rubbed my nose on her head below the fly mask down to her nose again and again while I rubbed the end of her bumpy, wrinkled nose with my hand. I talked in a private, comforting tone to her. I began talking to her about her life with us and the friend she had become to me. I told her everything I could remember beginning with the first day we saw her and bought her, and the day she was first brought to us and she floated about the pasture playing "catch me if you can." I told her she always loved to run, and she did it beautifully—just as she did everything. I told her she had been a prize winning racehorse. I told her about my fall from her, and what it had taught me. I told her about the loss of her twin foals, about the birth of Suzanne, how proud I was of her, and what a perfect mother she was. I told her I thought that she had definitely brought me closer to God because since I fell from her I had become more prayerful, and had come to realize that my sole purpose on earth is to get to heaven and take as many others with me as I can. I told Star she also taught me what motherhood should mean to every female, human or animal. She was so proud to be a mother and definitely was willing to lay down her life for her child. I told her over and over again throughout that day in my talks to her that we would meet again because in the Bible it says a victorious rider with a bow and a crown will come riding a white horse at the end of time. (Revelation 6:2) I told her she would be in His Company.

I walked alone with her in that springtime pasture—sometimes I ran to keep up with her because the pain made her walk so urgently, but I stayed with her. I talked to her, fed her sugar cubes, led her to water, and gave her extra grain. There was no danger treats would harm her today. Sometimes she stood still for long periods of time; she seemed to fall asleep standing there as I stroked her nose with my hand and her face with the side of my face. If it alleviated her pain, as I thought it might be doing, I felt I was accomplishing my mission of comforting her and being a friend to her this last day. She had to walk through the valley of death, but she would not go the whole way alone.

When the men came around 1:30 to dig the hole for Star's burial, to my amazement, Star insisted on going to the site and watching. In horses, curiosity is the opposite of fear—she kept her curiosity until the last day. We had wondered for the last two months just exactly how much she could see and hear; apparently she could see enough to satisfy her wonder. As the hole was dug, we stood there together some thirty feet away from them. I quietly talked to her as I stroked her; the backhoe did not frighten her, nor did the men. She stood there in her normal tall, lady-like stance, head lifted. I could not help but think of the tragic irony of watching while one's own grave was dug.

The men were country workers who all had animals; they quietly, compassionately expressed their regret at my loss of "a good animal." I was deeply grateful for their kind sympathies. When they finished their work, we wandered away, my precious horse and I. We walked together through the pasture until the designated time for the vet arrived. It was almost as if she knew it was time. With me still by her side, went and stood fairly near the just-dug gaping hole and stopped there. She stood there almost contemplatively for close to an hour; I continued to pet and talk to her and wait. Had the vet come then it would have been a simple thing for him to give her the first injection, and then lead her a little closer and give the second injection. It did not happen.

He was late, over two hours late because he had a flat tire; during our wait we checked our answering machine every half hour to see if he had tried to contact us, but he did not. This was not a time being late *did not* matter, but it could not helped, and it did give me two more hours with Star. We were standing near the barn when he finally drove up—Star had just taken a brisk, spur-of-the-moment walk into the hay field where Rod was mowing hay, and then returned to the narrow area between the garage and barn. I said my good-byes all day long, and continued to pray for her even as I stood there holding her lead rope, petting and talking to her, and waiting in those last minutes. As he finally drove up I gave her one last message: "This is good-bye, Star, but I hope I will see you again at the end of time."

I really believe Star remembered the sound of his truck and that he had given her a shot three days before. She was afraid. How I wished I could have changed the outcome or somehow made it less fearful for her.

The first shot was given quickly and we led her toward the gate which opened to the just completed hole. Star stumbled over a clump of hay and simply slept, never to wake up—never to see me or hug me again, never to so beautifully run again, but also never to have pain again, or know rejection of the other horses again. It was already over; her time with us was ended.

The doctor gave the final injection and made some small talk before he left. I went into the house and brought Rod some older linen tablecloths to put into the hole to rest Star upon, and to cover her with. Then I returned to the house and gathered some pictures children had drawn of her, her pedigree, a beautiful note card my good friend, Linda, had sent me for her, and wrote a note myself telling her she was a wonderful race horse, mother and friend, and that I would miss her. I put everything into a plastic bag and gave it to Rod to put into the grave with Star. He used the front end loader of our tractor and covered her up, and when she was completely buried, I went out and laid some of our beautiful white irises which were so plentiful that season, on her gravesite. When I returned with my camera, Shaggy was sitting on the site. I believe he understood what happened and he too already missed her.

For days, weeks, even months afterward I looked out the window for a grey horse, but she was not there. I missed her more than I even imagined possible; my heart physically ached. Everywhere I looked I was reminded of her—every corner of our farm had a special memory of Star and echoed her to me. I remembered her grace and beauty, our friendship, her dignity in her whole life, even in her suffering and pain. Everywhere I saw her dark eyes peering in at me; everywhere I looked for her following me. She had been my particular friend, and now she was gone. We still had four good horses, but Star was my out of the ordinary friend, and she had just recently become my favorite. We had formed an understanding, a bond back when she lost her twins and our friendship had slowly grown and become part of each of us. We had given each other the gift of friendship. I believe she looked for me and waited for me, just as I looked for her. We were "friends for life," as Equus Magazine had titled my *True Tale* when they printed it. Now her life was over and mine went on without her. It didn't seem like I should be here without her—she taught me so much.

She had just recently looked for me and liked to follow me; even before that she seemed to like to pose for me to take her picture. She knew I loved her, and I believe, as horses love, she loved me. I do not know that I shall ever completely get over the loss of Star; I still can get choked up, even tearful talking or writing about her. She left a hole in my soul and my life that cannot be filled. St. Paul wrote in 2 Corinthians 4:17-18: "For this slight momentary affliction is preparing us for an eternal weight of glory beyond all comparison, because we look not to the things that are seen but to the things that are unseen; for the things that are seen are transient but the things that are unseen are eternal."

Even in the seemingly trivial loss of an animal who was a friend can be offered to God, joined to His suffering on the cross, and thus sanctified. God can bring good out of evil; He brought our salvation out of the death of His Son who was completely innocent yet died as a criminal for us sinners. Like God's only Son, we all go to heaven by way of our own Good Fridays. Often over the months of losing Star, Rod reminded me in my times of deepest sadness that it could be either of us, one of our children or grandchildren we were losing.

I knew this, and I was grateful it was not one of these, but it made bearing the sorrow no easier.

Unexpectedly, so many people were so kind in offering sympathy in the loss of Star—many friends, near and far, sent cards, poems, and offered words of deep understanding. Words such as: "I was so sorry to hear about the death of your wonderful horse" and "that's almost like losing a family member" helped to comfort me and to dull the pain somewhat. I was so impressed with peoples' kindness; it was a lesson for me. A kind word is never lost or unwelcome even for things that may seem small or insignificant. Our seven year old granddaughter, Maria, profoundly touched my heart when she came up to me a month later at our daughter, Veronica's wedding and, hugging me, whispered: "Grandma, I am sorry about Star. She was my favorite." Tears came to my eyes, as they do now as I write, and my throat tightened; hugging her back tightly, I softly choked: "She was *my* favorite too, Maria! Thank you so much!" Her cousin, Michael, Catherine's oldest son, told me later: "What you maybe didn't know, Grandma, Star was everybody's favorite." Two friends sent me poems I had never read. One, a poem by Mary Oliver, "The Poet Goes to Indiana," reminded me of rubbing my face and nose on Star's face that last day, and reminded me of happier times when Star had indeed told me, as written in the poem, "that I was good." Even the inexpensive horse calendar in our utility room astonished me when it by coincidence had a memorial to Star and her Suzanne when I lifted the page for the month of June: a grey mare and her dark brown foal graced a green field. Star died May 22, the day our daughter Catherine was married ten years before.

Star lived with us for nine years. She has filled my thoughts and filled the pages of this book with her presence, and I have filled drawing papers and canvases with her likenesses. The art has been part of my healing process. In my heart and mind she will live forever. For a long time just the thought of her would bring a tremble to my lip, a lump in my throat, and easy tears. Even now tears can come as I read this.

I missed my dear friend daily, but the silky summer necks and the velvet soft nuzzling muzzles of the four remaining amid the glorious summer weather somewhat helped soften some of my sadness. The harshest pain of loss surfaced throughout the following winter when every day was a memory of her the year before on that

270

date, and every corner of our farm flashed her presence to my mind and heart. My mind saw her everywhere, I avoided her grave except in the early fall to plant white iris bulbs above her headstone. Daily I offered the haunting pain to God, and asked Him to bring some good from my small sacrifice. Finally, in the early days of May the following spring I believe God showed His blessing by allowing buds and then blooms of beautiful, huge white iris to grace Star's gravesite. I was alone the first day I saw them. Standing at her grave, I shed tears. I talked to my dear horse friend as I had not talked since the day she died. A few days later, as I returned from feeding the other four horses, I could see in the distance, the iris blossoms above the tall spring grasses that rippled in the wind like waves. I felt gratitude and peace; it was as if Star reached out to me from beyond the grave to tell me she was free and that the two of us would always be best friends.

There will never be another Star; the passage of time will eventually somewhat dull my loss. She left me with hope that I will always have a horse in my pasture, and the ability to spend time with such a miracle of creation. Fortunately, we still have four horses we can care for and love. I will continue to enjoy them all as much as I possibly can for all the days we all have left. None of us know what heaven will be like, whether there will be animals there, but we know we will be completely happy. St. Paul writes: "No eye has seen, nor ear heard, nor the heart of man conceived, what God has prepared for those who love him." (1 Corinthians 2: 9). The book of Revelation mentions several horses; I hope there will be horses in heaven. I truly hope that when I pass into the next life, the Just Judge with his crown and bow on His gleaming white horse will welcome me leading a rider-less grey mare and invite me to come to live where He is for Eternity.

Above: Star, in fly mask, last day. Below: Shaggy beside iris on Star's grave.

Mary Barbara and Rod with Star, last day

Irises grow on Star's grave in May, the year after she died.

Chapter 32
Life Goes On

When my brother called from the hospital to tell me of our mother's diagnosis of advanced lung cancer, he then passed the phone to mom so we could talk to one another. She greeted me: "Hi, Honey."

All I could eke out in a faltering voice was:

"Mom! You can't die!"

"Life goes on," mom said.

Her answer fit her; it was a hopeful answer. She was always a hopeful person, and she was exactly right. Life would go on for us without her; and her life would go on forever with God. We live forever. Mom knew that, it was part of who she was. That forever hope filled her entire being; she was 85. She was the perfect patient those days of the three weeks we cared for her. She knew she was dying. She accepted it. She kept her sense of humor until she stopped speaking a few days before she died. She was a gift and an example of how to live and how to die. Star was an example too. Life, indeed, does go on, but we have come to the end of this story of our exquisite horses and my personal growth and experience. These stories cannot continue forever, though my life with our horses continues.

Before Star died, I wondered how I would finish this book. What should be the final story? For a long while after Star died, I stopped writing. I was not ready to write about her passing because it affected me too deeply for words; it hurt too much to think or write about it. I could and did paint and draw many pictures of her. Finally I did write about Star's last days because I felt *I must*; her death was part of my life, my experience, my growth, though I truly wished it was not. Linda Graf read it and said it was my best. Even though years have now passed since losing Star I can barely read the story. I avoid the story, and cry when I read even parts of it. I don't like sad endings. Life goes on, as my mother said, and I did not want the story of my growth-filled years with horses to end in sadness and death, but to end in hope and life. I had to write this one final chapter.

I knew I would never fully "get over" the loss of Star. Every time I saw the other four running, she was absent and I wished she was still here for me, and running with them. She was the fastest and the best. She was my favorite. God put Star in my life, and He took her away. "The Lord gave, and the Lord has taken away." (Job 1:21) I think I am a better person because of my experiences with Star. Through the love I grew to have for Star and the love she showed me God taught me the beauty and joy of acceptance of life as it is given, and the gift of friendship from a wonderful animal. I think Star taught me how to be a better friend to people too.

Someone said that if God made anything more beautiful than the horse, He kept it for Himself. Star embodied that beauty—the beauty God gave her she gave back to Him by being what He made her to be perfectly. She was an exemplary mother, lady, and friend. Everything she did gave glory to God. Star increased my perception of God in the world and taught me how to give Him glory by trying to be the best of myself and by trying to accept with submission the joys and trials He allows in my life. Star changed my life. She was my special teacher, my particular friend, prized companion, and my distinct glimpse of God.

The other horses were not in the same field with Star most of those last months, and after the initial sniffing around the "new" north pasture when we first opened the gates, it seemed Star's nonappearance was not questioned or really noticed, though I thought I detected a slight recognition in Chaos, as Pascal's recognition of the shed upon his return to our farm.

The spring we lost Star, Rod sewed a legume into the brome grass to increase the protein and quality of our hay for our horses. He bought a sprayer and was able to better control the weeds. In previous years it was nearly impossible to find a company to spray our small field; either its sprayers were already all assigned, or the weather would not cooperate. Now he could pull his sprayer behind his tractor when he wanted.

We fought the summer rains which seemed to be increasing and struggled to get just *half* the hay in our field cut, baled and into the barn by the first of July—in our first years he had *all* the hay *in* the barn by the end of May or the first week of June. We finished the second half of the field in August, and that became a routine for us. This was one of our best hay crops. We felt thankful to have a barn full of decent feed for our good horses this year. Rod blamed Star's death on poor hay that year ruining her ability to throw off illness.

Winnie continued to be the thinnest; Rod still called her "poor" and was concerned about her health as fall and winter approached. Yet often times it was our dear oldest mare who still led the pack in the pasture races they held for our enjoyment and their own—being thin, she ran faster. She seemed to have plenty of energy. We began feeding Winnie a large coffee can full of a high fat grain twice a day. We opened the gate into the arena, and fed the others outside the arena in their pasture. Winnie walked straight to her bucket of grain. While she ate, we opened the gates into the mowed hay field. Our senior aristocrat knew *exactly* what we were about! When she finished her breakfast, she nibbled at the grass in the arena for a few minutes, then blissfully walked out into the hay field and never looked back at her three former pasture mates. Her best friend, Dorit, Chaos, and even her own baby, Stormy, seemed to suddenly not exist. She put her head down and let her legs carry her out to the lush green pasture of the re-growing hay field, and either simply did not hear, or intentionally ignored, the protests from the other three horses. Dorit's objections were the most intense and vehement.

Poor Dorit was absolutely beside herself without her beloved Winnie! She ran up and down the fences and nickered loudly. We could hear her thundering gallop and we watched in amazement as she charged from one end of the horse pasture to the other, a quarter mile each way, calling loudly to her friend while Winnie completely disregarded her. We had never seen Dorit run so fast. One might think she was training for the Kentucky Derby! Chaos and Storm watched for a while, but they did not run with her, and eventually they went off to nibble grass or hay, although they both stayed near the entrance to the hay field. None of the three left behind sought out the shade of the shed or even of the trees on those first hot August days while Winnie was in the hay field, though a couple times Stormy and Chaos did get into the pond for a quick cool-off. Our fattest horse soon became noticeably thinner, and we were able to remove her grazing muzzle. The exercise trimmed Dorit's formerly bulging body into a thin, athletic, beautiful figure we had not seen since before she foaled. "Winnie's Program of Diet and Exercise for Dorit" was better for achieving weight loss than any muzzle.

The three left behind commoners waited patiently in their pasture until Winnie had her fill of the delicious grass and solitude, and decided *it was time* to return to her herd—and dinner: another coffee can of grain we gave her in the late afternoon. Around three o'clock, Win would drift back toward the gate, stand near it, sometimes put her head over the fence and touch noses with her buddies—her first recognition of their presence all day. They "visited" until we returned to feed her and put her back with the others for the night. This return to the gate was her way of telling us our aristocrat "had enough" and was ready to leave her royally charmed, peaceful, solitary existence in the lush pasture to go back to the mundane surroundings of the "common" equines. I still fondly called Winnie "My Aristocrat" and tell her she truly has "that wide-eyed look of eagles." She always had a beautifully chiseled head; she lost none of her well-born charm even in her "old age."

When she was with Dorit, which was nearly always, they were almost "joined at the hip." Dorit seemed very possessive and seldom let Winnie out of her sight. Winnie, for her part, was submissive to Dorit, but when she was alone in the hay pasture, she was content with herself for perfect company. She seemed as if she would have been wholly satisfied to live the life of a solitary horse. Winnie definitely relished her pasture retreat, her private time to eat, to lie down in the sunshine, to roll in the warm summer grass, to meander about the empty hay field and stand in the morning shade of the trees that bordered the east fence without interference from anyone. She loved the freedom to be completely herself. Being true royalty, she seemed to feel she was "entitled" to these privileges; she loved and expected them as if she deserved them.

When all four horses were together, we still witnessed Dorit herding Winnie away from the pond when we knew Win wanted a drink of water, or shuttling her into the shed, or to the hay feeder, if that was her own current preference, with no regard for what Winnie wanted. Sometimes Winnie just stood by fasting while Dorit gorged herself. Even though we never saw her nip or kick at Winnie, Winnie became anxious if she was tied and Dorit was free. We never saw Dorit do anything except stand beside her if she were tied, and, of course, move in and eat her remaining feed without permission.

Every time, Winnie simply stepped back and meekly let Dorit eat all she wanted. Unlike her reaction to any other horse attempting to meddle in her space, Winnie never flattened her ears or tried to bite Dorit, never scowled at her with a mean look that would tell her: "Get out! This is *my* food!" We never knew whether Winnie regarded Dorit as a buddy, or as a dreaded enemy--a controller and manipulator of whom she was unable to rid herself except when she was ushered into the solitary paradise of the hay field. Perhaps these forced separations were her only solace. Our aristocrat seemed to *need* her time to herself spiritually and physically, and we gladly catered to her. Winnie seemed happy, and her bodily appearance improved. Dorit's seemingly unwavering loyalty to Winnie, and yet her total manipulation of her pasture mate amazed us as much as Winnie's love for solitude. In Winnie's case, the herd, especially Dorit, needed her more than she needed, or wanted, the herd except at night.

Strangely, Winnie became irritable and feisty if she were kept in a separate pasture overnight. We hoped we could keep her in the north pasture and let her have her *own* hay bale to eat without being pushed around by the others, and have her own shelter in our new barn. However, Winnie would have none of this arrangement. She wanted her solitude *when* she wanted her solitude, but she wanted her herd *when she wanted her herd.*

The three horses had the south horse pasture with the shed and the north pasture near the house while Winnie enjoyed the hay field. Our vegetable garden was fenced off at the far north end of the upper pasture near the house. Actually there were two strips of electric tape "fencing" the garden, but we did not electrify it. The horses left it alone all summer though occasionally I found Stormy quietly staring at me from the other side of the tape as I picked cucumbers. As she eyed the basket carefully, I laughingly said:

"Oh! I know! *You want some of these!*"

She surprised me the first few times by nickering loudly and once even bobbed her head up and down as if nodding and saying: "Yes! Of course I want a cucumber, Mom!" Naturally, I gave her a few. Sometimes Chaos saw Stormy get handouts, and joined her for some snacks. I was not surprised. Every night while Winnie ate her evening portion of grain, I fed pieces of watermelon rind and the overgrown cucumbers from our garden to Stormy, Chaos and Dorit so they did not feel completely left out at Winnie's "dinner time." Winnie also received several pieces of cold watermelon as dessert after her grain each summer night. They all looked forward to these cool treats on hot evenings, but all our horses ate cucumbers even right off the vine. In earlier years I trained the vines to climb the fence that separated the pasture from the yard near the house, and discovered my cucumbers were easily gobbled up as treats by all our horses. If I happened to be working in the garden, Star especially used to approach and quietly seem to politely ask: "Please, Mom, may I have a cucumber?" These are happy, friendly memories of our good horses.

Our mischievous Chaos must have watched me harvest seventeen ripe watermelons from our garden one evening early that September. I left two melons I hoped might mature a little further, and I decided I would pick them in a day or two. The next morning, before I went out to feed Winnie and put her in the hay field for the day, I saw Chaos *inside* the garden tape busily grabbing huge, greedy bites of one of the last two watermelons. She was undeterred by the whole round melon; she did not need it cut into pieces. The other horses were dejectedly watching her from the other side of the tape they dared not cross. I imagined they were thinking: "Why don't *we* get any?" I had to laugh and snap a picture or two. It was actually amazing it had not happened before since I am sure the horses could hear the tape electricity was turned off. I collected the broken melons, and led Chaos out under the tape, and made sure the other three ladies also had some watermelon for *their* breakfasts.

We thought since Winnie was aging, Dorit's undisputed leadership of the herd would surface when Star was no longer there to challenge any attempts she made to be head horse. In the beauty shop department, Dorit, like Pascal before her, demanded *she_be curried first,* and often repeatedly! Even after she had a turn at being groomed, she pushed another horse out of the way so she could be brushed again. Her mid back and rump were still her favorite spots, and she positioned herself so I was exactly lined up with those positions. Some days Dorit did, in fact, lead the others, but more often it was Winnie who was at the head of the queue, and at twenty-four, was still agilely winning the pasture races. Winnie's solitary senior privilege certainly demonstrated to us the loyalty and dependence the other three had for their beloved aging lady.

One evening I came with the cold treats after Rod had returned Winnie to the commoner's pasture in the late afternoon. Winnie was behind a large cedar tree in the east corner of the "commoner" pasture munching grass. I knew she enjoyed the treats as much as her friends did. When Dorit, Stormy, and Chaos came to the door of the barn to be fed, I asked them: "Where is Winnie?" Dorit actually turned her head toward the cedar trees in the southeast corner of the pasture and gave a loud nicker, as if to call: "Come on, Winnie! Treat time." Nothing happened. I called, but there predictably was no response from Winnie. I looked at Dorit and urged: "Go get Winnie!" Finally, knowing *they* did not get to eat *until* Winnie came, Dorit started to trot in Winnie's direction, and then all three galloped at top speed to the cedar trees. They edged Winnie from behind the huge cedars. All four ran west to the shed, and then they all charged full speed to the barn where I was waiting. This was an amusing one time occurrence.

Normally, if Winnie was in the shed, even though the other three saw me, at the barn and *knew* I had treats, no amount of my calling could compel them to dare leave her in the shed and come to eat without her. Even as an aging equine, Winnie maintained some authority over the others. Besides loving her shed, Winnie still had her annoying selective hearing trait, which meant if I wanted to give my spoiled ladies treats, I had to go down and coax them _all_ to the barn so Winnie could have her grain and treats, and the others just their treats.

These good horses are, and will continue to be my friends. They are my teachers, my companions, and my glimpse of God in nature. We bring each other joy and friendship and teach each other a great deal about life along the way. Winnie turned 30 in 2016. My hope is they all will stay here until they die, and will be buried here. There is a portrait of Winnie on her 30th birthday near the end of these pictures.

God has filled me with Himself through these horses whom I have come to know and love as friends.

At long last, our niece Rena sent a picture of Suzanne and her foal, *Silver.* I have placed it last of all the pictures to show: *Life, indeed, does go on.* There is always hope.

Above: Dorit, Stormy and Chaos jealously watch Winnie alone in the hay pasture.
Below: Chaos greedily gobbles a fresh watermelon.

Winnie enjoys her "senior privilege "in the mowed hay field.

(Above and below): Horses enjoy winter snow.

Suzanne with her filly Silver

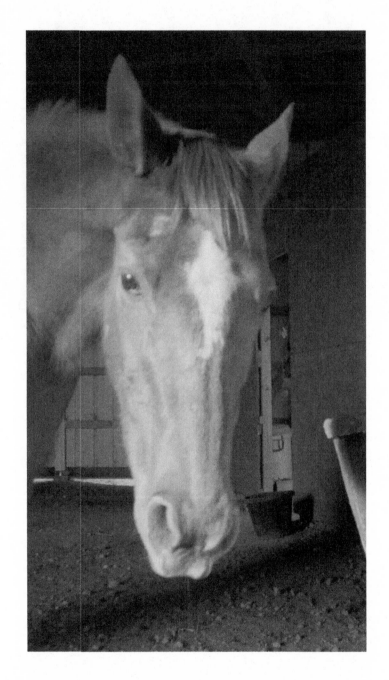

Winnie at 30

Postscript

Rod died unexpectedly in his sleep the night of February 14- 15, 2018. I knew one day one of us would be here alone. I could not know God would take Rod first. Death's finality has once again grasped me, this time with the deepest loss--that of my spouse, my life's partner. It does not seem I should be here without him. Truly part of me died and was buried with him.

"Life goes on," as my mother said, and as my faith, and my horses teach me. For Rod, life is changed, not ended. For me, life with Rod, as his wife, is ended, and my earthly life is forever changed. All the things Rod built, brought and lived here: the home, the farm improvements, and the animals continue without him. We see his reflection everywhere. He loved life deeply, and loved everyone in life deeply especially his family who were second only to God: his wife, his children and grandchildren, his brothers and sisters. Rod, the horses and I were, in a way, "a family" too. We all miss him.

People have been very kind and so helpful with daily chores, and to call to talk, to invite me to their homes and make me feel included. I have a strong religious faith which is my anchor. I know I will miss Rod the rest of my life; this is the price of love. God intends this daily sacrifice for my purification. Through this loss, God is teaching me to rely on Him even more than before and to seek to continue doing His will. I have the firm hope that one day I shall see Rod again.

My horse, Winspiration, passed away in July 2019 at the age of 33. She is buried on our farm.

In August 2019 I visited some of Rod's family. I felt completely at home and at ease with his brothers and sisters, their children and grandchildren. I was loved and welcomed. My niece, Rena, even took me to visit Suzanne whom she took from our farm 13 years before, and her daughter, Silver. I could sense Suzanne remembered me. She was very calm; she put her nose to my cheek and breathed on me, and even licked me, her hallmark sign of affection. I told her about her mother and about Rod. This meeting was a healing gift. Her daughter, Silver, looks like Star.

Rod always said "God built this place. I was just His instrument." I pray I too will be, as Rod was, His instrument as long as I am on this earth. God put Rod, His awesome animals and this amazing, beautiful world in my life to help point me toward heaven. I hope in reading these pages the reader gleans God loves us greatly, He is in control, and dreams can come true when we strive to put Him first each day.

Mary Barbara McKay

Above: Rod on Foxy Beau. Below: Mary Barbara with Suzanne

We need to find God and God

cannot be found in noise

and restlessness. God is the

friend of silence.

See how nature—trees and flowers

and grass—grow in silence.

See the stars, the moon and

the sun, how they move in silence.

The more we receive in silent

prayer, the more we can give

in our active life.

--St. Mother Teresa of Calcutta

Chaliha, jaya and Edward LE Joly. (Compiled by). <u>The Joy in Loving: A guide to Daily Living with Mother Teresa.</u> Penguin Books, USA, Inc. New York, NY., p. 228.

Acknowledgements

At different times in my life I sense God is in complete control of the events, and of everything needed to bring them to a beautiful final conclusion. In these instances it is my job to simply step back and let Him direct my work. So it is with this book. The good Lord was the Director from start to finish, and I thank Him.

I first acknowledge my husband of over 46 years, Rod McKay. He built our country home and provided the horses who made the stories and who became God's instruments to teach me His plan for my life. This book could not exist without Rod, his good mind, and his loving, hard work.

Next I gratefully acknowledge my friend of over 30 years, Linda Graf, who was truly my guiding genius, my Muse, in writing this book. She *insisted* I write it, and then she meticulously read my manuscript and made suggestions. The book would not exist without Linda's persistence and her never-ending encouragement.

Since I refer to our horses' illustrious ancestry in the text, The Jockey Club's free 5-X pedigrees for my horses are partially reproduced at the end for anyone desiring to see our horses' lineage. I am grateful The Jockey Club provides these pedigrees for free, and gladly give them credit.

Equus Magazine granted permission to reproduce their *True Tale* selection of my story of Star which they perceptively titled *Friends for Life* in their February 2004 Issue 316, pages 74-77.

I thank my friends, and especially my sister-in-law, Rena McKay Uhalde, who encouraged me through seeking publication. My thanks to those who gave permission for me to use their first names within my book. I especially thank my grandson, Michael, for his enthusiasm, belief in and eagerness for my book.

I thank my friend, Janalin Hood, artist, photographer, and horsewoman for her assistance with the cover design for my book. Janalin has a BFA from the University of Kansas.

Finally, I thank Newbookauthors.com for publishing my book and especially EM Hughes for guiding me through the process of formatting and cover selection.

--Mary Barbara McKay

References

Blazer, Eleanor. "To Longe, Lunge or Lounge?" The Way of Horses. Copyright 2011.

www.thewayofhorses.com/11_11_longe_lounge.html

Chaliha, jaya and Edward LE Joly. (Complied by). <u>The Joy in Loving: A guide to Daily Living with Mother Teresa.</u> Penguin Books, USA, Inc. New York, NY.1996.

Cooper, Page and Roger L. Treat. <u>Man O' War.</u> Julian Messener, Inc. 1950.2004 Westholme Publishing, Pennsylvania.1950 & 2004.

Dickon, Chris. <u>A Rendezvous with Death: Alan Seeger In Poetry, At War.</u> New Street Communications. 2017.

Harrison, G.B.,(Editor)., <u>Shakespeare: The Complete Works.</u> Harcourt, Brace & World, Inc., New York. 1950.

Hillenbrand, Laura. <u>Seabiscuit: An American Legend</u>. Random House, New York.2001.

"I Know a Place" (song). Source: Jubilee Songbook, Girl Guides of Canada. 1971.

Ives, S., Morgenstern, E., Ferrari, M., & Glenn, S. (2007). *American Experience: Seabiscuit* [Arlington, Va.]: PBS. http://www.contentreserve.com/TitleInfo.asp?ID={C40A0399-BEDB-4CF7-8B29-2CE4D362187E}&Format=35.

Longfellow, H. W., & Polley, R. L. <u>America the Beautiful in the Words of Henry Wadsworth Longfellow.</u> Country Beautiful Foundation, Waukesha, Wisconsin.1965.

Milne, A.A. <u>The Complete Tales and Poems of Winnie-the-Pooh,</u> (2001) Dutton Children's Books. Penguin Putnam Books for Young Readers, New York, NY.

Muggeridge, Malcolm. <u>Something Beautiful for God: Mother Teresa of Calcutta.</u> Image Books: A Division of Doubleday & Company, Inc. New York. 1977.

Oliver, Mary. <u>Why I Wake Early.</u> (2004). Beacon Press, Boston, Massachusetts.

Ours, Dorothy, <u>Man o' War: A Legend Like Lightning.</u> (2006). St. Martin's Press, New York.

Parelli, Pat, <u>Natural Horse-Man-Ship.</u> Western Horseman Inc.,Colorado Springs, Colorado.1993.

Swift, Sally. <u>Centered Riding.</u>(1985). St. Martin's Press. New York.

<u>The Holy Bible, Revised Standard Version, Ignatius Edition</u>. (2006). San Francisco. Ignatius Press.

Tolkien, J. R. R., <u>The Lord of the Rings Trilogy</u>: <u>The Fellowship of the Ring, The Two Towers, The Return of the King</u>. Ballatine Books, New York. 1965.

Williams, Oscar, (Editor). <u>Immortal Poems of the English Language: British and American Poetry from Chaucer's Time to the Present Day</u>. Washington Square Press, New York. 1961.

Partial Pedigrees for Horses I Have Owned

The following pedigrees for horses I have owned come from The Jockey Club website: http://www.equineline.com/Free-5X-Pedigree.cfm. They are reproduced in part here with permission and with the following disclaimer which applies to each pedigree copied here:

ATTENTION!

Data provided or compiled by The Jockey Club Information Systems, Inc. generally are accurate but errors and omissions occur as a result of incorrect data received from others, mistakes in processing and other causes. The Jockey Club Information Systems, Inc. shall have no liability or responsibility to you or to any other person or entity for the consequences, if any, of such errors, but would appreciate having any such errors called to their attention.

Little Dorit
Bay Mare; March 13,1996; 0 Starts; Unraced

Grand Alliance, 76 ch	*Vaguely Noble, 65 b	=Vienna (GB), 57 ch	=Aureole (GB), 50 ch	=Hyperion (GB), 30 ch
				=Angelola, 45 b
			=Turkish Blood (GB), 44 b	=Turkhan (GB), 37 b
				=Rusk (GB), 35 b
		=Noble Lassie, 56 b	=Nearco (ITY), 35 br	=Pharos (GB), 20 dk b/
				=Nogara (ITY), 28 b
			=Belle Sauvage (GB), 49 ch	=Big Game (GB), 39 b
				=Tropical Sun (GB), 40 ch
	Exclusive, 53 ch	Shut Out, 39 ch	Equipoise, 28 ch	Pennant, 11
				Swinging, 22 ch
			Goose Egg, 27 b	*Chicle, 13 b
				Oval, 21
		Good Example, 44 br	Pilate, 28 ch	Friar Rock, 13
				*Herodias, 16 gr
			Parade Girl, 33 b	Display, 23 b
				Panoply, 17 b
Tinkle Tina, 83 gr	Bushido, 66 dk b/	*Tudor Grey, 60 gr	*Tudor Minstrel, 44 br	=Owen Tudor (GB), 38 br
				=Sansonnet (GB), 33 b
			=Earnest Alice (GB), 54 gr	=Grey Sovereign (GB), 48 gr
				=Ardue (GB), 49 b
		Got Idea, 61 ch	Sub Fleet, 49 b	Count Fleet, 40 br
				Sub Rosa, 42 b
			Blue Lu, 36 b	Blue Larkspur, 26 b
				Lucille Wright, 30 b
	Tinkle Tinkle, 74 ro	Tinajero, 68 gr	Decidedly, 59 gr	Determine, 51 gr
				Gloire Fille, 49 dk b
			Queen City Miss, 62 b	Royal Union, 55 ch
				Foolspoint, 56 b
		Second the Motion, 65 ch	*Turn-to, 51 b	*Royal Charger, 42 ch
				*Source Sucree, 40 br
			Next Move, 47 br	Bull Lea, 35 br
				Now What, 37 ch

Noble Chaos
Chestnut Mare; July 13,2002; 0 Starts; Unraced

John's Sue, 99 ch	Master's Presence, 82 dk b/	Jacinto, 62 br	Bold Ruler, 54 dk b	*Nasrullah, 40 b
				Miss Disco, 44 b
			*Cascade II, 51 br	=Precipitation (GB), 33 ch
				=Marita (GB), 42 br
		Never Be Lonely, 69 dk b/	Windsor Ruler, 56 b	*Nasrullah, 40 b
				*Windsor Whisper, 45 br
			Miss Turner, 56 b	Blue Man, 49 b
				Admirals Wave, 50 ch
	Active Annie, 86 ch	Czaravich, 76 ch	Nijinsky II, 67 b	Northern Dancer, 61 b
				Flaming Page, 59 b
			*Black Satin II, 67 dk b/	=Linacre (GB), 60 br
				=Panaview (GB), 60 b
		Annie Active, 72 dk b/	Exceedingly, 63 b	Third Brother, 53 b
				Exceed, 58 b
			Action Station, 60 ch	Gun Shot, 53 ch
				High Station, 57 b
Little Dorit, 96 b	Grand Alliance, 76 ch	*Vaguely Noble, 65 b	=Vienna (GB), 57 ch	=Aureole (GB), 50 ch
				=Turkish Blood (GB), 44 b
			=Noble Lassie, 56 b	=Nearco (ITY), 35 br
				=Belle Sauvage (GB), 49 ch
		Exclusive, 53 ch	Shut Out, 39 ch	Equipoise, 28 ch
				Goose Egg, 27 b
			Good Example, 44 br	Pilate, 28 ch
				Parade Girl, 33 b
	Tinkle Tina, 83 gr	Bushido, 66 dk b/	*Tudor Grey, 60 gr	*Tudor Minstrel, 44 br
				=Earnest Alice (GB), 54 gr
			Got Idea, 61 ch	Sub Fleet, 49 b
				Blue Lu, 36 b
		Tinkle Tinkle, 74 ro	Tinajero, 68 gr	Decidedly, 59 gr
				Queen City Miss, 62 b
			Second the Motion, 65 ch	*Turn-to, 51 b
				Next Move, 47 br

296

Teeter On a Star
Roan Mare; March 11,1992; 15 Starts; Winner

- **Suzanne's Star, 77 ro**
  - Son Ange, 68 ch
    - Raise a Native, 61 ch
      - Native Dancer, 50 gr
        - Polynesian, 42 br
        - Geisha, 43 ro
      - Raise You, 46 ch
        - Case Ace, 34 b
        - Lady Glory, 34 br
    - Mon Ange, 62 ch
      - Tom Fool, 49 b
        - Menow, 35 dk b
        - Gaga, 42 b
      - Two Lea, 46 b
        - Bull Lea, 35 br
        - Two Bob, 33 b
  - Game Maid, 64 ro
    - Greek Game, 54 br
      - Olympia, 46 b
        - *Heliopolis, 36 b
        - Miss Dolphin, 34 ch
      - Sunday Supper, 41 b
        - Questionnaire, 27 lt b
        - Delicacy, 29 dk b
    - Ocean Maid, 61 ro
      - Sailor, 52 ch
        - Eight Thirty, 36 ch
        - Flota, 37 ch
      - *Hyperi, 55 gr
        - =Hyperion (GB), 30 ch
        - *Ranya, 47 gr
- **Sly Tee Tee, 84 b**
  - On the Sly, 73 dk b/
    - *Roi Dagobert, 64 dk b/
      - =Sicambre (FR), 48 br
        - =Prince Bio (FR), 41 b
        - =Sif (FR), 36 br
      - =Dame d'Atour (FR), 55 b
        - =Cranach (FR), 38 b
        - =Barley Corn (GB), 50 b
    - Trick Chick, 66 ch
      - Prince John, 53 ch
        - *Princequillo, 40 b
        - Not Afraid, 48 dk b
      - Fast Line, 58 b
        - Mr. Busher, 46 ch
        - Throttle Wide, 36 br
  - Red Cammy, 70 ch
    - Sailor, 52 ch
      - Eight Thirty, 36 ch
        - Pilate, 28 ch
        - Dinner Time, 29 ch
      - Flota, 37 ch
        - Jack High, 26 ch
        - Armada, 24 dk ch
    - On the Tee, 63 ch
      - On-and-On, 56 b
        - *Nasrullah, 40 b
        - Two Lea, 46 b
      - Pink Tea, 53 b
        - Rippey, 43 b
        - Garden Party, 44 br

Star's Suzanne
Gray or Roan Mare; April 13,2003; 0 Starts; Unraced

- **John's Sue, 99 ch**
  - Master's Presence, 82 dk b/
    - Jacinto, 62 br
      - Bold Ruler, 54 dk b
        - *Nasrullah, 40 b
        - Miss Disco, 44 b
      - *Cascade II, 51 br
        - =Precipitation (GB), 33 ch
        - =Marita (GB), 42 br
    - Never Be Lonely, 69 dk b/
      - Windsor Ruler, 56 b
        - *Nasrullah, 40 b
        - *Windsor Whisper, 45 br
      - Miss Turner, 56 b
        - Blue Man, 49 b
        - Admirals Wave, 50 ch
  - Active Annie, 86 ch
    - Czaravich, 76 ch
      - Nijinsky II, 67 b
        - Northern Dancer, 61 b
        - Flaming Page, 59 b
      - *Black Satin II, 67 dk b/
        - =Linacre (GB), 60 br
        - =Panaview (GB), 60 b
    - Annie Active, 72 dk b/
      - Exceedingly, 63 b
        - Third Brother, 53 b
        - Exceed, 58 b
      - Action Station, 60 ch
        - Gun Shot, 53 ch
        - High Station, 57 b
- **Teeter On a Star, 92 ro**
  - Suzanne's Star, 77 ro
    - Son Ange, 68 ch
      - Raise a Native, 61 ch
        - Native Dancer, 50 gr
        - Raise You, 46 ch
      - Mon Ange, 62 ch
        - Tom Fool, 49 b
        - Two Lea, 46 b
    - Game Maid, 64 ro
      - Greek Game, 54 br
        - Olympia, 46 b
        - Sunday Supper, 41 b
      - Ocean Maid, 61 ro
        - Sailor, 52 ch
        - *Hyperi, 55 gr
  - Sly Tee Tee, 84 b
    - On the Sly, 73 dk b/
      - *Roi Dagobert, 64 dk b/
        - =Sicambre (FR), 48 br
        - =Dame d'Atour (FR), 55 b
      - Trick Chick, 66 ch
        - Prince John, 53 ch
        - Fast Line, 58 b
    - Red Cammy, 70 ch
      - Sailor, 52 ch
        - Eight Thirty, 36 ch
        - Flota, 37 ch
      - On the Tee, 63 ch
        - On-and-On, 56 b
        - Pink Tea, 53 b

Winspiration
Chestnut Mare; February 28,1986; 13 Starts; Winner

Hot Words, 75 b	Verbatim, 65 dk b/	Speak John, 58 b	Prince John, 53 ch	*Princequillo, 40 b
				Not Afraid, 48 dk b
			*Nuit de Folies, 47 b	=Tornado (FR), 39 b
				=Folle Nuit (FR), 40 b
		Well Kept, 58 b	Never Say Die, 51 ch	*Nasrullah, 40 b
				Singing Grass, 44 ch
			*Bed o' Roses II, 50 b	=Preciptic (GB), 42 ch
				=Pasquinade (GB), 40 gr
	Napalm, 63 ch	*Nilo, 45 b	=Nearco (ITY), 35 br	=Pharos (GB), 20 dk b/
				=Nogara (ITY), 28 b
			*Dodoma II, 39 b	=Dastur (GB), 29 b
				=Mumtaz Begum (FR), 32 b
		Fire Falls, 42 b	*Bull Dog, 27 b/br	*Teddy, 13 b
				=Plucky Liege (GB), 12 b
			Stricken, 32 ch	Pennant, 11
				Moody Mary, 25 ch
Here's Linda, 75 ch	Black Mountain, 61 b	*Tudor Minstrel, 44 br	=Owen Tudor (GB), 38 br	=Hyperion (GB), 30 ch
				=Mary Tudor II (FR), 31 b
			=Sansonnet (GB), 33 b	=Sansovino (GB), 21 b
				=Lady Juror (GB), 19 b
		Portage, 52 b	War Admiral, 34 br	Man o' War, 17 ch
				Brushup, 29 b
			Carillon, 39 ch	Case Ace, 34 b
				Sunfeathers, 34 ch
	Hereby Jeanie, 71 ch	Platte County, 62 ch	Bolero, 46 ch	Eight Thirty, 36 ch
				Stepwisely, 41 br
			Red Carnation, 51 dk b	Sun Again, 39 ch
				Iron Maiden, 41 b
		Hereby, 53 ch	*Flushing II, 39 gr	*Mahmoud, 33 gr
				=Callandar (GB), 31 ch
			Cirzac, 41 ch	Zacaweista, 26 blk
				Circean, 30 ch

Dark Stormy Night
Chestnut Mare; May 09,2003; 0 Starts; Unraced

John's Sue, 99 ch	Master's Presence, 82 dk b/	Jacinto, 62 br	Bold Ruler, 54 dk b	*Nasrullah, 40 b
				Miss Disco, 44 b
			*Cascade II, 51 br	=Precipitation (GB), 33 ch
				=Marita (GB), 42 br
		Never Be Lonely, 69 dk b/	Windsor Ruler, 56 b	*Nasrullah, 40 b
				*Windsor Whisper, 45 br
			Miss Turner, 56 b	Blue Man, 49 b
				Admirals Wave, 50 ch
	Active Annie, 86 ch	Czaravich, 76 ch	Nijinsky II, 67 b	Northern Dancer, 61 b
				Flaming Page, 59 b
			*Black Satin II, 67 dk b/	=Linacre (GB), 60 br
				=Panaview (GB), 60 b
		Annie Active, 72 dk b/	Exceedingly, 63 b	Third Brother, 53 b
				Exceed, 58 b
			Action Station, 60 ch	Gun Shot, 53 ch
				High Station, 57 b
Winspiration, 86 ch	Hot Words, 75 b	Verbatim, 65 dk b/	Speak John, 58 b	Prince John, 53 ch
				*Nuit de Folies, 47 b
			Well Kept, 58 b	Never Say Die, 51 ch
				*Bed o' Roses II, 50 b
		Napalm, 63 ch	*Nilo, 45 b	=Nearco (ITY), 35 br
				*Dodoma II, 39 b
			Fire Falls, 42 b	*Bull Dog, 27 b/br
				Stricken, 32 ch
	Here's Linda, 75 ch	Black Mountain, 61 b	*Tudor Minstrel, 44 br	=Owen Tudor (GB), 38 br
				=Sansonnet (GB), 33 b
			Portage, 52 b	War Admiral, 34 br
				Carillon, 39 ch
		Hereby Jeanie, 71 ch	Platte County, 62 ch	Bolero, 46 ch
				Red Carnation, 51 dk b
			Hereby, 53 ch	*Flushing II, 39 gr
				Cirzac, 41 ch

298

John's Sue
Chestnut Gelding; April 25, 1999; 0 Starts; Unraced

				=Nearco (ITY), 35 br
Master's Presence, 82 dk b/	Jacinto, 62 br	Bold Ruler, 54 dk b	*Nasrullah, 40 b	=Mumtaz Begum (FR), 32 b
			Miss Disco, 44 b	Discovery, 31 ch
				Outdone, 36 b
		*Cascade II, 51 br	=Precipitation (GB), 33 ch	=Hurry On (GB), 13 ch
				=Double Life (IRE), 26 b
			=Marlta (GB), 42 br	=Dastur (GB), 29 b
				=Caerlissa (GB), 35 b
	Never Be Lonely, 69 dk b/	Windsor Ruler, 56 b	*Nasrullah, 40 b	=Nearco (ITY), 35 br
				=Mumtaz Begum (FR), 32 b
			*Windsor Whisper, 45 br	=Windsor Slipper (GB), 39 b
				=Inkling (GB), 32 br
		Miss Turner, 56 b	Blue Man, 49 b	Blue Swords, 40 b
				Poppycock, 39 br
			Admirals Wave, 50 ch	War Admiral, 34 br
				Fly Off, 43 ch
Active Annie, 86 ch	Czaravich, 76 ch	Nijinsky II, 67 b	Northern Dancer, 61 b	Nearctic, 54 br
				Natalma, 57 b
			Flaming Page, 59 b	Bull Page, 47 dk b
				Flaring Top, 47 ch
		*Black Satin II, 67 dk b/	=Linacre (GB), 60 br	=Rockefella (GB), 41 br
				=True Picture (IRE), 55 blk
			=Panaview (GB), 60 b	*Panaslipper, 52 ch
				=April View (GB), 49 b
	Annie Active, 72 dk b/	Exceedingly, 63 b	Third Brother, 53 b	*Princequillo, 40 b
				Hildene, 38 b
			Exceed, 58 b	Better Self, 45 b
				Vinina, 48 b
		Action Station, 60 ch	Gun Shot, 53 ch	=Hyperion (GB), 30 ch
				*Silence II, 42 br
			High Station, 57 b	*Royal Vale, 48 br
				Challequeen, 45 b

Pascal's Wager
Dark Bay or Brown Gelding; March 22, 1997; 0 Starts; Unraced

				Bold Reasoning, 68 dk b/
Slewidero, 93 ch	Slewacide Squeeze, 86 ch	Slewacide, 80 b	Seattle Slew, 74 dk b/	My Charmer, 69 b
			Evasive, 70 ch	Buckpasser, 63 b
				Summer Scandal, 62 ch
		Snoop's Legacy, 79 ch	King Emperor, 66 b	Bold Ruler, 54 dk b
				Irish Jay, 57 b
			Snoopstep, 65 dk b/	Watch Your Step, 56 ch
				Snoop, 53 dk b
	Anidera (ARG), 77 ch	=Alislos (ARG), 66 ch	=Court Harwell (GB), 54 br	=Prince Chevalier (FR), 43 b
				*Neutron, 48 ch
			=Squall, 60 b	*Tatan, 52 ch
				=Sudestada (ARG), 55 b
		=Redalera, 65 ch	=Redactor, 59 blk	=Jungle King (ARG), 51 b
				=Rupia, 50
			=Cotelera, 47 ch	=Barman II, 31
				=Contadina, 30
Twist of Knowledge, 87 dk b/	Fleet Twist, 74 b	Fleet Nasrullah, 55 dk b	*Nasrullah, 40 b	=Nearco (ITY), 35 br
				=Mumtaz Begum (FR), 32 b
			Happy Go Fleet, 50 b	Count Fleet, 40 br
				Draeh, 39 br
		Miss Twist, 61 ch	Prince John, 53 ch	*Princequillo, 40 b
				Not Afraid, 48 dk b
			Night Dance, 57 blk	*Cortil, 48 br
				*Nuit de Folies, 47 b
	Fashion Knowledge, 80 b	Tree of Knowledge, 70 b	Dr. Fager, 64 b	Rough'n Tumble, 48 b
				Aspidistra, 54 b
			Bent Twig, 59 dk b	*Nasrullah, 40 b
				Pines of Rome, 49 b
		Manner of Fashion, 68 dk b/	Comic, 59 b	Tom Fool, 49 b
				His Duchess, 50 lt br
			Lady in Mink, 61 b	*Noor, 45 br
				Extravagant, 55 ch